MARÍA FULLAONDO

Colors of Rhetoric

Places of Invention in the Visual Realm

T0344506

ar+d

APPLIED
RESEARCH
+DESIGN
PUBLISHING

Published by Applied Research and Design Publishing, an imprint of ORO Editions.
Gordon Goff: Publisher

www.appliedresearchanddesign.com
info@appliedresearchanddesign.com

USA, EUROPE, ASIA, MIDDLE EAST, SOUTH AMERICA

"Copyright © 2022 María Fullaondo. All rights reserved."

All rights reserved. No part of this book may be reproduced, stored in a retrieval system, or transmitted in any form or by any means, including electronic, mechanical, photocopying of microfilming, recording, or otherwise (except that copying permitted by Sections 107 and 108 of the U.S. Copyright Law and except by reviewers for the public press) without written permission from the publisher.

You must not circulate this book in any other binding or cover and you must impose this same condition on any acquirer.

Author: María Fullaondo
Preface: María López Díez and Diego Fullaondo
Book Design: María Fullaondo
Cover: María Fullaondo [Peter Weibel and VALIE EXPORT, *Aus der Mappe der Hundigkeit* (From the Portfolio of Doggedness), 1968]

10 9 8 7 6 5 4 3 2 1 First Edition

Library of Congress data available upon request. World Rights: Available

ISBN: 978-1-954081-30-7

Color Separations and Printing: ORO Group Ltd.
Printed in China.
International Distribution: www.appliedresearchanddesign.com/distribution

ORO Editions makes a continuous effort to minimize the overall carbon footprint of its publications. As part of this goal, ORO Editions, in association with Global ReLeaf, arranges to plant trees to replace those used in the manufacturing of the paper produced for its books. Global ReLeaf is an international campaign run by American Forests, one of the world's oldest nonprofit conservation organizations. Global ReLeaf is American Forests' education and action program that helps individuals, organizations, agencies, and corporations improve the local and global environment by planting and caring for trees.

A mi madre

Contents

THE TREACHERY OF IMAGES?
María López Díez

Dr. María López Díez (PhD Universidad Autónoma de Madrid, 2003) completed her doctoral thesis in the field of architecture of the 15th century. Since then, her research has focused on the architecture and development of the modern city and its image from a historical perspective. She currently teaches at NYU-Madrid, and Master's programs at ESNE (Escuela Universitaria de Diseño, Innovación y Tecnología), ETSAM (Escuela Técnica Superior de Arquitectura de Madrid), and EFTI (Centro Internacional de Fotografía y Cine), where she teaches various courses related to Urban Studies, City Development, Architecture, Art History, Photography, Contemporary Design, as well as others on heritage and Spanish culture. Also, she has started to collaborate with Observatorio Permanente del Hispanismo, dedicated to promoting Hispanic Culture.

Magritte once warned us of the deception concealed within images, thus questioning the credibility of such portrayals, associating this with language. Because figurative images do not suffice on their own, certain strategies must be resorted to by their creators in order to convey intended messages. However, this does not mean they contain outright falsehoods or deception, and even less so betrayal; instead we must learn to use certain procedures to establish an effective form of communication with them. These consist of a two-fold process of encoding and decoding, given that every representation is a visual code that must be known and recognized by both sender and receiver.

In order for this to work properly, it is advisable to create a space of shared understanding between the two, thereby enabling the exchange. The heart of the matter is how to negotiate this territory, reach agreement amongst differing subjectivities, and, moreover, take into account the complexity that arises when many role-players enter one stage, including every aspect from cultural references and social customs to, of course, ever-present politics. This leads us to search for a consensual yet compelling visual order able to articulate the image while ensuring effective communication.

Naturally, many *vantage points* have been proposed to deal with the urgency of systematizing the terms in which visual comprehension is attained, but to a great extent the most influential terms in contemporary discourses are those engaged in strategies for decoding, while also taking the relationships between text and image into consideration. The most widely accepted ideas on artistic interpretation in academia are those proposed by Erwin Panofsky (1892–1968) in his iconographic and iconological analyses of the *meaning* of works of art, in which he verifies the distance between form and content. Later, Roland Barthes (1915–1980), so much in line with structuralist and post-structuralist schools of thought, paid closer attention to the mechanisms of signification and to the symbol as a mediator between image and concept, placing a special emphasis on the active role played by the reader. Furthermore, unlike Panofsky's scholarly propositions, pop culture, consumerism, advertising, mass media, and other fields outside of the arts form part of his scope of analysis, thus constructing a *rhetoric of the image*. Taking this one step further, the importance assigned to context, to the autonomy of images, and to the flux in contemporary society would also be discussed by W.J.T. Mitchell (born in 1942).

This interest since modern times in analyzing and processing images is what led María Fullaondo to propose such a powerful visual system not only suitable for deciphering images, but also for providing a methodology to create them. Dismissing the now outdated myth of inspiration, the author has brilliantly and courageously proposed a set of "recipes" that allow anyone to produce effective images and facilitate an enhanced understanding of the visual universe in which we are immersed. To achieve this, she proposes a revision of the rhetoric that, though originating in literature—or perhaps for that very reason—acts as an efficient catalyst for the organization of visual representation.

But why focus on the rhetoric? In principle, it could be regarded as completely obsolete. In fact, however, it takes us back to Aristotle and then to scholastic education, a medieval study plan designed by Alcuin of York in which knowledge of the Liberal Arts was divided into *Trivium* and *Quadrivium*. The *Trivium*, consisting of grammar, logic, and rhetoric, prepared one to effect good communication based on knowledge about language, comparing opposing arguments and studying the ways in which we attempt to persuade those with whom we interact. And that is precisely what Fullaondo achieves in this book, using the teachings of classical rhetoric and taking them even further in order to enrich our relationship with images today.

Nevertheless, despite the initially apparent sophistication of this approach, *Colors of Rhetoric: Places of Invention in the Visual Realm* is really a practical, user-friendly handbook for anybody. The profound link between text and image lies at the heart of this publication, from both a conceptual and physical perspective. It hits the mark in explaining the great potential held by images through tropes and rhetorical figures, and in discussing how several may all be acting at the same time, thus showing that no image is free from rhetorical mechanisms.

Images do not betray us. And neither does this book.

THE SPEAKING IMAGE
Diego Fullaondo

Dr. Diego Fullaondo (PhD Universidad Politécnica de Madrid, 2012) is a Spanish-Australian practicing architect and architectural design academic. Both his professional work and his teaching & research interests have focused on articulating a better understanding of rational processes behind invention and creativity in Architecture, Art, and Design.

Inspiration, revelation, fantasy, imagination, oracle, epiphany, vision, aha or eureka moment, omen, afflatus, satori, genius, brainwave, and talent—these are some of the cryptic terms and concepts often used by all types of creators in the visual realm when asked to explain or describe their creative processes . It remains unclear if these typical yet enigmatic responses are thoughtless or deliberate; if they respond to an authentic lack of understanding of the creative processes or to a sophisticated defensive strategy of artists' most valuable secret; if they use silence to increase the magnetic attractiveness of the unknown or purposefully maintain an openness to the interpretation of their work. Regardless, the truth is that visual creators reveal very little about how they generate their work. Edward Hopper (1882–1967) said, "If I could say it in words, there would be no reason to paint."

Surprisingly, experts, critics, and researchers have also struggled to explain this mysterious instant of creation. At best, we must settle for a few vague clues comprising strictly individual methodologies and inspiring contexts or references (again, the same magic concept). Pablo Picasso's (1881–1973) famous quote, "Inspiration exists, but it has to find you working," adds little more than a claim for a rigorous work ethic while the artist waits for divine illumination. Even if we accept the existence of that enlightening moment, questions remain (i.e., Working on what? Working how?).

In María's work as an architect, artist, researcher, and, most importantly, as a teacher, she has focused on pursuing and sharing answers to these crucial questions. The inventory contained in *Colors of Rhetoric* summarizes more than 25 years of rigorous research and the validation of an initial hypothesis glimpsed during her early work as a designer in the visual realm: the processes and manipulations used to operate with visual language are similar to those of verbal language. While the culture of image is relatively young and has been thoroughly researched only in the last couple of centuries, rhetoric and figures of speech have been studied since Aristotle as means to create, generate, and persuade.

Therefore, María's intuitive proposition was as follows: if this hypothesis is valid, all knowledge, methodologies, and procedures of literary rhetoric apply to the visual realm, which implies a profound advancement in the understanding of the multiple creative disciplines related to it. The inventory presented in this work asserts and comprehensively demonstrates that this proposition is valid.

More than a hundred different figures of speech are presented in their traditional literary form. Each figure of speech is accompanied by a piece of work from the visual realm (e.g., art, film, photography, architecture) that is identified and explained in its fundamental generative operations to confirm a common thought or formal creative process. Both the quantity and quality of the examples are overwhelming. Advertising examples are extremely explicit in their correspondence to their literary references due to their relatively simple overall requirements (i.e., persuasion is the main objective). The artwork examples selected for the different figures of speech are also unambiguous. Moreover, some fascinating discoveries and coincidences can be found amongst the examples (for instance, similarities and relationships between works from different artists).

This book illustrates architectural correspondences (instead of final images or renders of projects) by focusing on initial and conceptual architectural drawings in which the architects have captured the raw drivers of their proposals. I must highlight the elegant and subtle criticism María has included in her inventory by including a blank page for the entry dedicated to the metaphor. As the most well-known figure of speech, the metaphor is unfortunately vastly overused by architecture students and even practicing architects around the world to justify the most simplistic approaches to some designs; this practice reduces their building designs to the mere resemblance of a shape or silhouette of a human torso, a butterfly, or any other supposedly inspiring reference.

Although the inventory is as rigorous and comprehensive as any extensive taxonomy should be to have any value, there is a sense of playfulness embedded in it. María humbly puts forward her own interpretation of the excellent pieces of work, which have been carefully curated and explained. For each work, in addition to the figure of speech it illustrates, the author lists a series of other tropes she has also identified. By doing this, María implicitly makes a double statement: firstly, every reader and observer should reflect on their own assessments in which a rhetorical figure or color was the real main trigger of the work discussed; secondly, these multiple interpretations that coexist in the same piece of work are not merely another symptom of the desirable openness (Umberto Eco, *Opera Aperta*, 1962) pursued by artists of any type through their work.

Finally, the multi-disciplinary approach taken in *Colors of Rhetoric* proves that all these creative disciplines—literature, advertising, and architecture—share a general thought process. Studying them together is not only possible but imperative for each one's progress. Blurring the boundaries between disciplines has proven to be a very fertile way of evolving. However, this transversality is possible only because this common ground exists as identified in *Colors of Rhetoric*.

As an architect myself, I am fully aware of the conflictive duality of my discipline, always swinging between its scientific and humanistic components. The response to this debate is not very relevant. Nevertheless, these days, with the scientific approach predominant, arguments like those made in *Colors of Rhetoric* remind us why architecture was firmly included as the first of the seven traditional *Beaux Arts*.

A parallel can be drawn between verbal and visual languages. *Colors of Rhetoric* identifies outstanding correspondences between literary rhetorical figures and the works of several designers, artists, and architects. This approach not only facilitates a profound understanding of the work for authors and audiences, but it also (more importantly) enables the establishment of systematic and objective methodologies to operate within the visual realm without having to rely exclusively on the emergence of elusive inspiration.

Introduction

This study explores the application of literary rhetorical mechanisms in a range of spatial practices and visual arts to facilitate creation and invention. It also offers alternative ways to understand the world around us by reflecting on the spatial and social dislocations in everyday contemporary life.

RHETORIC AS A CREATIVE DISCIPLINE

The new art of rhetoric is the art of discovery. It is not a heuristic method or a radical interpretation but an art of topics or a selection of elements which opens the way to the recognition of new facts and to the perception of unnoticed structures and sequences.

—Richard McKEON, *Rhetoric: Essays in Invention & Discovery*, 1987.

Rhetoric is a complex discipline with a long history and several overlapping meanings, concerns, and applications. It has been broadly defined as the art of persuasion, or the study of the means of persuasion available for a given situation. However, it can also be defined as the study of general relationships of unexpectedness. At one level, this is no more than a method of creation.

The core premise of this investigation emphasizes rhetoric as a creative discipline. *Colors of Rhetoric* reveals that the rhetorical system may be a useful descriptive and analytical instrument for dealing with phenomena related to creation. Rhetorical strategies and devices, by definition, defy the logic of discourse to the point of transformation; they are a set of diverse decontextualization mechanisms that allow us to search for unexpected relationships that do not yet exist or that no one has thought of yet.

If we think of the architect, designer, or artist primarily as an inventor of relationships, rhetorical methods and operations become a powerful tool in the creative process. Since rhetoric was established early in the fifth century BC, it has been concerned almost solely with verbal language, public speaking, and literature. However, this study explores the application of literary rhetorical mechanisms to a range of spatial practices and visual arts to facilitate the invention of new and unexpected relationships. Of note, the investigation focuses on the practical possibilities of applying rhetorical mechanisms to design disciplines rather than providing a comprehensive theory of rhetoric.

Rhetoric provides a repertoire of different methods for original and innovative creation by introducing notions of surprise, the unexpected, and conflict. The myths of "inspiration" and "the brilliant idea" dominate explanations of the genesis of many architectural and creative projects. Nevertheless, perhaps the most original ideas and innovative designs could be explained as transpositions of the classical figures or colors of rhetoric. This possibility brings up several questions. Is rhetoric a kind of repertoire of different ways in which one can be "original"? Can the creative process be facilitated and enriched if creators become more aware of the system that they often use intuitively? Do architects make conscious or unconscious use of some of the figures of thought, tropes, and schemes when creating and discussing architecture? Can metonymies, hyperbatons, oxymorons, antitheses, and puns, among many other rhetorical figures, be identified in spatial and visual disciplines? Can rhetorical mechanisms be applied to architecture to coordinate social action? These are some of the key questions addressed in this book, which revolves around an inventory of rhetorical figures found in architecture and visual arts.

This research constitutes an accessible "proto-manual" of rhetorical tools, strategies, and mechanisms by which architecture (among other design disciplines) might be thought of, elucidated, and communicated. Greater awareness of the system that architects use (often intuitively) would make the approach to the process of creation more secure, less arbitrary, and more inclusive of more alternatives. The present study adds a novel critical insight into specific spatial and visual works and, by extension, their design processes. In doing so, this study uncovers a particular methodology of creative disciplines beyond intuition and seemingly magical inspiration.

In this respect, *Colors of Rhetoric* maps the creative relationships between architecture and various figures of rhetoric. While some significant theoretical studies have investigated architecture as a language, there are very few comprehensive book-length studies that assess the potential use of a large number of rhetorical procedures as tools for architectural thought and creation. The present study is also intended to fill the existing gap in works that offer a categorization and detailed explanation of the architectural production over the last three decades from the point of view of the discipline itself—namely, architectural design.

This project responds to the present-day reality of design practices, in which the boundaries between fields are disappearing. The increasing number of intersections between disciplines, as well as a praxis based on multidisciplinary teams, indicate that the traditional frames, capacities, and ranges of all design fields are changing. As Jonathan Hill states, the most positive characteristic of architectural design is its ability to combine intuitive and rational thought and ideas from various disciplines.[1] The purpose of the present study is to demonstrate that rhetorical methods and operations could be a powerful tool for dealing with the phenomena of creation beyond specific design areas. The project also indicates that rhetorical mechanisms and figures might be the means by which all design disciplines converge. Thus, this research expands the traditional boundaries of architecture and design learning concerning all design disciplines while also providing evidence of the diversity of architectural and spatial practices.

... 1
Jonathan Hill, "Building a Drawing and Drawing a Building," *Nordisk Arkitekturforskning (NA Nordic Journal of Architectural Research)* 15, no. 4 (April 19, 2013).

RHETORIC AS THE ART OF PERSUASION

Rhetoric is communication that attempts to coordinate
social action. For this reason, rhetorical communication is
explicitly pragmatic. Its goal is to influence human choices
on specific matters that require immediate attention.
—Gerald A. HAUSER, *Introduction to Rhetorical Theory,* 2002.

Rhetoric, understood as the use of persuasive techniques, is the basis for
another significant line of argument within this research. Persuasion has
been used for many purposes throughout history. Unfortunately, over the
last two centuries, rhetoric has gained a negative reputation because it
has been deliberately overused to mislead and manipulate. The overuse
of empty promises and half-truths to fulfill the purposes of propaganda
and advertising has revealed the dangers of rhetoric. Manipulation has too
often become a synonym for persuasion and, by extension, of rhetoric. The
current study emphasizes the positive uses of rhetoric and its constructive
capacity for alerting people about social issues.

As Hauser states, rhetoric influences individual and collective
choices, focusing on the specific challenges to our societies and urban
environments that require immediate attention. Therefore, this book
argues that rhetorical figures are powerful interrogative and critical
tools that stimulate our social and collective conscience regarding critical
questions, challenges, and social issues. On the other hand, it also offers
alternative ways to understand the world around us. By investigating the
relationships among form, event, body, subject, matter, and space, the
present study reflects on the spatial and social conventions, contradictions,
and dislocations found in everyday contemporary life.

COLORS OR FIGURES OF RHETORIC

As defined by Richard A. Lanham, the term rhetorical "figure" (which
includes the metaphor, antithesis, and metonymy, among many others)
refers, in its most general sense, to any device or pattern of language in
which meaning or form is enhanced or changed.[2] Theorists have differed
in classifying and naming the **figures**, and, thus, any single classification
would be prescriptive; however, two fundamental ideas guide all
taxonomies: (1) distinctions between changes in **form** and **meaning**,
whether of a word, words, clause, speech, or writing; and (2) the size or
scope of the change.

In this sense, the broadest way to classify figures is to divide them into
"tropes" and "schemes." A *trope* (from the Greek, "turn") refers to the use
of a word or words to mean something other than its typical meaning. A
scheme (from the Greek, "form" or "figure") refers to words that preserve
their literal meaning but are placed in a significant arrangement of some
kind. Tropes operate at the semantic level, changing the meaning of a word
or words; schemes operate at the syntactic level and change the form,
shape, and organization of the information. Furthermore, in the context in
which "form" is an essential element of visual language, a change of form
usually (if not always) involves a change of meaning. Therefore, in this
frame, in which the image is the protagonist, the division between tropes
and schemes seems irrelevant.

... 2
Richard A. Lanham, *A Handlist of Rhetorical
Terms*, Second Edition (University of California
Press, 1991).

Color is a term that represents the visual and artistic world, as it (generally) refers to all the figures and (more specifically) to the figures of form. Since this book's central argument does not distinguish between figures of meaning and figures of form, the term "color" (of rhetoric) is used to refer to any rhetorical procedure, whether trope or scheme. Indeed, the title of this book includes "colors" and not "figures" due to the visual character of the term.

As Jacques Durand states, another way to understand a rhetorical color is as an artificial and conscious transgression of a norm, whether the norms of language, of morality, of society, of logic, or of physical reality.[3] As transgressions, the analysis of figures focuses on the notions of decontextualization, deviation, disjunction, and conflict. The current study extrapolates to different spatial and visual disciplines regarding what rhetoric does (which is no more than putting "things" together in alternative ways to create a new whole).

PRECEDENTS

To associate a theme with another diverse and unrelated reality through some link is a constant, sometimes unconscious, operation in any creative process. In 1976, as part of the collective exhibition *The MAN transFORMS*, curated by Hans Hollein at Cooper Hewitt Museum, Oswald Mathias Ungers proposed a method for designing using images and visual analogies rather than creating from scratch, assuming that the designer's mind was not a tabula rasa. In 1982, this notion that the imaginative processes of thinking and designing are a fundamental procedure of conceptualizing an unrelated, diverse reality using images, metaphors, and comparisons was collected in Ungers's *Morphologie: City Metaphors*.[4]

The book and the related exhibition explored the relationship between rhetoric and architecture as a method of creation. *City Metaphors* is composed of 50 cities expressed by a plan or diagram (as the architectural image). The urban schemes are associated and juxtaposed with 50 distant realities (natural organisms and networks, artifacts, or objects of everyday life as the associative image) that are not part of the original cities but have morphological affinities. A term describing the formal relationship and conceptual content of both images completes the comparison, or simile. After all, what the German architect and professor is offering is to think and create "architecture" through relations of similarity and three specific figures of rhetoric: analogy, simile, and metaphor.

Architecture has used (and often abused) the metaphor, usually to offer a partial explanation of the generation of a project, adding nothing besides a mere illustrative and direct comparison of resemblances. *City Metaphors* is one of the very few comprehensive and complete studies that assess the potential of using a large number of rhetorical procedures as tools of thought and creation in architecture and urbanism.

The present research can be understood as a continuation of Ungers's proposed method for thinking through images by expanding its scope to include additional rhetorical mechanisms. It extends the method proposed by Ungers to other types of relationships, such as difference, opposition, contiguity, double meaning, and contradiction, to provide possibilities of invention, imagination, and communication. At the same time, this study does not limit the methodology to three figures, as it examines more than a hundred rhetorical figures and their applications to the processes of architecture and visual arts.

... 3
Jacques Durand, "Rhetoric and the Advertising Image," *Australian Journal of Cultural Studies 1*, no. 2 (December 1983): 29–61.
... 4
Oswald Mathias Ungers, *Morphologie: City Metaphors* (Walther König, 2011).

From a theoretical and historical perspective, Emmanuel Petit's book *Irony; or, The Self-Critical Opacity of Postmodern Architecture*[5] reassesses postmodern architecture at the end of the 20th century through the concept of irony and the work of five architects: Peter Eisenman, Arata Isozaki, Rem Koolhaas, Stanley Tigerman, and Robert Venturi. As Petit explains, irony manifested in the work of these architects as an aesthetic tool as a form of existential comedy and cultural satire. Meanwhile, the present work concentrates on a greater number of rhetorical figures and extends the range of architecture and art works examined. In this way, this book completes the historical and social analysis of architectural production and provides new perspectives from which visual and spatial disciplines can be understood.

Concerning visual language, rhetoric seems to have taken refuge in advertising, as it is the only discipline that explicitly uses rhetorical figures as creative mechanisms. In that regard, Roland Barthes, in his celebrated article in visual semiotics, "Rhetoric of the Image," was the first to link images and rhetoric and to propose a method of analyzing images based on rhetorical concepts.[6] Until then, verbal language, whether written or spoken, consciously made the most use of this discipline. Barthes outlined the foundation of a rhetoric of the image, suggesting that "this rhetoric could only be established on the basis of a quite considerable inventory."

An essential reference of the expansion of rhetorical methods and concerns from language to images is Jacques Durand's study "Rhétorique et image publicitaire," originally published in 1970. "Rhetoric and the Advertising Image" (the English translation) was published in 1983 in the *Australian Journal of Cultural Studies.*[7] It was later republished as "Rhetorical Figures in the Advertising Image" in *Marketing and Semiotics.*[8]

In this study, following Barthes' in-depth analysis of an advertisement, Durand proposed an inventory of visual figures showing that not just some but all classical figures of rhetoric can be found in advertising images. He stated that most of the creative ideas behind the most effective advertisements can be interpreted as transpositions of classical figures. Similarly, we consider that rhetoric contributes to architecture, as almost all rhetorical figures may generate new ideas.

Colors of Rhetoric replicates Durand's methodology, applying it to architecture and visual arts. Jacques Durand's research on advertisement is re-examined in Chapter Eight ("The rhetoric of advertising") in Gillian Dyer's book *Advertising as Communication,*[9] which understands advertising as a form of communication in contemporary society and places it in its broader cultural and economic context. In this vein, Gui Bonsiepe's study "Visual/Verbal Rhetoric," published in the *Journal of the Ulm School of Design*, explains how a modern system of rhetoric might help address advertising by analyzing various figures of rhetoric appearing in print advertisements.[10]

The Language of Landscape[11] by Anne Whiston Spirn is a crucial text in landscape theory and has had a broad influence in numerous fields outside design, from history to choreography to poetry. By combining theory and practice; discussions of the thoughts of renowned landscape authors; and analyses of urban, rural, and natural landscapes, the book argues that "the language of landscape exists with its own syntax, grammar, and metaphors" and that "we imperil ourselves by failing to learn to read and speak this language."

... 5
Emmanuel Petit, *Irony; or, the Self-Critical Opacity of Postmodern Architecture* (New Haven: Yale University Press, 2013).
... 6
Roland Barthes, "Rhetoric of the Image," in *Image-Music-Text: Essays*, trans. Stephen Heath (London: Fontana, 1977), 32–51. ("Rhétorique de l'image," *Communications 4* [1964]).
... 7
"Rhétorique et image publicitaire" by Jacques Durand was originally published in *Communications* no. 15, (Paris: Editions du Seuil, 1970). The translation to English was done by Theo van Leeuwen, and published in *Australian Journal of Cultural Studies 1*, no. 2, (Perth, December 1983): 29–61.
... 8
Jacques Durand, "Rhetorical Figures in the Advertising Image," in *Marketing and Semiotics*, ed. Jean Umiker-Sebeok, 77 vols., Approaches to Semiotics (De Gruyter Mouton, 1987), 295–318.
... 9
Gillian Dyer, *Advertising as Communication*, Studies in Communication. (Methuen & Co, 1982; Routledge, 1988).
... 10
Gui Bonsiepe, "Visuell-verbale Rhetorik /Visual-verbal Rhetoric," *Journal of the Ulm School of Design*, no. 14–16 (1965): 23–40.
... 11
Anne Whiston Spirn, *The Language of Landscape* (Yale University Press, 1998).

The book is very useful for the current project owing to its didactic and interdisciplinary nature; emphasis on photography; analysis of a wide range of landscapes and landscape authors; integration of practice and theory; and, above all, the visual thinking that drives the integration of all these aspects. Spirn states that "landscape is pragmatic, poetic, rhetorical, polemical. It is language." In this regard, it needs to be clarified that the current investigation does not focus on demonstrating whether architecture is or is not a language, as explained in these pages. The focus is on the mechanisms of rhetorical devices as generative, creative, and persuasive tools.

BOOK STRUCTURE AND CONTENTS

In addition to this introduction on the research topic and approach, this book is structured into three parts.

Part 1: Understanding the system and its elements

This part outlines the role of rhetoric in verbal language and examines the rhetorical elements while addressing the main differences between verbal and visual language. It frames the meaning of rhetorical figures as the feigned transgressions of a norm. The profusions of classical figures are categorized into a few fundamental operations and relations. These mechanisms are explained first according to the form of expression, the nature of the operation, or the category of change applied to the elements. They are then re-explained according to the nature of the relationship linking the elements of the proposition.

Regarding rhetorical play and language, at the most basic level, two elements exist: form and content. As mentioned before, this division is not accurate enough to be transposed to architecture. This is because the content of architecture, in most (if not all) cases, deals with form. Hence, this part also identifies the rhetorical components in architecture and clusters them into three broad categories: context, content, and concept.

Part 2: Inventory of Colors of rhetoric

The second and core part of the book includes an alphabetical taxonomy of more than a hundred rhetorical figures found in architecture and visual arts. In most cases, one or two double pages describe each rhetorical mechanism through a wide range of examples of spatial practices. The first page of each term introduces the rhetorical figure by providing its verbal meaning and root. The figure is then exemplified with a short passage chosen from literature, film, music, or public speech.

In the following pages, the mechanism is observed in one, two, or three different visual and spatial disciplines—architecture, art, and drawing. Together with the illustration of the work, the inventory includes a brief analysis of how the main rhetorical figure is understood in the visual realm. Whenever there is more than one visual work that expresses a rhetorical figure, the chosen visual examples usually share formal similarities. Additionally, most of the visual examples work with more than one figure; all secondary figures are listed next to the work to establish relationships among various strategies and works.

All the rhetorical figures in the inventory are examined to create a sense of parallelism between verbal and visual language. The identification of figures operating in various works facilitates a comprehensive understanding of the methodology of creation and, consequently, their potential and future application. (1) The literary figures are chosen from renowned examples of oratory, poetry, drama, prose, music, and film. The visual study-cases are grouped into three broad categories: (2) "architecture" (which includes urbanism, landscape, art, and interior or industrial design, among other spatial practices); (3) "art" (including photography, painting, film, television, advertising, and graphic design, among other media); and (4) "drawing" and graphical works (such as projections, music notations, maps, and diagrams) while emphasizing the communication phase of the creative process.

In this sense, the graphical works and drawings allow for a more specific exploration of the traditional capacity of these figures to serve as tools of persuasion. The selection criteria for the iconic works that drive the inventory are also governed by the potential of the images to raise questions about contemporary and social issues. An attempt is made to include and express the complete spectrum of experience, from the individual to the collective. However, the inventory could also emphasize the individual human scale of the theme.

Damien Hirst claims that the collage is the greatest idea of the 20th century and that he understands everything as a collage. Something similar occurs in the current project, as collages work primarily with the operations of decontextualization. Collages select certain existing objects and reuse them by re-contextualizing them in a new environment—the artwork. Each element and fragment that makes up a collage (and the collage itself) acquire a new meaning due to the combination, integration, and interaction of all of the elements, which synthesizes how rhetorical mechanisms work (indeed, this study might be expanded to focus solely on collages). Therefore, in this study, the collage—as a concept, technique, and outcome—constitutes a critical manifestation of the direct visual expression of rhetorical mechanisms. Thus, collages and hybrid drawings were preferred when creating the visual inventory of figures.

Interdisciplinary examples and case studies are taken from various parts of the world, art and design fields, and periods, thus ensuring that the book will interest a diverse international audience, from practicing architects and designers to academics and students.

This book is intended to serve as something of a practical guide to creative and persuasive mechanisms in architecture, spatial practices, and visual arts with multiple layers and different levels of reading. As such, this book is highly accessible to students from the undergraduate to postgraduate level, as well as practitioners, academics, and researchers of design and visual culture. Modern and contemporary case studies are drawn from many visual disciplines and from all around the world to ensure this book's relevance to a diverse audience of readers who are interested in the processes of creation and communication.

As listed in the bibliography at the end of the book, regarding verbal language, many sources have been consulted to realize the inventory of the colors of rhetoric. However, two primary sources—*A Handlist of Rhetorical Terms* by Richard A. Lanham and Gideon Burton's website "Silva rhetoricae" (http://rhetroci.byu.edu)—have been followed for the production of this inventory and the definitions of the rhetorical terms.

Finally, in the inventory, the "Metaphor" entry has intentionally been left blank given the overuse of this figure to explain the genesis or result of many architectural projects. Besides, most (if not all) rhetorical figures may be understood as subtypes of the metaphor.

Part 3: Classifications, indexes, and bibliography

The final section includes some classical categorizations of the figures of rhetoric and diverse arrays of indexes and lists. Thus, this section contains cross-references of the works and mechanisms proposed throughout the book.

SUMMARY

Colors of Rhetoric analyzes a large and heterogeneous group of visual and spatial examples—for example, buildings, architectural projects, cities, landscapes, photographs, paintings, sculptures, performances, interiors, furniture, films, advertisements, drawings, maps. In doing so, this book identifies more than a hundred "turns" through which the creative process can be approached. Thus, this book expands the comprehension of the thought processes that underly design. This project expands the traditional borders of architecture and design by responding to the current reality surrounding design disciplines in which the limits between fields are becoming increasingly blurred. This book presents an effective way of understanding creativity in the visual realm based on evidence of the diversity of architecture and spatial practices.

The current research aims to accomplish the following:

(1) Reveal and address a series of systematic design strategies to enrich the creative spectrum of architectural and spatial practices.

(2) Bring some transparency to the design process to reduce the degree of subjectivity and uncertainty associated with the creative disciplines.

(3) Provide a new way to understand and read paradigmatic works of modern and contemporary architecture and art.

(4) Contribute to architectural education by inviting and motivating students to learn and apply these rhetorical procedures and devices as methods of creation and communication.

(5) Awaken the general awareness of several social challenges in our society by highlighting the role of rhetorical figures as drivers for social change and action.

ILLUSTRATIONS

Every effort has been made to identify copyright holders and obtain their permission for the use of copyright material. The author and publishers apologize for any errors and omissions, and, if notified, will endeavor to correct these at the earliest available opportunity.

Part 1

Understanding the system and its elements

VERBAL AND ICONIC LANGUAGE

Some basic ideas of language and the main differences between verbal and visual language need to be explained before addressing the study on rhetorical mechanisms applied to the visual and spatial world.

Concerning language, the first question to be addressed deals with the meaning of the term "sign." All languages are systems of signs governed by codes. A *sign* is an object, phenomenon, or material action that represents or replaces another by nature or convention. It consists of two inseparable parts: the *signifier* (the perceivable part of the sign and the material form perceptible by the senses, for example, the letters h-a-t) and the *signified* (the understandable part of the sign or the semantic content associated with the signifier). In other words, the signified is essentially the concept or idea evoked by the signifier, for example, the meaning of the word *hat*. The signified, or meaning, is determined by the system and the context.

In the Aristotelian tradition, the sign is broken down into three parts: (1) the signifier; (2) the signified; and (3) the *referent* (the concrete thing to which the sign refers, for example, a real hat). The referent is the being or object of reality beyond the linguistic element that the sign refers to. Charles Sanders Pierce also incorporates (4) the *interpreter* as another major element of a sign.

In short, a linguistic sign is a reality that can be perceived by one or more senses and refers to another real plane that is not present. It consists of a signifier, a signified, and a referent, all of which are inextricably linked by significance. The relationship between the signifier and signified determines one of the many ways to classify the different types of signs. From this viewpoint, signs can be divided into two classes: iconic (commonly known as visual, representational, non-arbitrary) and verbal (digital, non-representational, arbitrary).

As Professor Ana García-Valcárcel Muñoz-Repiso explains in "Didactic use of iconic media," the previous classification highlights the first difference between visual and verbal language. Each language uses different types of signs—visual language uses **iconic** signs, while verbal uses **digital** signs.

To understand what a digital sign is, consider two watches—an analog wristwatch with hands and a digital watch in which a number represents the time. The main difference between the two representations of time is that the analog clock conveys a sense of continuity (think of the seconds hand); that is, the present is represented to the future and the past. By contrast, the digital clock represents time in an exact way in the present. The representation of time is produced in intervals as the numbers change; thus, it seems that time is broken into discontinuous units. Similarly, the "digital" qualifier refers to this discontinuity condition, the "either this/or that" of the verbal signs.

Peirce explains that an iconic sign bears some resemblance to the object to which it refers. The sign is iconic when it either has at least one of the properties of the represented object or denoted properties. However, the relationship between signifier and meaning in verbal signals is **arbitrary**, as there is no correspondence between the parts of the sign.

Consider, for example, /dog/. The sequence of these three letters in English has no resemblance or natural relationship with the reality it represents; it is expressed through a convention. In fact, the same referent is designated very differently across languages: /dog/perro/chien/. For this reason, verbal signs are considered arbitrary. If you think of the rhetorical figure known as "onomatopoeias," a remote connection between the signifier and the object they refer to is detectable despite being verbal signs. These signs mimic the sound of something to signify it.

In iconic signs, there is a visual isomorphism relationship between the signifier and meaning. In other words, the representation is interesting and reveals its close (almost literal) formal relationship with the reality to which it refers. Depending on the degree of similarity between the sign and the object it refers to, three successive levels of iconicity can be established from conventional drawing elements: image, shape (line), and text. From this point of view, the image or photograph is the most iconic, followed by line drawing and text.

Signs that make verbal language are arbitrary and considered **trivial** signs, in the sense that their meaning, not their "form," matters. As their aspect appearance is unimportant, they are classified as **transparent**. In this regard, it should be clarified that any sign can assume different roles simultaneously. A sign can work as a digital and visual sign at the same time. This explains the basic and generic properties of the two languages separately and in opposition to each other. However, when a letter, a word, or a sentence is included in any piece of visual art, the verbal element also functions as a visual sign that assumes the same role as all other graphic elements.

Imagine you are in a restaurant in South Korea. You speak no Korean and want an apple. Probably the quickest way to communicate the information to your Korean waiter, who speaks no other language, is to draw an apple. The reason is simple: instead of using a verbal sign (it is necessary to know the code to interpret or understand the message), you are using a visual sign that does not require any **code**. To the waiter or receiver of the message, the more the drawing (sign) of the apple looks like the reality (less arbitrarily) of the apple (reference), the easier it is to understand that you want an apple.

VERBAL LANGUAGE (TEXT)	ICONIC LANGUAGE (IMAGE)
ARBITRARY signs	NON-ARBITRARY signs
TRIVIAL | TRANSPARENT signs	OPAQUE | INTERESTING signs
CODE	NON-CODE
FINITE set of elements | Coded by a finite set of rules (phonological system, grammar)	INFINITE set of elements | Ordinations un-coded
LESS NOISE | The intended message is conveyed more accurately	MORE NOISE | It is easier for some details to distract from the fundamental communication message
MONOSEMIC | Less ambiguous language	POLYSEMIC | More ambiguous language
Easy to refer to CONCEPTS | Ideas	Easy to refer to CONCRETE objects
Provides CONCEPTUAL information (principles, ideas)	Provides SENSORY data (shape, texture, color...)
Easy to give meaning to certain types of expressions	Limited meaning for certain types of expressions (all, much, little, pretty, enough, is, should be, was...)
LINEAR | SEQUENTIAL element presentation	NONLINEAR | SIMULTANEOUS element presentation
DISCONTINUITY	CONTINUITY
TIME | Temporary dimension	SPACE | Space dimension

This fact leads directly to another aspect that distinguishes the two types of language. A finite number of rules govern verbal language. Thus, you need to know the rules or code to understand the message. Iconic language, however, is an un-coded system consisting of a virtually infinite set of elements. A brief set of rules governs architectural drawings, representational systems, and architectural graphic standards. Once these rules are learned, their application or omission provides a richer expressive language.

Furthermore, iconic language is much more open, polysemous, and indeterminate than verbal language. In principle, the picture of an apple can raise many more meanings than the word *apple*. Note that when decoding an image, the receiver's experiences or personal universe are a determinant factor. This experience triggers numerous interpretative differences, meaning that different receivers can read the same image differently.

The main properties and differences between both languages—as well as the concept of signs and their components, the material form (signifier) and the semantic content (signified)—allow a much clearer understanding of what the rhetorical figures are.

CLASSIFICATION OF COLORS OF RHETORIC

As mentioned in the introduction, theorists have presented various definitions for the term "figure" and its various types. Most classification methods distinguish between changes in form, changes in meaning, or the size or scope of the change. In general, the term "figure" or "color" refers to any device or pattern of language by which meaning or form is enhanced or changed. The term has two subcategories: colors of words and colors of thought, which are outlined below.

1. Colors or figures of words:

- *Trope*: The use of a word to mean something other than its ordinary meaning (e.g., a metaphor).
- *Scheme*:
    i.   Any kind of figure or pattern of words.
    ii. A figure of arranging words such that the literal sense of the word is not affected by the arrangement.

2. Colors or figures of thought: A large-scale trope or scheme, or a combination of both (e.g., an allegory).

However, this categorization is prescriptive since all terms have been used interchangeably at one time or another to refer to the numerous linguistic devices.

In this context, it is essential to understand how the rhetorical devices work and how the relevant elements are affected and modified by them. Rhetorical figures have also been defined as artificial and conscious transgressions of norms of language, morality, society, logic, or physical reality. In this sense, Durand gives a straightforward and clarifying example:

> In a letter to the "Dear Abby" column of the women's magazine *Bonnes Soirees* (11 February, 1968) a reader writes: "I married a bear." If we were to take this proposition literally, it would tell of a transgression of the social, sexual and legal order: in our society it is illegal to marry animals. This transgression plays a double role. Firstly, its

implausibility in the given context warns the readers that they should not take it literally and induces them to reduce it to its initial, simple form: "My husband is (as brutal as) a bear," or simply "My husband is a brute." But it also, even if only feigned, brings the satisfaction of a repressed desire, a satisfaction which, precisely because it is feigned, can be enjoyed with impunity.

Therefore, from a general point of view, rhetorical figures can be understood as deviations, decontextualizations, disjunctions, conflicts, transgressions, or departures from an accepted standard to generate new, unexpected relationships. From this perspective, all of these terms are synonyms for the term "figure" and, thus, are subjects of this investigation. Therefore, definitions for these terms are provided below:

Deviation. The action of departing from an established course or accepted standard in ways that are unexpected and far from anticipated or common modes.

Decontextualization. Out of context. Divergence. A serious incompatibility between two or more opinions, principles, or interests. To take an element from its usual context and put it in a different one, thereby changing/transforming its original meaning.

Disjunction. The act of disjoining or the condition of being disjoined. Separation, disunion. The relationship between the terms of a disjunctive proposition. A lack of correspondence or consistency.

Conflict. Competitive or opposing actions of incompatibles. A situation in which it is difficult for two things to coexist or be true at the same time. Regarding architecture, Bernard Tschumi defines the relationship of conflict between spaces and activities as follows: "Most relations, of course, are more complex. You can also sleep in the kitchen. And fight and love. Such shifts are not without meaning."

Transgression. An act, process, or instance of going beyond set or prescribed limits.

Distortion. The act of twisting or altering something from its true, natural, or original state.

Ambiguity. The quality or state of being understood in two or more possible senses, especially in meaning. A word or expression that can be understood in two or more ways. Semiotically speaking, ambiguity is a mode by which the rules of the code are violated. Messages can also be totally ambiguous by violating both phonetic and lexical rules.

RHETORICAL OPERATIONS AND RELATIONS

Following ancient tradition, rhetoric involves two (opposite) levels of speech: "literal" and "figurative." Literal language always means exactly what it says. Meanwhile, figurative language uses words, phrases, sentences, and clauses to convey a message without directly saying it; thus, it departs from the literal use of words. Since rhetorical figures are operations and strategies that allow the passage from one level to another, figurative, expressive, and creative language uses various rhetorical colors to convey meaning in unusual and creative ways.

Consequently, rhetorical devices can be thought of as operations that start from simple propositions to modify certain elements to make the message more expressive and persuasive. Following this logic, Jacques Durand's taxonomy organizes such devices into two dimensions:

— The nature of the operation (1) or the category of change. These operations involve the form of the sign or expression (the signifier).
— The nature of the relation (2) linking the elements of the proposition, sentence, paragraph, clauses, or expressions. Relations involve the form of content or meaning (the signified).

On the contrary, in "Figures of Rhetoric in Advertising Language," Edward F. McQuarrie and David Glen Nick propose a classification of rhetorical figures in advertising based on the gradient of deviation:[1]

— Rhetorical operation
— The size (3) or scope of the change or deviation

In both classifications, a limited number of rhetorical operations serve to classify and order the large number of existing figures. In 1983, Duran distinguished four main operations: adjunction, deletion, substitution, and rearrangement. Adjunction and deletion are fundamental operations, while substitution and rearrangement are combinations of adjunction and deletion. In 1996, McQuarrie and Nick again used four categories of change, but two of these are different from their previously described operations: repetition, reversal, substitution, and destabilization.

A. *Adjunction*, or addition, occurs when one or more elements are added to a proposition. Repetition is a special case, as it is the adjunction of identical elements.

B. *Deletion*, subtraction, or omission occurs when one or more elements are deleted from a proposition.

C. *Substitution* (deletion + adjunction) is a deletion followed by an adjunction. In other words, an element is taken out and replaced by another.[2]

D. *Rearrangement*, or permutation, consists of two reciprocal substitutions; thus, it is the exchange of two elements of the proposition.

E. *Reversal*, or inversion, is a particular case of rearrangement in which one or more elements are arranged in an unusual way.

F. *Destabilization* occurs when one or more elements make a proposition unstable.

Within the context of advertising, Durand classifies figures in advertising into the following five relations: identity, similarity, opposition, difference, and false homology. Durand further divides the last relation into double meaning and paradox. Since a paradox is a rhetorical figure, the term "contradiction" will be used to refer to paradoxical relations to avoid confusion instead.

The first four relationships can be encompassed under the umbrella of broader notions, such as the *contiguity* relationship. Proximity or contiguity must be included as one of the rhetorical relationships since there are two theories of rhetorical figures. One group of theorists consider the METAPHOR the mother of all figures. Others opine that METONYMY serves this function.

A metaphor works exclusively with similar relationships, while metonymy uses a much broader spectrum of relationships. Metonymy replaces one

... 1
Edward F. McQuarrie and David Glen Mick, "Figures of Rhetoric in Advertising Language," *Journal of Consumer Research* 22, no. 4 (1996): 424–438.

... 2
Nicolas Ruwet proposes two additional operations: "expansion" and "reduction;" but these are subcategories of substitution ("majorative" and "minorative" substitutions) differing according to the nature of the relation. Nicolas Ruwet, *Introduction à La Grammaire Générative*. (Librairie PLON, 1969, pp. 250–251).

word, phrase, or clause with another that has a relationship (spatial, temporal, or casual contiguity) with the first. The association between the elements is based on contiguity in metonymy, while the substitution is based on similarity in a metaphor. In fact, from this point of view, the metaphor could be understood as a kind of metonymy since similarity is included within contiguity (but not the other way around).

Taxonomy of Rhetorical Figures in Advertising, Jacques Durand, 1970.

RELATION between elements		Rhetorical OPERATION			
		A Adjunction [Addition, amplification]	B Deletion [Subtraction, Omission]	C Substitution [Replacement, Exchange]	D Rearrangement [Transposition, Permutation]
1 Identity		Repetition	● **Ellipsis** [053]	● **Hyperbole** [067]	Inversion
2 Similarity	of Form	Rhyme	Circumlocution	Allusion	Hendiadys
	of Content	● **Simile** [092]		● METAPHOR [074]	Homology
3 Difference		● **Accumulation** [001]	Suspension	● METONYMY [075]	● **Asyndeton** [038]
4 Opposition	of Form	Anachronism	Dubitation	Periphrasis	● **Anacoluthon** [012]
	of Content	● **Antithesis** [031]	Reticence	Euphemism	● **Chiasmus** [043]
5 False homology	Double Meaning	● **Antanaclasis** [020]	Tautology	● **Calembour** (PUN) [088]	● **Antimetabole** [026]
	Paradox	● PARADOX [079]	Preteriton	● **Antiphrasis** [028]	● **Antilogy** [025]

Taxonomy of Rhetorical Figures in Advertising, McQuarrie and Nick, 1996.

I. Figuration

**All rhetorical figures
(artful deviations)**

II. Figurative mode

Scheme
(excess regularity)

Less   COMPLEX   More

Trope
(irregularity)

Less   COMPLEX   More

III. Rhetorical Operation

REPETITION	REVERSAL	SUBSTITUTION	DESTABILIZATION
Rhyme Chime ● **Alliteration** [008]	● **Antimetabole** [026]	● **Hyperbole** [067]	● METAPHOR [074]
● **Anaphora** [016] Epistrophe Epanalepsis Anadiplosis	● **Antithesis** [031]	● **Ellipsis** [053]	● PUN [088]
● Parison (**Isocolon**) [071]		● Epanorthosis (**Correctio**) [048] ● **Rethorical Question** [059]	● IRONY [070]
		● METONYMY [075]	● PARADOX [079]

Lower   GRADIENT OF DEVIATION   Higher

Therefore, at a basic level, rhetorical mechanisms can be categorized into seven relationships:

A. CONTIGUITY:
1. *Identity*
2. *Similarity*
3. *Difference*
4. *Opposition*
5. Proximity or *contiguity*

B. FALSE HOMOLOGY
6. *Double Meaning*
7. *Contradiction*

Rhetorical Colors based on Jacques Durand's classification

RELATION	Rhetorical **OPERATION** (Category of Change)				
	A **Addition** [Adjunction, Multiplication]		B **Deletion** [Subtraction, Omission]	C **Substitution** [Replacement, Exchange]	D **Rearrangement** [Transposition, Permutation]
	Repetition	Amplification			
1. CONTIGUITY	Apomnemonysis [034]	Aetiologia [005] ● AMPLIFICATIO [011] Apodixis [033] Auxesis [039] ● Climax [044]		● **Alleotheta** [007] ● **Anamnesis** [014] Anthypallage [024] Antiprosopopoeia [029] Antonomasia [032] ● METONYMY [075] Prosopopoeia [085] Proverb [086].	Anthimeria [023]
1.1 Identity	● **Alliteration** [008] ● **Anaphora** [016] Assonance [036] Conduplicatio [046]		● **Ellipsis** [053]	● **Hyperbole** [067]	Anastrophe [017] Anoiconometon [019] ● HYPERBATON [066]
1.2 Similarity	Analogy [013] Antapodosis [021] Epicrisis [057] Isocolon [071] Polyptoton [082] ● Simile [092]	● **Accumulatio** [001] Congeries [047] Epexegesis [056] Epitheton [058] Scesis onomaton [090] Synonymia [098]	● Erotesis [059] Expeditio [061]	Allegory [006] Ecphonesis [052] Fable [062] Fictio [063] Image [069] ● METAPHOR [074] Onomatopoeia [076]	Parenthesis [080]
1.3 Difference	Commoratio [045] Correctio [048] Disjunctio [051] Exergasia [060] Polysyndeton [084]	Alloiosis [009] Anatomy [018] Appositio [035] Bomphiologia [040] Diallage [049] Dinumeratio [050] ● ENARGIA [055] Pragmatographia [084] Systrophe [099] Topographia [100] Topothesia [101]	● **Asyndeton** [038]	Antiptosis [030] ● ENALLAGE [054] Hypallage [065] Syllepsis [093] Synaeresis [094] Synecdoche [096]	Cacosyntheton [041] Hysterologia [068] Hysteron Proteron [068]
1.3.1 Opposition	● **Antithesis** [031]	Syncrisis [095]	Anantapodoton [015]	Antenantiosis [022] Horismus [064]	● **Anacoluthon** [012] ● **Chiasmus** [043]
2. FALSE HOMOLOGY					
2.1 Double Meaning	● **Antanaclasis** [020] Ploce [081]	Acrostic [002] Adianoeta [003] Sarcasmus [089]	Meiosis [073] ● **Significatio** [091]	Amphibologia [010] Asteismus [037] Paronomasia [081] ● PUN [088]	● **Antimetabole** [026] Palindrome [078]
2.2 Contradiction	Antinomy [027] Charientismus [042]	Adynaton [004] Oxymoron [077] ● PARADOX [079] Synoeciosis [097]	Litotes [072]	● **Antiphrasis** [028] ● IRONY [070]	● **Antilogy** [025]

CONCEPT, CONTENT, AND CONTEXT

Colors of rhetoric are changes, deviations, disorders, distortions, transgressions, departures, conflicts, dysfunctions, or violations of any element of verbal language. These are strategies for the manipulation and variation of discourse across a vast array of linguistic levels, including word forms, word meanings, word arrangements, sentence and clause orders, grammatical rules, syntactical norms and functions, the delivery of a speech, the style of a written piece, and emotional appeals.

The transfer of these word mechanisms to the world of images makes it necessary to first frame and define (even if only generally) which elements are susceptible to deviation and manipulation. Just as letters, syllables, words, phrases, clauses, and text pieces make up verbal language, four essential groups of elements embody visual language. The first of these is the norms and rules that govern descriptive geometry, architectural drawing, and specific techniques of each artistic medium. The three additional categories summarize the visual elements involved in visual rhetoric:

— Visual and graphic rules and norms.
— Concept: the idea(s), meaning, purpose, and conceptual elements of a work.
— Content: the formal and visual elements of a work.
— Context: the physical, social, economic, and cultural background of a work.

At the most basic level, only two elements exist (form and meaning), both of which are implicit in all four groups listed above. At the same time, concept, context, and content are generic enough to cover all the protagonist disciplines of this study. Artful, expressive, and creative transgressions can be particularized and defined in detail, especially concerning the differences in the content of various spatial and visual disciplines. For example, in architecture, rhetorical mechanisms can operate and manipulate space, material, program, function, distribution, organization, color, facade, circulation, level of privacy, structure, facilities, and location, just to name a few elements.

Part 2
Inventory of
Colors of rhetoric

You put together two things that have not been put together
before. And the world is changed. People may not notice at
the time but that doesn't matter. The world has been changed
nonetheless.

—Julian BARNES, *Levels of Life,* 2013.

AMPLIFICATIO(N)
● Techniques of argument
● REPETITIO(N)
● AMPLIFICATIO(N)

Operation:
AMPLIFICATION
Relation:
SIMILARITY

— Synathrouesmus
(G. "collection, union").

See also
Congeries [047].

L. "heaping up"

Accumulatio

Heaping up praise or accusation to emphasize or summarize points or inferences already made.

Thither the extremely large wains bring foison of the fields, flaskets of cauliflowers, floats of spinach, pineapple chunks, Rangoon beans, strikes of tomatoes, drums of figs, drills of Swedes, spherical potatoes and tallies of iridescent kale, York and Savoy, and trays of onions, pearls of the earth, and punnets of mushrooms and custard marrows and fat vetches and bere and rape and red green yellow brown russet sweet big bitter ripe pomellated apples and chips of strawberries and sieves of gooseberries, pulpy and pelurious, and strawberries fit for the princes and raspberries from their canes.

—James JOYCE, *Ulysses*, 1920.

Accumulatio is a color of rhetoric that gathers points, elements, and words correlative to their meaning (synonyms or antonyms), form (syllables and letters), or grammatical function (e.g., whether the word is a verb, adverb, adjective, etc.). In other words, accumulatio lists similar terms or elements together. Thus, it creates a sense of force, amplifying the core idea of the topic and expressing it with increased specificity. It also provides details and interpretations of topics by increasing clarity as much as possible. Accumulatio can also be used to summarize a broad argument. This device often involves some repetition, especially **anaphora** [016] (the repetition of a word or phrase at the beginning of successive clauses or verses).

Bogusław Schaeffer (1929–2019), a prolific Polish composer, musicologist, professor, playwright, and graphic artist, was concerned with the visual and graphic aspects of music. He became famous for his experiments in graphic notation. Varied practices, including the collage, surrealism, and performance-art techniques, inspired his experimental work.

Bogusław SCHAEFFER (1929–2019),
Partytura PR -1⁸, n.d.
© Fundacja Przyjaciół Sztuk AUREA PORTA and
Muzeum Sztuki, Łódź

Schaeffer's innovations in contemporary music included musical scores without notes, scores that used alternative forms of notation such as pictures, blocks of color, diagrams, typescript, decomposition, assemblages, and collages.

Thus, Schaeffer's experimental music scores might be understood as visual transpositions of accumulatio. *Partytura PR -I⁸* is divided into similar boxes or frames scattered on the paper, following a hidden structure. Each of these islands contains a mixture of graphic elements of different sizes and natures. The graphic elements have a uniform density and cover the full support. All clusters (most of which are rectangular collections of elements) gather five or six types of notations (line clouds, ellipsis, circles, curves, line trees, etc.). The families of elements are juxtaposed and framed, generating a kind of labyrinth.

Irena Galanos's ready-mades are another notable example of this figure. Galanos's constructions imply an enumeration of elements that create an unordered collection of grammatical units, all of which express a similar content. This enumeration may be either chaotic or gradual (i.e., following an ascending or descending order). These drawings, part of the project *Metronomics or an asynchronous count. A [Dis]continuous Theater,* represent a small sample of the final step of Galanos's design process in the Master Advanced Design Studio, "Rear Window." Her ready-mades were generated over one semester, and they record the different phases of the design process. Their development began with the count of four elements found in a specific site of Melbourne CBD: Brick, Body, Paver, and Step. Galanos performed in the studio every week, and the wall became a temporary, sporadic, and provisional new site for her project. The wall supported the accumulation of the various elements that made up this theater. As the author states: "Ready-Mades as the final step of the design process. Four counts and their peculiar count-constructions. This is a project that is as close as possible to being entirely about itself."

Six void abstractions and six tactical proposals became the architectural layers to the *[Dis]continuous Theater* designed by Marcella Palma. Human rights, in keeping with "Border +, Control," drove the research. The accumulation and collages of images, drawings, texts, and notations depicting protest, suppression, time, geography, or geology questioned prominent societal structures that had created a space for human rights to be breached.

The theater was a superimposition and accumulation of all the work that had been completed over 14 weeks. The main room of this vertical urban theater represents the three primary actions synthesized in "to take away a fundamental part for no apparent reason." This event was a response to the action of climbing under extreme circumstances. As the author claims, "Border+, Control as a discontinuous theater vibrates, cracks, dislocates, extracts, binds, and depends on the new Cartesian tolerance."

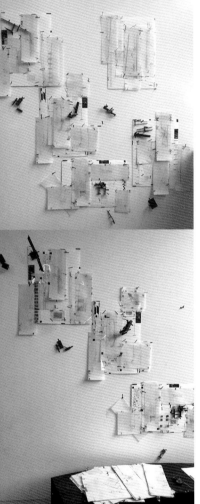

Irena GALANOS, *Metronomics or an asynchronous count. A [Dis]continuous Theater,* 2019, Melbourne, Australia.

Ready-mades.

"Rear Window" Master Advanced Design Studio and Studies Unit by María Fullaondo, First Semester 2019, Monash Art Design Architecture (MADA), Monash University.

Courtesy of Irena Galanos

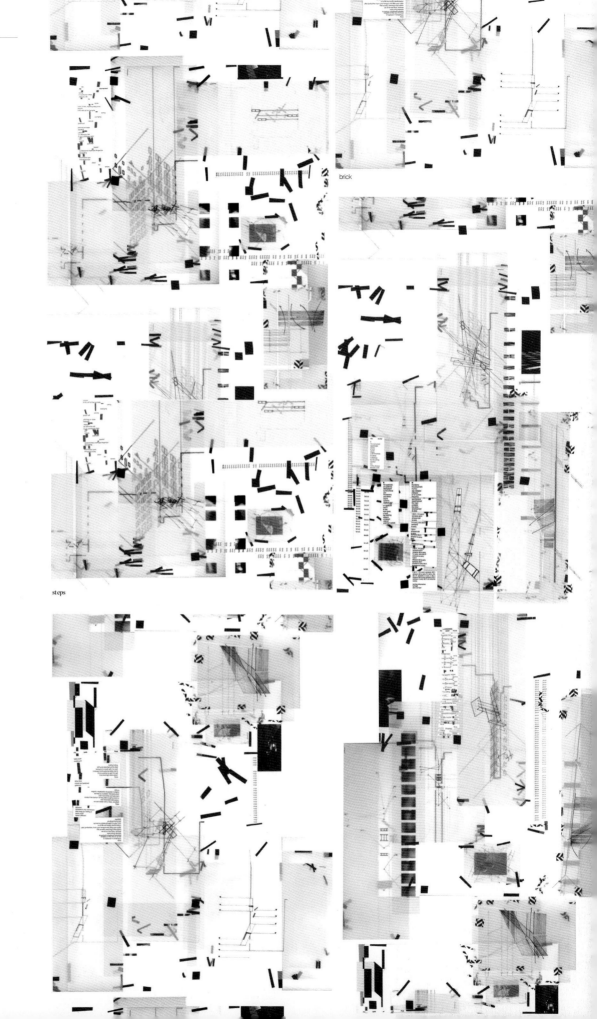

brick

steps

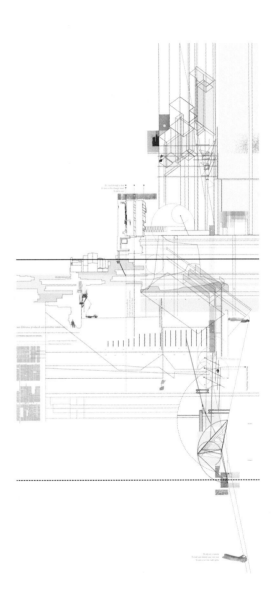

Marcella PALMA, *Border +, Control. A [Dis]continuous Theater,* 2019, Melbourne, Australia.

Final hybrid drawings.

"Rear Window" Master Advanced Design Studio and Studies Unit by María Fullaondo, First Semester 2019, Monash Art Design Architecture (MADA), Monash University.

Courtesy of Marcella Palma

[001] Accumulatio; [003] Adianoeta; [006] Allegory; [009] Alloiosis; [010] Amphibologia; [011] AMPLIFICATIO; Augendi Causa; [039] Auxesis; [046] Conduplicatio; [047] Congeries; Consonance; Emphasis; [067] Hyperbole; [069] METAPHOR; [075] METONYMY; REPETITIO(N); [091] Significatio; [101] Topothesia.

G. "row, line"

Acrostic

A series of lines in which certain letters form a name when read in sequence.

```
                                        abOut 1948 or 50 the number of people
                                        liVing
                          all at oncE
                  equaled the numbeR who had ever lived at any time all added together
                              the Present as far as numbers
                                  gO
                  became equal to the Past
                  we are now in the fUture
                                  hAs
                              iT doubled
                          has It qualrupled
                  all we nOw
                          kNow for sure is
                      the deAd
                      are iN the minority
              they are outnumbereD by us who're living
                          whAt does this do to
                          ouR
                  way of communicaTing...
                  mail's rarely frOm people we know
                  i spend time saVing it
                          to sEnd it to
                  wesleyan noRthwestern or santa cruz
              for fungi'n'arts a Picture's thus given
                              Of this moment in history
                          ePhemera give it
              rest of the mail's bUreacratic fundraising by institutions concerned
                          with heaLth
                              And
                  environmenT
                          iNefficiency
                  glaringly exhibiteD
                              All
                          thRown away
                              Triplate
                              ...
```

—John Cage, *Overpopulation and Art*, 1992.

ARM Architecture (Howard RAGGATT),
Barak Building, 2015, 553 Swanston St,
Melbourne, Australia.

An **acrostic** is a series of lines in which certain letters form a name or a message when read in sequence. There are five types of acrostic poems based on the position of the message.

An example of this in architecture is the *Barak Building* in Melbourne CBD by ARM Architecture. The southern and eastern facades of this 32-story apartment feature a portrait of William Barak, the last traditional 'Elder' of the Wurundjeri-Willam Aboriginal Australian clan. As in acrostic poems, the face is hidden and only comes into view from a distance. As you move closer to the building, the face of William Barak fades from view, and the effect of curved, carved balconies becomes increasingly apparent.

IRONY
●METAPHORICAL &
METONYMIC Substitution
●IRONY
●AMPLIFICATIO(N)

Operation:
AMPLIFICATION
Relation:
DOUBLE MEANING

G. "unintelligible"

Adianoeta

An expression that has an obvious meaning and an unsuspected secret one beneath.

"Come," I said with decision, "we will go back; your health is precious. You are rich, respected, admired, beloved; you are happy, as I once was. You are a man to be missed. For me it is no matter. We will go back; you will be ill, and I cannot be responsible…"
"Enough," he said; "the cough is a mere nothing; it will not kill me. I shall not die of a cough."
"True – true," I replied.

—Edgar Allan POE, *The Cask of Amontillado*, 1846.

An **adianoeta** is a figure of speech dealing with hidden meaning. The word is derived from the ancient Greek *adianoetos*, meaning "unintelligible," "not noticed," or "not understanding." An adianoeta occurs when an expression conveys an additional, subtle meaning hidden underneath its obvious surface meaning. It is a form of IRONY [070], as the hidden meaning often opposes the explicit meaning.

Facsimile by Diller Scofidio + Renfro is an excellent architectural example of a visual adianoeta. The installation's name provides a clue about ambiguity, irony, and a double entendre. The word "facsimile," borrowed from Latin and meaning "to make alike," is any exact copy or reproduction of an old book, manuscript, map, art print, or other items of historical value that are as true to the source as possible. In this work, the American architects play with the ambiguity of what is real, virtual, copied, and imagined today. The project questions the nature of reality by reflecting on the role of the Internet and the effects of a world in which images and information are available everywhere, thus blurring the boundaries between virtual and real.

Facsimile is a screen that travels around the facade of the Moscone Convention Center in San Francisco. It consists of a large monitor suspended on a glass building that moves very slowly along the facade, recording the activity inside the lobby on the second level of the convention center and documenting it as a live video. A screen facing the street broadcasts 24-hour activity and events that happen inside the building.

However, fiction and non-fiction are mixed. Footage of the events going on inside the building is combined with fictional pre-recorded videos. False and imaginary people and events are mixed with actual building occupants, interior spaces, and the natural course of activities. As the architects explain,

> The apparatus could be seen as a scanning device, a magnifying lens, a periscope (a camera at a high elevation looks toward the city), and as an instrument of deception substituting impostors for actual building occupants and spaces.

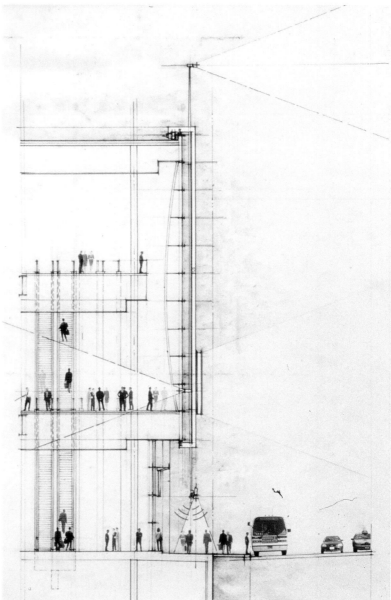

DILLER SCOFIDIO + RENFRO,
Facsimile, 2004, Moscone Convention
Center, San Francisco, United States.

Corner detail and section.

In collaboration with Ben Rubin of
Ear Studios and Mark Hansen.
Photo: John Louie
Courtesy of Diller Scofidio + Renfro

[DS + R: Elizabeth DILLER, Ricardo
SCOFIDIO, Charles RENFRO]

PARADOX
● METAPHORICAL &
METONYMIC Substitution
● PARADOX
● ENARGIA
● Ungrammatical, illogical,
or unusual uses of language
● Techniques of argument
● AMPLIFICATIO(N)
● Emotional appeals

Operation:
AMPLIFICATION
Relation:
CONTRADICTION

— Adynata;
Impossibilia.

G. "powerless" L. "impossibility"

Adynaton

A stringing together of impossibilities.

O brawling love! O loving hate! Love that
comes from nothing! Sad happiness! Serious
foolishness! Beautiful things muddled together
into an ugly mess! Love is heavy and light, bright
and dark, hot and cold, sick and healthy, asleep
and awake—it's everything except what it is! This
is the love I feel, though no one loves me back.
Are you laughing?

—William SHAKESPEARE, *Romeo and Juliet*, (1596).

An **adynaton** is a rhetorical device that encompasses fictional and impossible poetic creation. It is a form of exaggeration by which impossibility is expressed by reversing the logic of the real.

A visual example is René Magritte's *The Listening Room*, which features an apple in a pink room with a white ceiling, wooden floors, and a white-trimmed window with a view. This adynaton implies a statement so extreme as to imply that it is impossible. In this painting, the apple is represented as being large enough to fill an entire room. Or, is the apple of normal size while the room is impossibly small? Such an extreme level of exaggeration is used to emphasize a point or show the intensity of something. It is used for comparison and contrast.

Adynaton is also very clear in Superstudio's collage "The New York Extrusion Project" from *The Continuous Monument* series. This collage depicts a top view

of Manhattan with a monumental extrusion of the cityscape's profile. Superstudio created powerful drawings, photomontages, and projects while searching for the ideal city of the future. Most of these visions string several impossibilities together.

In Natalini's words, *The Continuous Monument* is

> a single piece of architecture to be extended over the whole world. [Its] static perfection moves the world through the love that it creates, [through] serenity and calm [and through its] sweet tyranny.

The group was founded in Florence in 1966 by Cristiano Toraldo di Francia and Adolfo Natalini, who were then joined by Gian Piero Frassinelli, Alessandro Magris, Roberto Magris, and, later, Alessandro Poli. In 1978 Superstudio ended their ventures as a group, though its members continue to develop their ideas independently through their writing, teaching, architecture, and design projects.

SUPERSTUDIO, *The Continuous Monument:*
New York Extrusion Project, 1969,
New York, United States.

Aerial perspective.

Museum of Modern Art (MoMA). Graphite, color
pencil, and cut-and-pasted printed paper on board,
38 x 25.75 in. (96.5 x 65.4 cm). Gift of The Howard
Gilman Foundation. Acc. n.: 313.2000.
© 2022. Digital image, The Museum of Modern Art,
New York/Scala, Florence

[Superstudio (1966–1978): Adolfo
NATALINI, Cristiano TORALDO DI FRANCIA,
Gian Piero FRASSINELLI, Alessandro MAGRIS,
Roberto MAGRIS, Alessandro POLI]

René MAGRITTE (1898–1967), *La Chambre*
d'Écoute (The Listening Room), 1958.

Christie's Images Limited. Oil on canvas.
14.76 x 18 in. (37.5 x 45.7 cm).
© 2022. Christie's Images, London/Scala, Florence

Magritte made two versions of this painting. The
first version was painted in 1952 (part of the Menil
Collection in Houston, Texas). The 1958 version
was painted for the cover of the album *Beck-Ola* by
British rock band The Jeff Beck Group. This version
is held in a private collection.

005

TECHNIQUES OF
ARGUMENT
● Techniques of argument
● AMPLIFICATIO(N)

Operation:
AMPLIFICATION
Relation:
CONTIGUITY

Etiologia, Etiology
— Enthymeme
(G. "thought, piece
of reasoning");
Reason Rend
(Puttenham's term);
Redditio causae;
Tell Cause.

G. "giving a cause"

Aetiologia

Given a cause or reason.

As Caesar loved me, I weep for him; as he was fortunate, I rejoice at it; as he was valiant, I honor him; but as he was ambitious, I slew him. There is tears for his love; joy for his fortune; honor for his valor; and death for his ambition.

—William SHAKESPEARE, *Julius Caesar*, (1599).

Aetiologia is an explanation for a claim or statement by showing cause and effect. As Richard A. Lanham explains, an inverted abbreviated syllogism is sometimes created by giving a cause first and a result after. This is the case of Hamlet on the players: "Let them be well us'd; for they are abstract and brief chronicles of the time."

In 1999 Francis Alÿs, in collaboration with Rafael Ortega, created *Zócalo*, a 12-hour documentary focused on the flagpole of the main square of Mexico City known as the Plaza del Zócalo. The filming with the same name as the plaza—redesigned as a setting for massive demonstrations and to express public discontent—constitutes a visual equivalent of this rhetorical color. *Zócalo* begins at dawn with the flag-raising ceremony and ends at dusk with the flag's descent. The camera follows the progression of the flagpole's shadow over the day, registering the effect of the sun and changes on the square. People take advantage of a bit of shade from the sun. The accumulation of people standing in the shadow may be understood as part of the artwork, although nothing was planned. On the contrary, the work highlights changes in the density of people around the flagpole and different positions of the public within this space. Thus, the documentary demonstrates how random social encounters and activities can sometimes be perceived as artistic situations.

[005] Aetiologia, [011] AMPLIFICATIO, [018] Anatomy, [035] Appositio, Brevitas, Demonstratio, Emphasis, [055] ENARGIA, [069] Image, Metalepsis, [100] Topographia.

Francis ALŸS in collaboration with Rafael ORTEGA, *Zócalo, May 22, 1999*, 1999, Mexico City, Mexico.

Video. Duration 12 hours.

© Centre Pompidou, MNAM-CCI, Dist. RMN-Grand Palais / Philippe Migeat
Courtesy of the Artist/ADGP, Paris

G. "speaking otherwise than one seems to speak"

Allegory

Extending a metaphor through an entire speech or passage.

METAPHORICAL
& METONYMIC
Substitution

● METAPHORICAL &
METONYMIC Substitution
● Techniques of argument
● AMPLIFICATIO(N)
● Emotional appeals

Operation:
SUBSTITUTION
Relation:
SIMILARITY

—False Semblant;
Inversio
(L. "inversion");
Permutatio
(L. "change,
substitution").

See also
METAPHOR [074].

No one believes more firmly than Comrade Napoleon that all animals are equal. He would be only too happy to let you make your decisions for yourselves. But sometimes you might make the wrong decisions, comrades, and then where should we be?

—George ORWELL, *Animal Farm*, 1945.

Georgia COLLINS, *Garden of Earthly Delights. Permutations and combinations*, 2017, Melbourne, Australia.
The garden script and the pleasure device at the scale of the body.

"The Garden of Earthly Delights. A Social Condenser of Contemporary Pleasures," Second-Year Design Studio by María Fullaondo and Joseph Gauci-Seddon, First Semester 2017, Monash Art Design Architecture (MADA), Monash University.
Courtesy of Georgia Collins

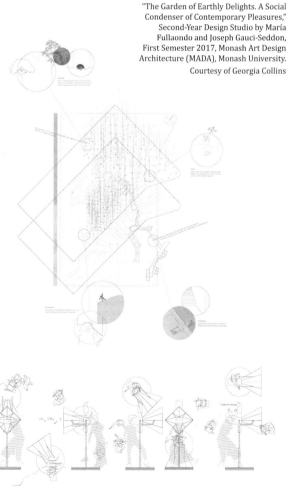

An **allegory** is a rhetorical strategy by which a METAPHOR [074] is extended across sentences or even throughout an entire discourse. Thus, it is a longer description, illustration, **analogy** [013], or comparison than a **simile** [092] or a metaphor, and it contains extensive symbolism. The word comes from Greek and means "description of one thing under the image of another." Allegories are also known as *inversio*, *permutatio*, and *false semblant* (Puttenham's term).

The famous triptych *The Garden of Earthly Delights* by Hieronymus Bosch (1450–1516) is a vivid example of a visual allegory. Three main scenes (Paradise, Earth [from which the triptych derives its name], and Hell) linked by a common denominator (sin), which creates an ambiguous and enigmatic world of multiple narratives and micro and macro readings.

The triptych moves away from the exclusive, conclusive, and determined, as well as unique meaning. It shows a clear vocation of openness in which the viewer reinvents and adds to the painting in collaboration with the author. The painting constantly changes according to the interpreter. To some extent, Bosch's triptych is the apotheosis of open work as discussed by Eco in that it proposes a broader range of interpretive possibilities, a configuration of stimuli whose substantial indeterminacy allows for several possible readings. In other words, it is a constellation of elements that lend themselves to all sorts of reciprocal relationships.

The painting was the conceptual scenery for a second-year design studio at Monash University titled *The Garden of Earthly Delights: A Social Condenser of Contemporary Pleasures*. All the proposals of the studio use allegory to develop the gardens or social condensers of contemporary pleasures. For instance, in the first briefing of the studio (the catalog of pleasures), students were asked to reflect on how current society transferring to our social context in the form of a "pleasurable event," thus addressing some of the questions raised by the triptych. Those pleasurable events served as the programmatic content for the social condenser.

The idea of sin—as an excess of pleasure or the fragility of happiness and delight in the sinful desires—is ambiguously conveyed in the painting, providing a useful framework for embracing critical thinking from different lenses. Images of egg shelters, tree tents, flower canopies, transparent capsules, giant inhabitable mussels and lobsters, palaces, animal boats, mobile pods, blimp fishes, killer ears, and so on offered an endless imaginative repertoire of artifacts and spatial suggestions. At the same time, the richness and range of characters, men and women of various races, animals, fantastic beasts, demihumans, and over-scaled creatures performed countless and provocative activities, both individually and in groups. These characters thus act as an incredible visual stimulus that generates a broad spectrum of diverse architectural approaches that align with contemporary social challenges in terms of space and activity.

Hieronymus BOSCH (1450–1516),
The Garden of Earthly Delights Triptych,
1490–1500.

Grisaille, oil on oak panel,
80.9 x 151.5 in. (205.5 x 384.9 cm).
© Archivo Fotográfico Museo Nacional del Prado

Anna LEKANIDIS, *The Garden of Earthly Delights*, 2019, New York, United States.

The Screaming Institute and contemporary pleasures.

"The Garden of Earthly Delights. A Social Condenser of Contemporary Pleasures," Advanced Design Studio by María Fullaondo,
The Bernard & Anne Spitzer School of Architecture, The City College of New York.

Courtesy of Anna Lekanidis

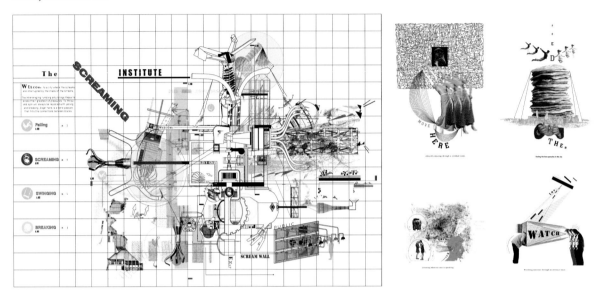

Ngawang TENZIN, *The Garden of Earthly Delights*,
2019, New York, United States.

Superimposed plan and tactical proposal.

"The Garden of Earthly Delights. A Social Condenser of
Contemporary Pleasures," Advanced Design Studio by María
Fullaondo, The Bernard & Anne Spitzer School of Architecture,
The City College of New York.

Courtesy of Ngawang Tenzin

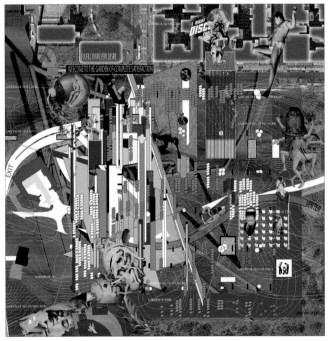

Alleotheta

Substitution of one case, gender, number, tense, or mood for another.

Mr. A — is frequently spoken of as "one of our most industrious writers;" and, in fact, when we consider how much he has written, we perceive, at once, that he *must* have been industrious, or he could never (like an honest **woman** as **he** is) have so thoroughly succeeded in keeping himself from being "talked about."

—Edgar Allan POE, "Fifty Suggestions," 1849.

"Bees Bicycle Seat" *Postcard,* 1967.
Postcard from Meret OPPENHEIM (1913–1985) to
Carl Frederik REUTERSWAERD (1934–2016).
Hannover, Sprengel Museum
Photo: Michael Herling/Aline Gwose
© 2022. Photo Scala, Florence/bpk, Bildagentur fuer Kunst,
Kultur und Geschichte, Berlin
© OPPENHEIM MERET

Touch and Tap Cinema is an excellent example of several decontextualization strategies. One such strategy is **alleotheta**: a rhetorical color that works as an ENALLAGE [054], or a substitution of one case, person, gender, number, tense, mood, or part of speech, for another. **Anthimeria** [023], **anthypallage** [024], **antiptosis** [030], and **hypallage** [065] also belong to this cluster since they are all based on the substitution of grammatically different but semantically equivalent constructions.

In speech, the use of one grammatical form in place of another—for example, using the plural form instead of the singular, the present tense instead of the past, an adjective instead of an adverb, or the masculine instead of the feminine—usually does not imply a change in meaning. Conversely, in iconic language, a replacement of, for example, material, size, scale, function, program, context, or user, significantly changes the meaning of a piece.

Peter WEIBEL and VALIE EXPORT,
Tapp und Tastkino (Touch and Tap
Cinema), 1968, Munich, Germany.

The action happened during the
*1. Europäisches Treffen unabhängiger
Filmemacher* (1st European Meeting of
Independent Filmmakers) in Munich on
November 14, 1968. Video (black and
white, sound); 1:11 min.
© 2022 Archive Peter Weibel
Courtesy of Peter Weibel

In this sense, *Touch and Tap Cinema*—the 1968 performance by VALIE
EXPORT and Peter Weibel documented as a short video—works on several
levels. EXPORT entered a crowded Munich square wearing a specially
constructed box over her nude torso. She stood silently while Peter Weibel
used a megaphone to invite people to reach inside the box for 30 seconds
at a time. By challenging the public to engage with a real woman instead
of images on a screen, the performance redefines the notion of traditional
cinema and illustrates the idea of an "expanded cinema," in which film is
produced without celluloid. Instead of watching, the tactile reception or
touching experience becomes the film. Collective and "public" accessibility
is reframed with an individual experience—restricted to half a minute per
person—that is noisily proclaimed by Peter Weibel. Defined as the "first
immediate women's film," it challenges and substitutes the traditional
stereotypes of cinema and social engagement.

Substituting a standard or expected material with another to create singular
relationships is a common decontextualization strategy in the art world.
Another form of alleotheta focuses on providing unusual and surprising
associations and replacements of "materials" of everyday objects. An example
of such material exchange is this postcard sent from Meret Oppenheim
(1913–1985) to Carl Frederik Reuterswaerd (1934–2016) of a bee-covered
bicycle seat.

Alliteration

Repetition of the same letter or sound within nearby words.

It dates from day
Of his going in Galilee;
Warm-laid grave of a womb-life grey;
Manger, maiden's knee..

—Gerard Manley HOPKINS, *The Wreck of the Deutschland*, (1875).

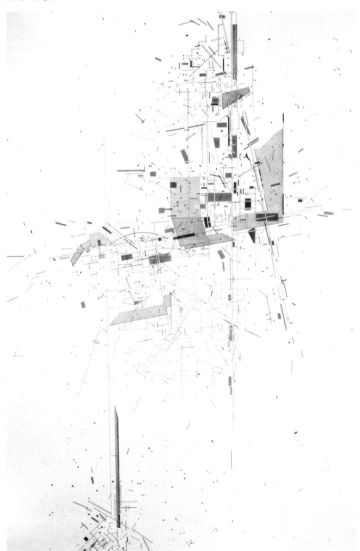

Alliteration was originally defined as the recurrence of an initial consonant sound (making it a type of consonance), but now sometimes also includes the repetition of vowel sounds (making it overlap with **assonance** [036]). The phrase "kids' coats" is alliterative (though the words begin with different consonants, they produce the same consonant sound). Examples of alliteration in popular culture include Dunkin' Donuts, PayPal, Best Buy, Coca-Cola, Life Lock, Park Place, American Apparel, American Airlines, Chuck E. Cheese, Bed Bath & Beyond, and Krispy Kreme.

Iconic language lacks vowels, consonants, and letters. As such, the equivalent of alliteration is much broader in the visual world than in verbal language. Many alliterative examples can be seen in architectural drawings, such as in this graphic interpretation of a private residence in Tamagawagakuen— "Experience in Material #12"—by Japanese architect Ryoji Suzuki. This drawing is an excellent example of the repetition of similar shapes, lines, rectangles, curves, colors, and patterns.

Ryoji SUZUKI, *House in Tamagawagakuen*, "Experience in Material #12," 1986, Tokyo, Japan.
Courtesy of Ryoji Suzuki

009

G. "difference, alteration"

Alloiosis

Highlighting differences by dividing a subject into alternatives.

Ah ha, my lord, this prince is not an Edward.
He is not lulling on a lewd love-bed,
But on his knees at meditation;
Not dallying with a brace of courtesans,
But meditating with two deep divines;
Not sleeping, to engross his idle body,
But praying, to enrich his watchful soul.

—William SHAKESPEARE, *King Richard III*, (1633).

Alloiosis means "change" and "alteration." This ancient Greek term does not refer to changes of quantity; instead, it implies a qualitative form of alteration. As Quintilian describes, the device points out "the differences between men, things, and deeds" by breaking down a subject into alternatives (Lanham 1991, p. 7).

16 different configurations of *Mora House* by the Spanish architects Iñaki Ábalos and Juan Herreros illustrate the possible applications of this figure in architecture. These variations of the plan highlight the central concept of this spatial research regarding the possible organization of a contemporary domestic space without any reference to the modern open floor model or the traditional model of corridors and rooms. As the architects state,

It is thought as an additive system of indoor and outdoor rooms, with similar proportions, to be organized in a grid of rectangular proportions and labyrinthine paths and a collection of objects, —furniture, works of art, vegetation—, which give the ensemble character and functional sense, identifying each room. Diagonal movements and visions, differentiated room lights, and the sum of climatic and visual factors—guidance, wind regime,

panoramic views, energetic use of sun, wind, and water—complete the scheme which always avoids figuratively expressing its technical complexity.

The plan depicts a 30×18 m rectangle subdivided into five horizontal sectors, which are later crossed by thin walls hosting the house functions, punctuated by small patios. The rooms share a surface, and they are juxtaposed or related directly by doors. The project drawings include several configurations of the plan to show a set of changes in the position of the rooms—for example, the library, dining room, study, living room, and bedrooms.

Following the procedure of alloiosis, the project emphasizes the differences in the plan by dividing the configuration of the depicted domestic space into alternatives. However, these variations do not change the project's character; on the contrary, they demonstrate the basic characteristics of this experiment on domestic space. That is, they highlight the genericity of the spaces and the absence of hierarchy in the distribution of the rooms.

The artist book *Brutus Killed Caesar* designed by American conceptual artist John Baldessari (1931–2020) expresses the use of this strategy in the art world.

ÁBALOS & HERREROS, *Casa Mora* (Mora House), 2002–2003, Cádiz, Spain.
Collaborators: Jacob Hense, Renata Sentkiewicz, Dries Vande Velde, Wouter van Daele.
© Ábalos & Herreros

[Ábalos & Herreros (1985–2008): Iñaki ÁBALOS, Juan HERREROS]

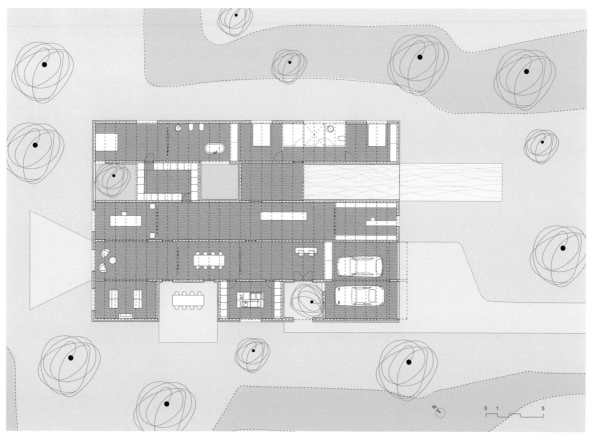

Baldessari is known for pioneering the use of appropriated imagery. For example, in *Brutus Killed Caesar,* one of his earliest printed artist books, he interprets the iconic historical event of "Brutus killing Caesar" through a set of triptychs describing several murder weapons. Baldessari juxtaposes three images representing each "actor" in columns: (1) Brutus on the left, (2) the weapon in the center, and (3) Caesar on the right. The artist uses two identical photographic portraits of the young Brutus and an older man, Caesar, facing each other for all the triptychs. The variations and changes in this work focus on the photograph between them; the murder weapon is expressed as an ordinary household object. Each triptych shows a different everyday object such as a kitchen knife, a shoe, a match, a banana peel, an apple, a revolver, a cue ball, a briefcase, a wire coat hanger, toilet paper—in total, 33 possible weapons that Brutus could have used to kill Caesar.

John BALDESSARI (1931–2020), *Brutus Killed Caesar*, 1976.

Black-and-white photographs, in three parts.
Each part: 107.25 x 32.75 in. (272.4 x 83.2 cm).
© John Baldessari (1976).
Courtesy Estate of John Baldessari © 2022
Courtesy Sprüth Magers

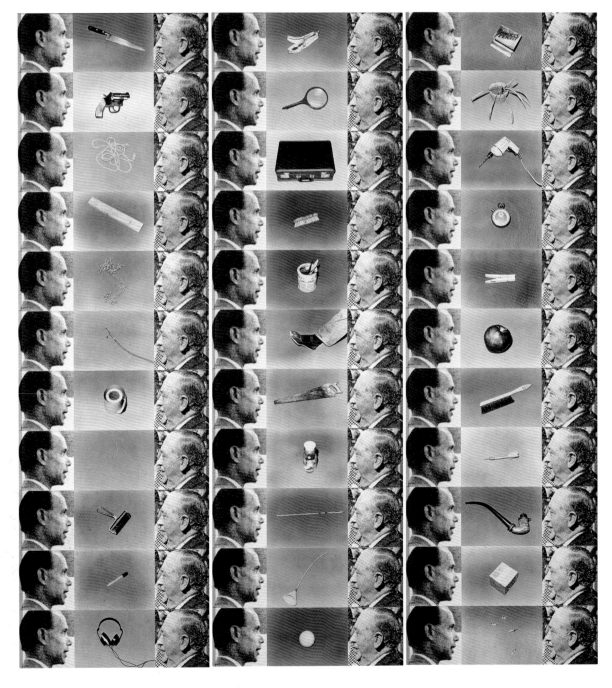

Operation:
SUBSTITUTION
Relation:
DOUBLE MEANING

Amphibolia —
Ambiguous.

G. "ambiguity"

Amphibologia

Ambiguity, either intended or inadvertent.

Cassio. Dost thou hear, my honest friend?
Clown. No, I hear not your honest friend. I hear you.

—William SHAKESPEARE, *Othello*, (1604).

Ernest CORMIER (1885–1980),
*Photograph of a Model for the
Montreal Courthouse Annex,*
1925, Montreal, Canada.

Unknown photographer.
Contemporary print from nitrate
negative. 9.96 x 7.91 in. (25.3 × 20.1 cm).
ARCH250494

Ernest Cormier fonds
Canadian Centre for Architecture

John HEJDUK (1929–2000),
The Lancaster/Hanover Masque, 1980–1982.

Sketches of the "Court House" and
"Prison House."

Black felt-tip pen with green, brown, and
blue watercolour on laid paper. 10.67 x 11 in.
(21.7 x 28 cm). DR1988:0291 :033.
10.67 x 13.11 in. (27.1 x 33.3 cm).
DR1988:0291 :038
John Hejduk fonds
Canadian Centre for Architecture
© Estate of John Hejduk

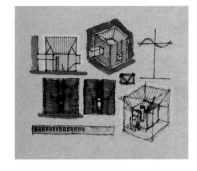
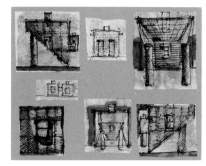

For *The Lancaster/
Hanover Masque* see also
Anoiconometon [019];
Synaeresis [094].

Amphibologia, or *amphibolia*, refers to ambiguity in grammatical structure, usually achieved by mispunctuation. It is also an overarching term used to describe anything that is unclear, usually resulting in a misunderstanding. Quintilian uses this term to mean "ambiguity" and explains that its forms are innumerable; among them, presumably, are PUNS [088] and IRONY [070]. Lanham gives the following example: "In accordance with instructions, I have given birth to twins in the enclosed envelope" instead of "In accordance with instructions in the enclosed envelope, I notify you."

The photograph of a model for the *Montreal Courthouse Annex* by Canadian architect and engineer Ernest Cormier (1885–1980) is a visual equivalent of amphibologia. The ambiguity regarding the size and scale of the courthouse is evident in this photograph.

American architect John Hejduk's drawing of the "Court House" and "Prison House" in *The Lancaster/Hanover Masque* illustrates another interesting example of visual amphibologia. In this graphic document, John Hejduk (1929–2000) creates an ambiguous and hybrid projection of these houses. Traditionally, the views are displayed by juxtaposing orthographic projections (plans, sections, and vertical views). However, in this drawing, the section and plan of both houses are overlapped instead of being placed on top of each other.

Moreover, a cube's vertical and horizontal projections are a square, and the envelope of the "Court" and "Prison" Houses is a cube of the same size. In this way, Hejduk intentionally overlaps both projections—plan and section—making the interpretation of the houses ambiguous since both boundaries are square. The fact that the "Court House" and "Prison House" are connected by a bridge on the same support increases the drawing's ambiguity. Are we facing two projections of the same building, or are we facing several projections of different buildings?

John HEJDUK (1929–2000),
The Lancaster/Hanover Masque,
1980–1982.

Plan and section of the "Court House" and
"Prison House."

Graphite with green, brown, blue, and
gray pencil on paper. 32.10 x 50.95 in.
(81.5 x 129.4 cm). DR1988:0291 :044
John Hejduk fonds
Canadian Centre for Architecture
© Estate of John Hejduk

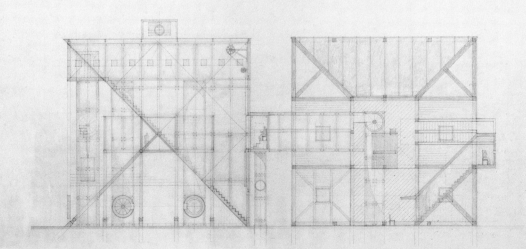

G. "enlargement"

AMPLIFICATIO

Rhetorical device used to expand a simple statement.

AMPLIFICATIO(N)

● Techniques of argument
● AMPLIFICATIO(N)
● Emotional appeals

Operation:
AMPLIFICATION
Relation:
CONTIGUITY

"More light." Ever since we crawled out of that primordial slime, that's been our unifying cry: "More light." Sunlight. Torchlight. Candlelight. Neon. Incandescent. Lights that banish the darkness from our caves, to illuminate our roads, the insides of our refrigerators. Big floods for the night games at Soldier's field. Little tiny flashlight for those books we read under the covers when we're supposed to be asleep. Light is more than watts and footcandles. Light is metaphor. Thy word is a lamp unto my feet. Rage, rage against the dying of the light. Lead, Kindly Light, amid the encircling gloom, Lead Thou me on! The night is dark, and I am far from home—Lead Thou me on! Arise, shine, for thy light has come. Light is knowledge. Light is life. Light is light.

—Chris STEVENS, *Northern Exposure*, 1992.

AMPLIFICATIO is a rhetorical term for all the ways that an argument, explanation, or description can be expanded and enriched. Quintilian subdivides it into *incrementum, comparatio, raticinatio,* and *congeries.* Hoskyns isolated five means of amplification (comparison, division, accumulation, intimation, progression) and the following figures that amplify: **Accumulatio** [001]; **Correctio** [048]; Divisio; **Exclamatio** [052]; **Hyperbole** [067]; **Interrogatio** [059]; Paralepsis; Setentia; **Synoeciosis** [097].

Richard A. Lanham highlights the following figures: Accumulatio; **Aetiologia** [005]; Apophasis; Apoplanesis; Asianism; **Auxesis** [039]; **Bomphiologia** [040]; Cohortatio; **Congeries** [047]; Diaeresis; **Diallage** [049]; Digestion; **Dinumeratio** [050]; Dirimens copulatio; Distinctio; Divisio; Epanodos; **Epexegesis** [056]; **Epicrisis** [057]; **Epitheton** [058]; **Expeditio** [061]; Macrologia; Megaloprepeia; Metanoia; Palilogia; Paradiegesis; **Parenthesis** [080]; Periergia; Periphrasis; Peristasis; **Synonymia** [098]; **Systrophe** [099].

Walter DE MARIA (1935–2013), *The Lightning Field*, 1977, Quemado, New Mexico, United States.

Photo: John Cliett
© Estate of Walter De Maria, courtesy of the Walter De Maria Archive

Stainless steel
Permanent earth sculpture consisting of 400 stainless steel poles spaced 220 feet apart in a rectangular grid array (16 poles wide by 25 poles long) The average pole height is 20 feet 7 inches. Solid-steel pointed tips on the poles form an even plane covering an area of one mile by one kilometer. Commissioned and maintained by the Dia Art Foundation, New York.

The Lightning Field by American sculptor Walter De Maria (1935–2013) illustrates many rhetorical figures, making it a fitting example of AMPLIFICATIO—a generic term that encompasses many creative strategies.

The Lightning Field (commissioned by Dia Art Foundation) is internationally recognized as one of the late-20th century's most significant works of art. It is a work of Land Art situated in a remote area of the high desert of western New Mexico. This art project's nature and scale exceed the limits that are typical of traditional museums or galleries. It comprises 400 polished stainless-steel poles installed in a 16-by-25 grid measuring one mile by one kilometer. The poles—five centimeters in diameter and averaging six meters and 19 centimeters in height— are spaced 61 meters apart, taking up a vast horizontal plane.

This land artwork falls somewhere between architecture, sculpture, installation, and even performance of nature. It is conceived to be both walked in and viewed. As Dia Art Foundation explains, *The Lightning Field* is to be experienced over an extended period. Lightning is not needed for *The Lightning Field* to be experienced thoroughly, and visitors are encouraged to spend as much time as possible in the field, especially when the sun is rising or setting.

UNGRAMMATICAL,
ILLOGICAL, OR
UNUSUAL USES OF
LANGUAGE.

● Ungrammatical, illogical,
or unusual uses of language
● AMPLIFICATIO(N)
● Omission
● Emotional appeals

Operation:
REARRANGEMENT
Relation:
OPPOSITION

The second meaning
of this figure is
Anantapodoton [015] or
anapodoton: a kind of
ellipsis [053] in which
the second member of a
correlative expression is
left unstated.

G. "inconsistent, anomalous"

Anacoluthon

Ending a sentence with a different grammatical structure from that with which it began.

I will have such revenges on you both
That all the world shall—I will do such things—
What they are yet I know not, but they shall be

—William SHAKESPEARE, *King Lear*, (1606).

Anacoluthon (also known as a syntactic blend) is defined as an abrupt change in the syntax or grammar of a statement. Thus, it is a syntactic deviation, an interruption within a sentence in which one structure is abruptly replaced with another. In other words, the grammatical flow of sentences is interrupted to begin more sentences. Gertrude Stein uses this device in *A Portrait of Mabel Dodge*: "A plank that was dry was not disturbing the smell of burning and altogether there was the best kind of sitting there could never be all the edging that the largest chair was having." She starts by talking about a plank and its smell. Then, more sentences are added in a way that changes the grammatical order of the phrases.

Anacoluthon can be both a vice and a device. Richard A. Lanham clarifies this double role of anacoluthon using an example from Bergin Evans's *A Dictionary of Contemporary American Usage*. In the King James Version, there is an anacoluthon that has been corrected in the Revised Standard Version:

King James Version: And he charged him to tell no *man*; but go, and *shew thyself* to the priest.

Revised Standard Version: And he charged him to tell no one; but "go and show yourself to the priest."

Mona Hatoum's photograph *Performance Still* can be considered a translation in the visual world of anacoluthon—the ungrammatical, illogical, or unusual use of language. In 1985, this Briton of Palestinian origin performed *Roadworks*, a one-hour performance during which she walked through the streets of Brixton in London. Ten years later, Hatoum extracted a still picture from the video, cropped it, and printed it as a black-and-white photograph. The image depicts the bottom half of the artist's legs as she walked barefoot through the streets but gives no clear context of the original Brixton. The unusual characteristic of the performance that has attracted attention is the Doc Marten boots. The artist does not wear the boots (which are usually worn by police officers, punks, and skinheads). Instead, they are on the pavement, tied to her ankles by their laces. The composition plays with dualities and accentuates the fragility of the bare feet in comparison to the roughness of the street and the heavy boots.

Performance Still visually expresses an anacoluthon in several ways. First, people do not often walk barefoot through the streets; this visual, combined with the boots attached to the legs as they walk by, creates an anomalous, inconsistent, unexpected, and powerful image. The image represents other rhetorical deviations besides anacoluthon. For one, it is a visual HYPERBATON [066] regarding the unusual orientation of the boots towards the feet. Also, the composition shows the artist's body's bottom half only, which is a visual **synecdoche** [096], as the artist's full body is substituted for her legs.

Between 1919 and 1927, multifaceted architect El Lissitzky (1890–1941) produced a large body of paintings, prints, and drawings that he referred to, using the word "Proun," an acronym for "project for the affirmation of the new" in Russian. Any of these *Prouns* can be understood as visual anacoluthons. These abstract works portray the architect training Lissitzky received in Germany before World War I and the influence of Kazimir Malevich (1878–1935), a fellow teacher at the Vitebsk art school.

Lissitzky applies the Suprematist lexicon by combining monochromatic forms, surfaces, elementary structures, linear vectors, geometric shapes, and spatial elements. The artist constructs a new formal landscape between the bi-dimensional and tri-dimensional world in which the movement of the composition seems to predominate. The systems of projection that he uses to render these constructions do not follow the standard rules of architectural representation. *Prouns* combine various elements drawn in perspective, oblique, and orthographic projections that amplify the dimensional space and break the boundaries between the coherent and impossible.

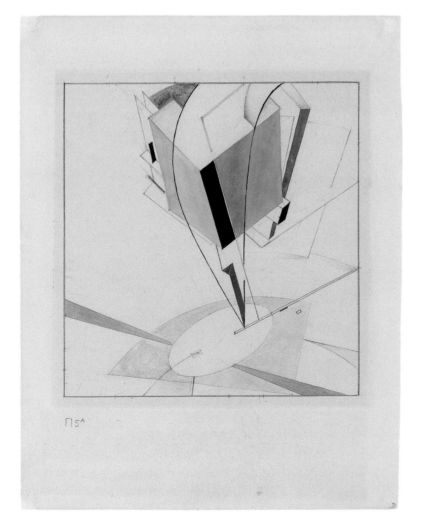

Π5ᴬ

El LISSITZKY (Eleazar Lissitzky 1890–1941), *Proun 5 A*, 1919.

Madrid, Museo Nacional Thyssen-Bornemisza. Pencil and gouache on paper, 8.66 x 6.89 in. (22 x 17.5 cm). 25.20 x 22.64 x 0.79 in. with frame (64 x 57.5 x 2 cm). INV.: 650 (1977.103)

© 2022. Museo Nacional Thyssen-Bornemisza/ Scala, Florence

Mona HATOUM, *Performance Still*, 1985,
1995, London, United Kingdom.

Gelatin silver print on paper, mounted on
aluminium, image: 30.07 x 44.72 x 0.16 in. (764 x
1,136 x 4 mm). Inv.: P80087. London, Tate Gallery.

© 2022. Tate, London./ Photo Scala, Florence.
© Mona Hatoum

013

TECHNIQUES OF
ARGUMENT
● METAPHORICAL &
METONYMIC Substitution
● Techniques of argument
● Example, allusion, and
citation of authority
● REPETITIO(N)
● Balance
● Omission

Operation:
REPETITION
Relation:
SIMILARITY

—Proportio
(L. "proportion,
symmetry;
analogy").

See also
Simile [092].

G. "equality of ratios, proportion"

Analogy

Reasoning or arguing from parallel cases.

They crowded very close about him, with their
hands always on him in a careful, caressing grip,
as though all the while feeling him to make sure he
was there. It was like men handling a fish which is
still alive and may jump back into the water.

—George ORWELL, *A Hanging*, 1931.

Oswald Mathias UNGERS (1926–2007),
City Metaphors: "Duplication" and
"Similarity," 1976.

Morphologie: City Metaphors, (Cologne, Germany:
Buchhandlung Walther König, 2011), 24–25; 66–67.
[1976, 1982]
Courtesy of Ungers Archiv für
Architekturwissenschaft (UAA)

Duplication: GANT, *Plan of Manheim*, 1606
Similarity: Ivan LEONIDOV, *Town of Magnitogorsk*, 1930

Duplication   Verdoppelung

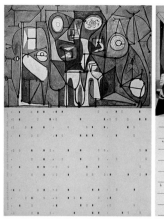 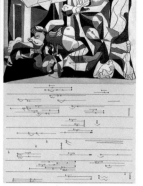

FRAGMENTATION   INTEGRATION

George MELLOS, *Music Analogies,*
"Integration" and "Fragmentation,"
2017, Melbourne, Australia.

The garden script (process).

"The Garden of Earthly Delights. A Social
Condenser of Contemporary Pleasures,"
Second-Year Design Studio by María Fullaondo
and Joseph Gauci-Seddon, First Semester
2017, Monash Art Design Architecture
(MADA), Monash University.
Courtesy of George Mellos

Integration: Analogy comparing *The Charnel
House* by Pablo Picasso (1944–1945), and
music score by Toshi Ichiyanagi, (name and
date unknown).
Fragmentation: Analogy comparing *The
Kitchen* by Pablo Picasso (1948) and *IBM for
Mere Cunningham* by Toshi Ichiyanagi (1960).

Oswald Mathias Ungers (1926–2007) in *Morphologie:
City Metaphors* (Cologne, Germany: Buchhandlung
Walther König, 2011) develops a design methodology
focused on creating visual analogies or thinking in
images. The German architect "makes you see" some
of the concepts and ideas governing past and present
of city planning. The book includes 50 visual analogies
that compare city plans to familiar objects or images,
linked by descriptive words that define abstract
spatial concepts.

Two of these analogies are reproduced here. One
analogy compares the plan of Manheim—a city in
southwest Germany—to a photo of two horses (a mare
and her foal) running through a field. Meanwhile,
"Duplication" synthesizes the urban scheme and the
photograph. Formal similarities and morphology are
the most apparent criteria governing the comparison.
However, the comparison also acts in at least two other
parallel planes, as it defines two distant realities, as well
as factual, perceived, and conceptual realities (i.e., a
city, a familiar object, and a word). The second analogy
compares the details of a competition proposal for
the Town of Magnitogorsk designed in 1930 by Ivan
Leonidov (1902–1959) to a top view of a chess game,
linking them by "Similarity."

This method of "thinking in images" was tested at
Monash University in a second-year architectural
design studio. Students of "The Garden of Earthly
Delights" produced a set of visual analogies comparing
contemporary music scores, art precedents, and/or
imagery connected by an abstract notion. This was
done as a form of structure generation (almost like
choreography) using Ungers's method of comparing two
distant realities. For example, George Mellos created
six analogies associating cubism art and music scores.
Whereas Ungers utilized similarity as the relationship
between the elements of the diptych, Mellos' analogies
are governed by contiguity or difference.

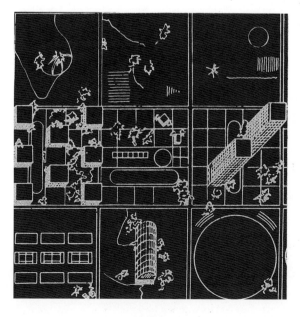 

Similarity   Gleichartigkeit

EXAMPLE,
ALLUSION, AND
CITATION OF
AUTHORITY

● Techniques of argument
● Example, allusion, and
citation of authority
● REPETITIO(N)
● AMPLIFICATIO(N)
● Emotional appeals

Operation:
SUBSTITUTION
Relation:
CONTIGUITY

—Recordatio
(L. "recalling to
mind.")

See also
Dinumeratio [050].

G. "remembrance"

Anamnesis

Recalling ideas, events, or persons of the past.

You who have lived during the period from 1915 to 1822 may remember that this country was never in a more uneasy position. The sufferings of the working-classes were beyond description; and the difficulties and struggles and bankruptcies of the middle-classes were such as few persons have a just idea of.

—John BRIGHT in *The Elements of Rhetoric* by James DE MILLE, 1878.

OMA (Rem KOOLHAAS),
La Casa Palestra, "The Domestic
Project," 1985–1986, Seventh Triennial
of Milan, Milan, Italy.
Images courtesy of OMA

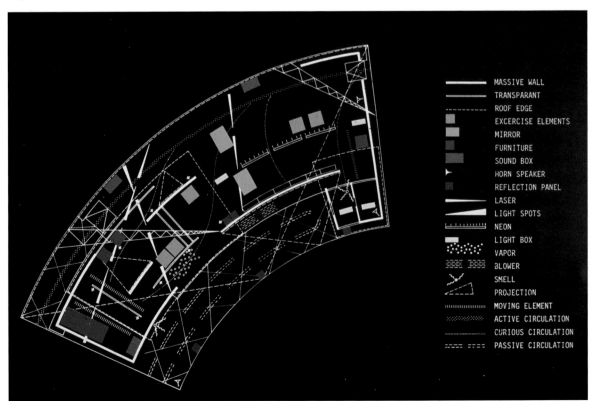

MASSIVE WALL
TRANSPARANT
ROOF EDGE
EXCERCISE ELEMENTS
MIRROR
FURNITURE
SOUND BOX
HORN SPEAKER
REFLECTION PANEL
LASER
LIGHT SPOTS
NEON
LIGHT BOX
VAPOR
BLOWER
SMELL
PROJECTION
MOVING ELEMENT
ACTIVE CIRCULATION
CURIOUS CIRCULATION
PASSIVE CIRCULATION

Anamnesis (*recordatio* in Latin) is a rhetorical procedure that calls past matters to memory. Specifically, it involves citing another author's words from memory. Reference is made to the past by bringing up old associations to produce an effect via a stated or implied contrast with the present. Anamnesis helps establish ethos since it conveys that the speaker or writer understands the wisdom of previous authors.

An excellent example of this strategy in architecture is the exhibition pavilion *La Casa Palestra*, presented by the Office for Metropolitan Architecture (OMA) in the XVII Milan Triennale. For this exhibition, 26 architectural firms were asked to re-frame domestic situations under the theme of "The Domestic Project." The iconic *Barcelona Pavilion* designed in 1929 by Mies van der Rohe (1886–1969) was the protagonist of the OMA proposal, and the original design was revisited. First, the Barcelona plan was bent within the exhibition building to fit the curve of the site. Second, Mies's pavilion was inhabited by gymnasts, bodybuilders, and exercise equipment since its original program was transformed into a gym or body-building home

"somewhere in the ambiguous zone between exercise and sexual pleasure."

As Beatriz Colomina states, *La Casa Palestra* is an homage to the *Barcelona Pavilion* and modern architecture in general. As such, this architectural project is a pure transposition of anamnesis. Also, the work makes multiple references to the modern movement. According to Colomina,

> The project alludes to the tradition of the body building house in modern architecture: from Marcel Breuer's bedroom for Erwin Piscator in Berlin (1927) to Walter Gropius's gym in his apartment for the German Building Exhibition in Berlin (1931), to Richard Döcker's gym on the roof at the Weissenhofsiedlung in Stuttgart (1927), to the 1000-meter running track that Le Corbusier proposed for the roof of his Immeuble Villas (1922), to Richard Neutra's Lovell House (1929), and even to the transformation in the 1960s of Mies's Tugendhat House in Brno into a children's gym by Communist bureaucrats (Buckley, "Manifesto Architecture," 40–81).

OMA (Rem KOOLHAAS), *La Casa Palestra*, "The Domestic Project," 1985–1986, Seventh Triennial of Milan, Milan, Italy.
Images courtesy of OMA

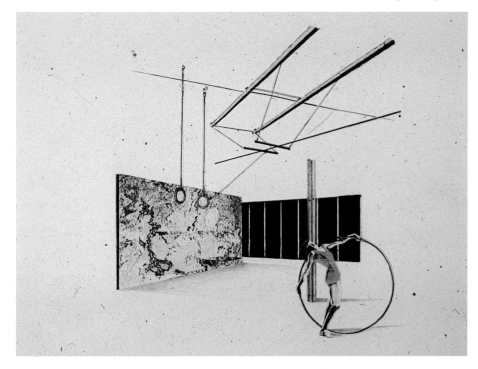

Operation:
OMISSION
Relation:
OPPOSITION

—Anapodoton

See also
Anacoluthon [012];
Ellipsis [053].

G. "without apodosis; hypothetical proposition wanting the consequent clause"

Anantapodoton

Omission of a correlative clause from a sentence.

If you eat the bear, you have become a man;
if the bear eats you, well then...

—Richard A. LANHAM, *A Handlist of Rhetorical Terms*, 1991.

Anantapodoton, also called *anapodoton*, is a figure of omission containing some properties of **anacoluthon** [012], as it also involves the interruption of grammatical expectations. In this sense, this device belongs to the category of ungrammatical, illogical, or unusual language usage. Specifically, anatapodoton occurs when the main clause of a sentence is omitted because the speaker or writer interrupts it to revise their thought. As a result, the initial clause remains grammatically unresolved. A visual equivalent of this strategy is André Kertész's photograph *Disappearing Act*, where the upper part of a body disappears.

André KERTÉSZ (1894–1985),
Disappearing Act, 1955, New York,
United States.
Photo © Ministère de la Culture
-Médiathèque de l'architecture et du
patrimoine, Dist. RMN-Grand
Palais / André Kertész

REPETITIO(N)
● Techniques of argument
● REPETITIO(N)
● AMPLIFICATIO(N)

Operation:
REPETITION
Relation:
IDENTITY

—Epanaphora
(G. "carrying
back"); Epembasis
(G. "attack,
advance"); Iteratio
(L. "repetition");
Relatio (G. "bringing
back, return");
Repetitio; Report.

G. "carrying back"

Anaphora

The repetition of the same word at the beginning of successive clauses.

The sweetness of affiance! Show men dutiful?
Why, so didst thou. Seem they grave and learned?
Why, so didst thou. Come they of noble family?
Why, so didst thou. Seem they religious?
Why, so didst thou.

—William SHAKESPEARE, *Henry V*, (1599).

Anaphora is a rhetorical color that features repetition of a word or phrase at the beginning of successive sentences, phrases, or clauses. This diagram, which revolves around the notion of flexibility in contemporary libraries, is an example of visual anaphora, as it repeats the same "image" at the beginning of successive clauses. The scheme describes the arrangement chosen in *The Seattle Central Library* as explained in the competition proposal:

> Flexibility in contemporary libraries is conceived as the creation of generic floors on which almost any activity can occur. Programs are not separated, rooms or individual spaces not given unique characters. In practice, this means that bookcases define generous (though nondescript) reading areas on opening day, but, through the collection's relentless expansion, inevitably come to encroach on the public space... Instead of its current ambiguous flexibility, the library should cultivate a more refined approach by organizing itself into spatial compartments, each dedicated to, and equipped for, specific duties. Tailored flexibility remains possible within each compartment, but without the threat of one section hindering the others.

The diagram links two aspects of the library. First, the reading areas are represented by a rectangular grid of bookcases. All other spaces are expressed by the fresco *The School of Athens* (1509–1510) painted by Raphael Sanzio (1483–1520). The Italian painting represents the libraries of those times—all the greatest mathematicians, philosophers, and scientists from classical antiquity are gathered together in a generic space, sharing their ideas and learning from each other. Meanwhile, a photograph of what seems to be an Asian stock exchange floor depicts spatial compartments.

The block containing the bookshelves and painting is repeated vertically and horizontally at the beginning of the diagram. *The School of Athens* represents the generic spaces of a library, and the stock image represents the spatial sections devoted to specific activities. They can be interpreted in two ways. When looking at it horizontally, one can make a time comparison between the opening and the future of the library. The uniform flexibility of traditional libraries (unstable) can also be compared with the compartmentalized flexibility (stable) proposed by OMA.

OMA (Rem KOOLHAAS),
Seattle Central Library,
"Flexibility Diagram,"
2004, Seattle, United
States.
Courtesy of OMA

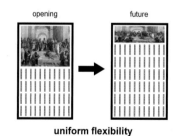

uniform flexibility

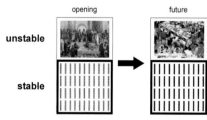

compartmentalized flexibility

017

HYPERBATON
●Ungrammatical, illogical, or
unusual uses of language
●HYPERBATON
●Emotional appeals

Operation:
REARRANGEMENT
Relation:
IDENTITY

—Perversio
(L."inversion");
Reversio.

See also
HYPERBATON [066].

G. "turning back"

Anastrophe

Unusual arrangement of words or clauses within a sentence.

It is the cause. Yet I'll not shed her blood,
Nor scar that whiter skin of hers than snow.

—William SHAKESPEARE, *Othello*, (1604).

Anastrophe is a rhetorical mechanism that explores how words or clauses can be rearranged within a sentence, often for metrical convenience or to produce a poetic effect. Anastrophe is often considered a synonym for HYPERBATON [066] (the changing of the position of a single word within a sentence). Richard A. Lanham notes that "Quintilian would confine anastrophe to a transposition of two words only, a pattern Puttenham mocks with 'In my years lusty, many a deed doughty did.'"

A widely known architectural example that uses anastrophe is the *Centre Georges Pompidou* by architects Richard Rogers (1933–2021) and Renzo Piano for an international competition in 1970 launched by the French Ministry of Culture. The task was to create an interdisciplinary cultural institution where contemporary art was accompanied by literature, design, music, and cinema. For this reason, the Center includes the Public Information Library, the National Museum of Modern Art, IRCAM, and a center for music and acoustic research. The Italian and English architects proposed a cultural center that would revolutionize the

architectural panorama of the moment by bringing all the facilities, services, and installations to the facade. The east facade, above all, is structured around the facilities and guts of the building. This architectural element was kept hidden until this project. It was unveiled because it was considered ignoble and inelegant. Each color stands for a particular function: blue for ventilation, green for water, red for automated elevators, yellow for electricity. The main structure is white. All services and the secondary structure—for example, service stairs and passageways—are gray.

Kari Kleinmann proposes a garden of contemporary pleasures for New York full of rhetorical strategies. In this sense, beyond the figures of departure from element order, it should be noted the use of figures of allusion and citation of well-known architectural projects such as **anamnesis** [014] or **epicrisis** [057]. The concept of the proposal is an interpretation of the theorical project *No-Stop City* (1969) by Archizoom.

No Stop Garden is a boundless experience of pleasure without borders. The garden's organization is borne from a series of tactical layers

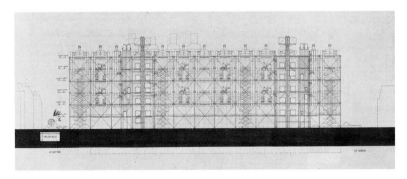

Studio Piano & Rogers architects
(Renzo PIANO and Richard ROGERS),
*Centre Georges Pompidou,*1971–1977,
Paris, France.

East elevation.

© Fondazione Renzo Piano -Rogers Stirk
Harbour & P.
Courtesy of Fondazione Renzo Piano

● 62

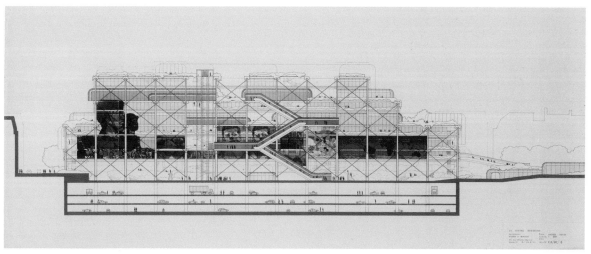

Studio Piano & Rogers architects (Renzo
PIANO and Richard ROGERS), *Centre Georges
Pompidou,*1971–1977, Paris, France.

West elevation and section parking.

© Fondazione Renzo Piano-Rogers Stirk Harbour & P.
Courtesy of Fondazione Renzo Piano

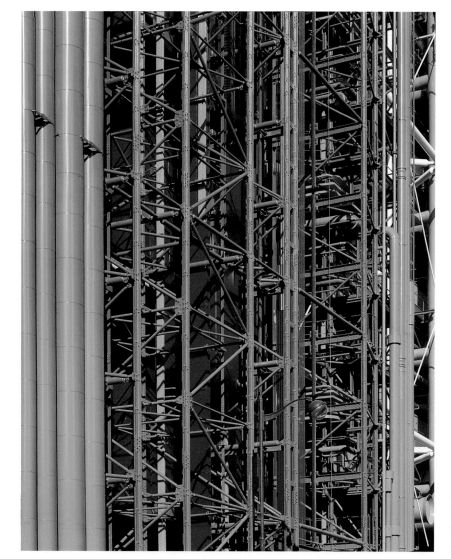

Studio Piano & Rogers architects
(Renzo PIANO and Richard
ROGERS), *Centre Georges Pompidou,*
1971–1977, Paris, France.

Detail of east facade. Pipes and
structure.

Photo: Michel Denancé
© Michel Denancé
Courtesy of Fondazione Renzo Piano

Competition: 1970–1971
Construction: 1972–1977
Renovation: 1996–2000

which is inspired by the schema of Archizoom's, *No-Stop City*, John Cage's musical compositions, and various pleasures as nodes of activity connect to create circulation. The pleasures have no conceptual relationship to each other, as the variety of pleasures are limitless, and users can freely create and establish their own. *No Stop Garden* is a continues landscape of pleasurable service and device which welcomes everyone to participate and creates a new typology of community. While *No-Stop City* is based on the idea of advanced technology aiding in decentralizing metropolis, *No Stop Garden* relies on an anarchistic user enriched landscape of endless and hedonist pleasures, imagined a post labour society. Archizoom's proposal speaks more to a continuous interior landscape, while *No Stop Garden* populates and moves through the city, receiving its continuity and coherence through pleasure (Kari Kleinmann).

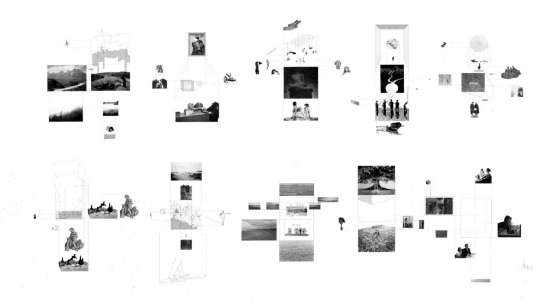

Kari KLEINMANN, *No Stop Garden*, 2019, New York, United States.
Tactical proposals and pleasures.

"The Garden of Earthly Delights. A Social Condenser of Contemporary Pleasures," Advanced Design Studio by María Fullaondo, The Bernard & Anne Spitzer School of Architecture, The City College of New York.
Courtesy of Kari Kleinmann

G. "cutting up, dissection"

ANATOMY

The analysis of an issue into its constituent parts, for ease of discussion or clarity of exegesis.

Although ANATOMY is not a traditional figure, it has been increasingly used as a generic term for a technique that includes the traditional dividing and particularizing of figures. The term anatomy comes from the Greek meaning "cutting up, dissection," as Japanese architect Takefumi Aida does in this drawing. This type of drawing is called an "Okoshie drawing," "Okoshi-Ezu," or "Tate-Ezu," and it defines and dissects the *Nirvana House* in a non-standard way. The employed technique involves unfolding and showing all the orthographic projections of a building in a single drawing. It is very familiar to most Japanese architects and has been used often to represent tea houses. It is original in that it shows and defines both the exterior and interior in a single drawing.

Takefumi AIDA, *Nirvana House*, 1972, Katase, Fujisawa city, Kanagawa, Japan.
"Okoshie Drawing." (Unfolded orthographic projections).

© Aida-Doi-Architects
Courtesy of Aida-Doi-Architects

first floor
reflected
ceiling plan

roof

west interior
elevation

south elevation

second floor

north interior
elevation

east interior
elevation

south interior
elevation

east elevation

north elevation

west elevation

second floor
reflected
ceiling plan

first floor plan

west interior elevation

- - - - - - - - convex fold
— — — — concave fold

019

HYPERBATON
● Ungrammatical, illogical, or unusual uses of language
● HYPERBATON
● Techniques of argument
● AMPLIFICATIO(N)
● Emotional appeals

Operation:
REARRANGEMENT
Relation:
IDENTITY

See also
HYPERBATON [066].

For *The Lancaster/ Hannover Masque see also* Amphibologia [010]; Synaeresis [094].

G. "not set in order"

Anoiconometon

Improper arrangement of words.

It was a perfect title ...
"In considering this strangely neglected topic," it began. This what neglected topic? This strangely what topic? This strangely neglected what?

—Kingsley AMIS, *Lucky Jim*, 1954.

This drawing for *The Lancaster/Hannover Masque* by John Hejduk (1929–2000) summarizes the structures that constitute the masque and illustrates this form of HYPERBATON [066] known as **anoiconometon**. In *A Treatise of Schemes and Tropes* (1550), Richard Sherry defines the deviation as follows: "When there is no good disposition of the words, but all are confused up and down and set without order" (Lanham 1991, p. 12).

The term means "without order," and the device consists of the improper arrangement of words. Precisely, Hejduk depicts the masque with an unorthodox layout. Without apparent or specific order, a single drawing presents a masque with more than 45 characters, among which are the "Court House," "Church House," "Prison House," "Animal Hospital," "Death House," "Market," "Harmony House," "Cemetery," "Scandal House," "Store House," and "Hotel." Some buildings are displayed only in plan, while others are displayed only in elevation or section; a few are represented in a horizontal and vertical view.

Meanwhile, the scale is constant in all projections. This allows buildings' sizes to be compared. In any case, even though there is no apparent order, there is a clear sense of organizational and graphic criterion, as is evident from the exemplary uses of color, scale, views, and composition, which make the drawing perfectly fulfill its role of presenting the project. Thanks to Hejduk's graphic mastery, the superimposition and juxtaposition between structures and houses create a hyperdense drawing that perfectly synthesizes the complex nature of this work.

Parasitic Urban Playscapes, Isaac Catón's final project for "Children & Elders' Games" design Studio, explores the city as a highly saturated environment dominated by business and politics and with no room for playing. By using the existing generic urban fabric as the primary structure, the proposal responds to the hostile environment with a series of parasitic vertical playgrounds representing the city's guts. The purpose of this is to reveal the city's inhabitants and users in their most primal form.

This detailed hybrid drawing works as a map defining the overarching urban strategy as a radial network. It also defines one of the proposed playscapes and the most notable aspects of the project on-site by using the design process as supporting elements. Like Hejduk's "Presentation drawing" for *The Lancaster/ Hanover Masque*, Catón's drawing works on many levels. For instance, the order and combination of the elements are not conventional per the rules and norms of architectural language. The drawing reveals many graphic strategies that separate it from the traditional architectural mode of representation. The drawing is valuable in itself regardless of its communicative and representative functions; it is remarkable how the author masters the combination and mix of different elements without using color as a graphic variable to increase the density of information: representation systems (plan, elevation, and perspective); conventional graphic elements (image, line, and text); representations of different natures (sketches, views, diagrams, and details); and the juxtaposition of several scales from general views to minute details. The radial-network urban strategy is defined through the composition and layout of the drawing.

John HEJDUK (1929–2000), *The Lancaster/Hanover Masque*, 1980–1982.

Presentation drawing.

Colored pencil and graphite on translucent paper. 36.38 x 60.43 in. (92.4 x 153.5 cm).
DR1988:0291:049

John Hejduk fonds
Canadian Centre for Architecture
© Estate of John Hejduk

Isaac CATÓN RASINES, *Parasitic Urban Playscapes,* 2020, Melbourne, Australia.

Site map with context and overarching strategy.

"Children & Elders' Games" Advanced Design Studio and "Open Secrets" Studies Unit by Ciro Márquez and María Fullaondo, Monash Art Design Architecture (MADA), Monash University.
Courtesy of Isaac Catón Rasines

[006] Allegory, [009] Alloiosis, [011] AMPLIFICATIO, [012] Anacoluthon, [018] ANATOMY, [019] Anoiconometon, [039] Auxesis, [040] Bomphiologia, [049] Diallage, [050] Dinumeratio, [052] Ecphonesis, [054] ENALLAGE, [055] ENARGIA, [066] HYPERBATON, [074] METAPHOR, [075] METONYMY, [091] Significatio, [093] Syllepsis, [100] Topographia, [101] Topothesia.

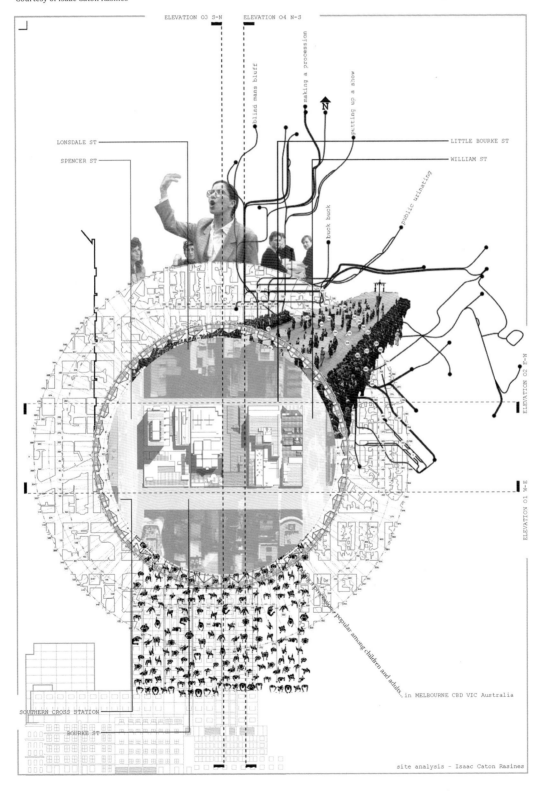

Operation:
REPETITION
Relation:
DOUBLE MEANING

—Anaclasis
(G. "bending back");
PUN; Rebounde;
Reciprocatio
(L. "alternation");
Refractio
(L. "breaking open");
Transplacement.

See also
Paronomasia [081].

G. "reflection, bending back"

Antanaclasis

One word used in two contrasting, usually comic, senses.

Put out the light, then put out the light...

—William SHAKESPEARE, *Othello,* (1604).

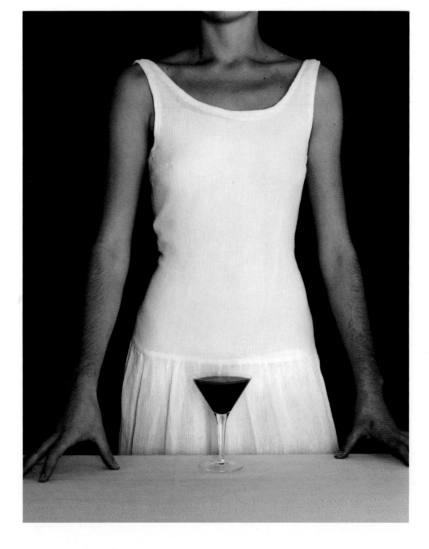

Chema MADOZ, *Untitled*
(Wine), 1980–1989
© Chema Madoz

Antanaclasis is a PUN [088] (or wordplay) with three similar meanings. The first one is the classical term closest to a plain English pun, as in Shakespeare's example from *Othello*: "Put out the light, then put out the light." The first use of "put out the light" means that Othello will extinguish a candle; the second use means that he will end Desdemona's life.

"Your argument is sound ... all sound," a quote from Benjamin Franklin, is another example of this kind of wordplay. The meaning of "sound" first appears to be solid or reasonable; however, its repetition means something very different: all air or empty.

The second meaning of antanaclasis is a homonymic pun, as when Lady Diana Cooper, in one of her famous misspellings, sent someone a recipe for "Souls in Sauce." Finally, antanaclasis can also manifest as a punning **ploce** [082] (the repetition of a word or a name with a new signification after the intervention of other words). An example is the following quote by Lewis Mumford: "The goods of life rather than the good life."

Spanish artist Chema Madoz creates a new and unexpected world by playing with the meaning and ambiguity of the elements in his photographs. His transposition of verbal puns into the visual world is evident in many pieces. This iconic image works with the gender of the model as Madoz plays with the composition and frame of the photo, the dress of the model, the model herself, and strategically places a

glass of red wine to create an ambiguous image. It is an open work that plays with the form and meaning of the elements displayed.

As Peter Eisenman explains,

> A small, 2,000-square-foot weekend house on a small rural site in northwestern Connecticut, *House VI* attempted to provide a sensuous and playful environment, full of continuous changing light, shadows, color and textures for a photographer and his wife. The house was to be a studio landscape providing an abstract background for the photography of still life and people.
>
> *House VI* is not an object in the traditional sense — that is, the result of a process — but more accurately a record of a process. Like the set of diagrammed transformations on which its design is based, the house is a series of film stills compressed in time and space.

House VI combines antanaclasis and HYPERBATON [066]. As seen in these two diagrams, the weekend house has a green and a red staircase, and Eisenman plays with the stairs' position, function, and meaning. The green staircase is placed in a standard position within the house and connects several levels. In contrast, the red staircase is placed upside down, creating an impossible and useless set of stairs that does not fulfill its usual function of connecting two different levels.

Peter EISENMAN,
House VI, 1972–1975,
Cornwall, United States.

Fourteen transformations (detail). Oblique projections.

New York, Museum of Modern Art (MoMA). Zipatone and laminated colored paper with ink on paper, each: 19.75 x 23.87 in. (50.2 x 60.6 cm). David Childs, Tracy Gardner, Barbara Jakobson, and Jeffrey P. Klein Purchase Funds. Acc. n.: 2366.2001.1-14 (2366.2001.14). © 2022. Digital image, The Museum of Modern Art, New York/Scala, Florence

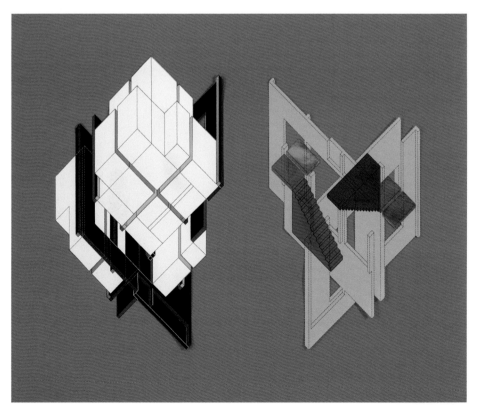

Operation:
REPETITION
Relation:
SIMILARITY

—Redditio
contraria.

See also
Simile [092].

G. "giving back in return"

Antapodosis

A simile in which the objects compared correspond in several aspects.

As they say that those, among the Greek musicians, who cannot become players on the lyre, many become players on the flute, so we see that those who cannot become orators betake themselves to the study of law.

—CICERO, *Pro Murena,* (63 BC).

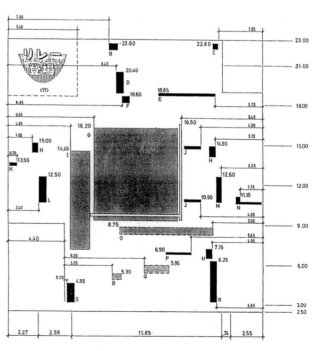

BOLLES+WILSON, *Cosmos Commercial Building,* 1989, Cosmos Street, Tokyo, Japan.

Left: Newspaper article on which the facade of the Cosmos Building was based.
Right: Analysis of voids and interstitial spaces.

© BOLLES+WILSON

[BOLLES+WILSON: Peter L. WILSON and Julia B. BOLLES-WILSON]

In 1989, BOLLES+WILSON were invited to design a "spectacular" building in Cosmos Street in Tokyo to raise the value of the neighborhood. The architects, confronted by a lack of restrictions, solved the facade via a homologous translation of a newspaper article about Mr. Nakamura, who had commissioned the project:

> Mr 'N' intended to raise the value of neighboring sites with a spectacular building – no program. A square newspaper article with Mr 'N' at the center was measured, and enlarged as wrapper/facade (text neutralised, voids as windows). Surface of inscription as interface/facade – surface of the earth as parking ramp with electronic rocks – interior with earthquake resistant Ninja columns (BOLLES+WILSON).

The square photograph of the client in the center of the newspaper page was transformed into a large square window presiding over the building's main facade. The gaps and voids inserted between the paragraphs of text serve as the windows of this project.

This project—particularly the way the facade is generated, is an excellent example of **antapodosis**—a **simile** [092] in which the objects being compared (in this case, a newspaper article and the Cosmos facade) are related in several ways.

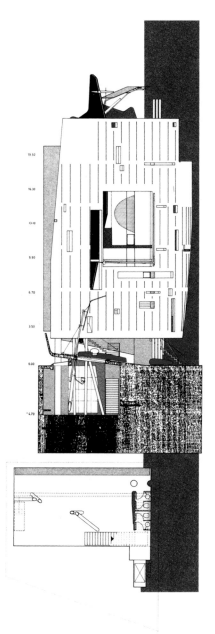

BOLLES+WILSON, *Cosmos Commercial Building,* 1989, Cosmos Street, Tokyo, Japan.

Elevation, plan, and model.

© BOLLES+WILSON

[BOLLES+WILSON: Peter L. WILSON and Julia B. BOLLES-WILSON]

G. "positive statement made in a negative form"

Antenantiosis

Deliberate understatement, especially when expressing a thought by denying its opposite.

We made a difference. We made the city stronger, we made the city freer, and we left her in good hands. All in all, not bad, not bad at all.

—Ronald REAGAN, *Farewell Address to the Nation*, January 20, 1989.

In 1971, John Baldessari (1931–2019) was invited to exhibit his work at the Nova Scotia College of Art and Design in Canada. Instead of sending his work to the school, the American artist decided to send the instructions for the exhibition in a letter. The letter read in part,

> The piece is this, from floor to ceiling should be written by one or more people, one sentence under another, the following statement: I will not make any more boring art.

> At least one column of the sentence should be done floor to ceiling before the exhibit opens and the writing of the sentence should continue everyday, if possible, for the length of the exhibit. I would appreciate it if you could tell me how many times the sentence has been written after the exhibit closes. It should be hand written, clearly written with correct spelling...

Although Baldessari was not present at the exhibition, the students covered the gallery's walls with his statement of sacrificial punishment for the exhibition's duration (April 1–10, 1971). In his notebook, Baldessari had written to himself the phrase, "I Will Not Make Any More Boring Art." The artist also sent the phrase to the students to create a lithograph that they could use for a fundraising program.

After the show's completion, Baldessari copied his version of the piece on a videotape. The exhibition and video demonstrate **antenantiosis** and John Baldessari's thinking and dissatisfaction with traditional painting limitations in the early 1970s. It also shows his interest in conceptual art, image and text, collage, and questions about painterly conventions, authorship, and the artist's role.

John Baldessari (1931–2020), *I Will Not Make Any More Boring Art*, 1971.

Black-and-white video, sound 31:17 minutes.

© John Baldessari (1971) Courtesy Estate of John Baldessari © (2022) Courtesy Sprüth Magers

G. "one part for another"

Anthimeria

Functional shift, using one part of speech for another.

His complexion is perfect gallows.

—William SHAKESPEARE, *The Tempest*, (1611).

Adalberto LIBERA (1903–1963),
Villa Malaparte, 1937, Capri, Italy.
Photograph Günther FÖRG, "Villa Malaparte, Capri,
1983." Gelatine silver print. 10.70 x 7.08 in. (27.2 x
18 cm). Part of the work: "Italienbilder, Fotografien
1982–1992," 1992. 250 parts. Edition of 3
Collection Stedelijk Museum Amsterdam.
© Estate Günther Förg, Suisse / (VEGAP, 2021)

Anthimeria implies a functional shift by using one part of speech for another—for example, "Lord Angelo dukes it well" (W. Shakespeare, *Measure for Measure*). Anthimeria is a particular case of ENALLAGE [054] such as **alleotheta** [007], **anthypallage** [024], and **antiptosis** [030].

In 1937, Rationalist architect Adalberto Libera (1903–1963) designed and built a house in the Isle of Capri for Italian writer Curzio Malaparte. *Villa Malaparte*, as this house is known, is a perfect example of anthimeria. Above the house, a large staircase leads to a solarium that seems to emerge from the landscape. As a continuation of the cliff, the staircase connects the new floor or solarium directly with the site extending the house toward the horizon. This space remains utterly oblivious to the rest of the house and is not accessible from its interior. The main staircase, as any staircase does, connects two different levels, the landscape and the house. However, in *Villa Malaparte,* the steps are also the roof—a function not so common for a staircase.

Another iconic building exemplifying a functional shift is *The Fiat Lingotto Factory* in Turin, designed by architect and engineer Giacomo Mattè-Trucco (1869–1934). The construction of this vertical urban factory started in 1916, and the building opened in 1923. Hired by Giovanni Agnelli, Mattè-Trucco created what was the largest car factory in the world at the time. It had five floors. The raw materials entered the building on the ground floor, and production progressed at each subsequent floor. The most unusual and recognizable feature of this building is the roof, where finished cars emerged; there was also a kilometer-long banked test track on the roof.

Giacomo MATTÈ-TRUCCO (1869–1934),
The Fiat Lingotto Factory, 1916–1923,
Turin, Italy.

Exterior, roof racetrack, central view.
Vespa Racing.

© Damiano Levati/Red Bull

024

G. "substitution"

Anthypallage

Change of grammatical case for emphasis.

As in Homer's line:

And the twin rocks—one of the twain with its peak towers up to the skies.
(And the twin rocks one with its peak towers up to the skies.)

—DEMETRIUS, *On Style*, (400–300 BC).

Anthypallage is a rhetorical device involving a change in grammatical case for emphasis. It belongs to the ENALLAGE [054] family. As an example,

> Demetrius cites *Odyssey* 12.73, where Homer adds some vowel music by case-change, as an instance of how the high style is created. This one of those figures which really make sense only in an inflected language like Latin or Greek (Lanham 1991, p. 15).

The two works displayed in these pages can be understood as an expression of this cluster. Both use the same decontextualization strategy—that is, they both replace the usual material of a car.

In *Car*, Saul Steinberg (1914–1999) uses bread to build a car. A photograph of a bagel or croissant constitutes the central fragment of this photomontage of a car traveling along the main street of a small town in the Midwest region of the US. Steinberg simulates this unusual vision of an American landscape by focusing on a "rare" graphic material and combining very few elements.

Meanwhile, in *Concrete Traffic*, commissioned by the Museum of Contemporary Art Chicago (MCA), a concrete rendering of a 1957 Cadillac de Ville was parked for several months in a busy Chicago commuter parking lot, starting on the morning of January 16, 1970. The creator of the piece, Fluxus artist Wolf Vostell (1932–1998), conceived this monumental concrete sculpture as an "instant happening" and an "event sculpture."

Wolf VOSTELL (1932–1998),
Concrete Traffic, 1970, [2016], Chicago, United States.
Created and originally installed 1970. Reinstalled 2016.
Concrete, 1957 Cadillac Series 62 Sedan de Ville. Width: 89.5 in. (173.99 cm). Length: 231 in. (25.4 cm). Weight: 16.2 tons.
© Wolf Vostell

Saul STEINBERG (1914–1999), *Car*, 1953.
Conté crayon over gelatin silver print, 10.75 x 13.25 in. (27.30 x 33.65 cm).
Private collection
© The Saul Steinberg Foundation

025

G. "controversy"

Antilogy

Two or more opposed speeches on the same topic.

Unfortunately robots capable of manufacturing robots do not exist. That would be the philosopher's stone, the squaring of the circle.

—Ernst JÜNGER, *The Glass Bees*, 1957.

Antilogy (derived from the Greek *anti*, "against," and *logia*, "speaking") means "controversy." It is a type of PARADOX [079] that exemplifies the basic rhetorical theory that two contrary arguments can be given about everything. Antilogy and **oxymoron** [077] combine apparently contradictory elements in the same proposition (for example, "obscure clarity"). Contradictions between words or passages in discourse or speech can occur either in terms or ideas.

Bernard Marie Dupriez's *Dictionary of Literary Devices* gives some verbal examples: "A two-sided triangle, a virtuous tyrant" (*Oxford English Dictionary*); "Even if it's true, it's false" (H. Michaux, *Tranches de savoir*, in *L'Espace du dedans*, p. 339); "On the stroke of five thirty-six o'clock" (R. Queneau, *Pierrot mon ami*, p. 32).

Antilogy also refers to words with two possible (opposite) meanings. An example is "clip," which can mean "to bring together," as in a hair clip or barrette, or "to separate" as in to cut hair with scissors.

In the *Buildings Made of Sky* series, American artist Peter Wegner creates a new vision of New York City in a visual depiction of antilogy. Opposing elements and meanings related to the city—such as air and earth, solids and voids, positive and negative spaces, light and dark colors, sky and buildings, architecture and no architecture—redefine the silhouettes of skyscrapers and Manhattan's skyline.

Peter WEGNER, *Buildings Made of Sky IX*, 2012, New York, United States.
Pigment print mounted and framed, 43.63 x 70 x 2 in. (110.8 x 177.8 x 5.1 cm).
Courtesy of Peter Wegner

As Wegner explained when he first began to exhibit this series in 2004,

> There are two Manhattans. One is a city of tall buildings; the other is a city of no buildings. This city begins where the architecture leaves off. It's a city cast in the die of Manhattan, a perfect complement to the built city, a kind of anti-Manhattan. This parallel city has an architecture all its own. It is the architecture of air, the space defined by the edges of everything else, its map redrawn by pigeons and pedestrians, barricades and scaffolding, cranes, trucks, taxis. It's the city we assume but cannot name. In this city, the buildings are made of sky. It's the Manhattan that isn't – without which there could be no Manhattan.

Wegner takes photographs from the street, pointed up at tall buildings, and turns them upside down, creating a new image of the city. The sky becomes the buildings, and the buildings become the sky. Two opposing arguments are given about the form and space of New York City's skyline, thereby amplifying and enriching our perspective of the city.

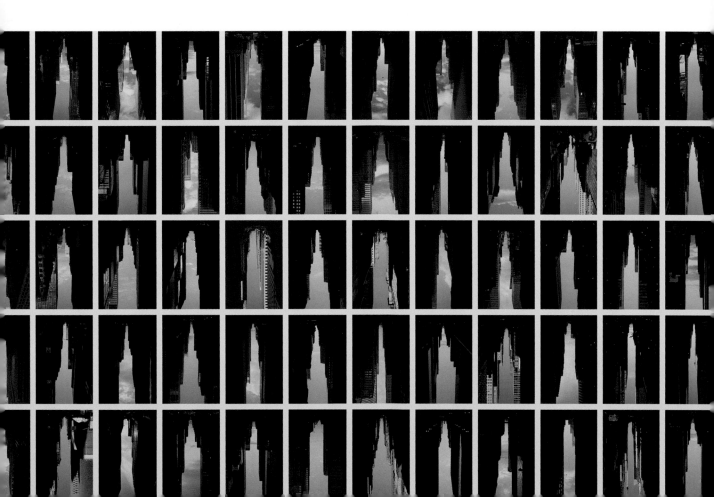

G. "turning about"

Antimetabole

Repetition of words in reverse order in successive clauses, thus forming an ABBA pattern.

Madam, I swear I use no art at all.
That he is mad, 'tis true. 'Tis true, 'tis pity,
And pity 'tis 'tis true—a foolish figure!

—William SHAKESPEARE, *Hamlet*, (1600).

In English, **antimetabole** is the repetition of words in successive clauses while inverting the order, using the scheme ABBA. Usually, this device is used to sharpen the meaning, contrast the ideas conveyed, or both. It is related to (and sometimes considered a special case of) **chiasmus** [043].

> The Latin use of the term was slightly different from the English and not precisely synonymous with chiasmus. Quintilian, for example, defines it: **Antithesis** [031] may also be affected by employing that *figure*, known as [antimetabole], by which words are repeated in different cases, tenses, moods, etc., as for instance when we say, *non ut edam, vivo, sed ut vivam, edo* [I do not live to east, but to eat to live] (*Instituto oratoria*). Chiasmus implies a more precise balance and reversal, antimetabole a looser, but they are virtual synonyms (Lanham 1991, p. 14).

Olafur Eliasson created a gigantic installation for the Turbine Hall of Tate Modern in London in 2003. The Danish artist describes this installation, titled *The weather project*, as follows:

> This site-specific installation employed a semi-circular screen, a ceiling of mirrors, and artificial mist to create the illusion of a sun. Aluminum frames lined with mirror foil were suspended from the ceiling to create a giant mirror that visually doubled the volume of the hall – along with the semi-circular screen mounted on the far wall, its long edge abutting the mirror ceiling.

Since the beginning of his career, Eliasson's artwork expressed his keen interest in kaleidoscopic reflections, light projections, mirrors, and geometric shapes that challenge the spectator's perceptions. In this regard, *The weather project* could be viewed as a visual antimetabole in which many elements, particularly the space, sun, and audience, are repeated in an inverse order.

Dan GRAHAM, *Public Space / Two Audiences*, "Ambiente Arte," 1976, 37th Venice Biennale, Venice, Italy.

Installation view: *Public Space / Two Audiences*, February 7– May 1, 2006, MACBA Museum, Barcelona, Spain
Photo and diagram: Ciro Márquez

Many of Eliasson's installations operate based on procedures very similar to rhetorical figures, such as antimetabole and chiasmus. While creating optical illusions, the artist manages to modify the perception of space and its experience altogether. In this sense, the result and effect of the mirrors on the ceiling of the Turbine Hall amplify and duplicate an already unusually large interior space. On the other hand, the contrast of this colossal scale with the human scale provided by the visitors (repeated twice by the reflection on the ceiling) makes the experience even more magical.

Dan Graham's famous *Public Space / Two Audiences* was produced for the 1976 Venice Biennale. This pavilion mixes the media of architecture, sculpture, and performance. The audience involvement is critical to completing the work. Like *The weather project*, *Public Space / Two Audiences* plays with the reflection and repeats some aspects in reverse order.

As explained in this diagram, the installation consists of one small room divided by a massive glass panel with two separate doors and a mirror wall on one far end. Spectators can enter the work through one of two entrances. The installation divides the audience into two parts so that each group sees the other group, as well as its own reflection. The glass panels and mirrors of various transparencies and reflectivities force spectators to participate. The mirror wall doubles the visual size of the space and puts the audience in a state of directional confusion. Performers become spectators, and spectators become performers.

As Graham states,

> Each audience sees the other audience's visual behavior, but is isolated from their aural behavior. Each audience is made more aware of its own verbal communications. It is assumed that after a time, each audience will develop a social cohesion and group identity.

Spectators watch themselves; spectators watch others; spectators watch others being watched; and spectators watch themselves being watched.

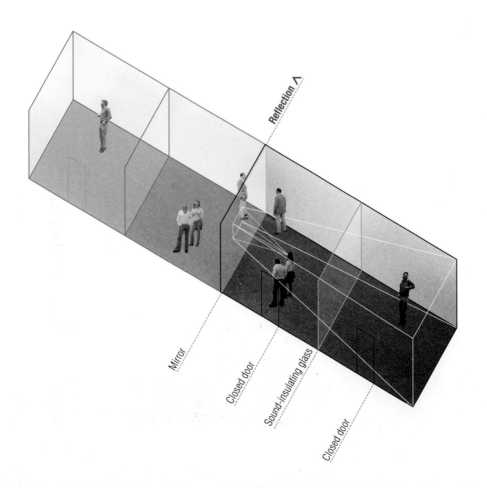

Olafur ELIASSON, *The weather project*, 2003,
London, United Kingdom.

Mono-frequency lights, projection foil, haze
machines, mirror foil, aluminum, scaffolding,
87.6 x 73.16 x 509.73 f. (26.7 x 22.3 x 155.44 m).
Installation view: Tate Modern, London, 2003
Photo: Andrew Dunkley and Marcus Leith

Courtesy of the Artist; neugerriemschneider, Berlin;
Tanya Bonakdar Gallery, New York / Los Angeles
© 2003 Olafur Eliasson

Operation:
REPETITION
Relation:
CONTRADICTION

G. "opposition of law; ambiguity in law"

Antinomy

Comparing one law, or a part of a law to another.

For *Casa Mora see also* Alloiosis [009]; Ellipsis [053].

Anything else, even the truth, would be an invention.

—Paul AUSTER, *The New York Trilogy*, "City of Glass," 1985.

In philosophy, **antinomy** refers to a contradiction, either real or apparent, between two principles or conclusions that seem equally justified. This term is nearly synonymous with PARADOX [079]. A self-contradictory phrase such as "There is no absolute truth" can be considered an antinomy because this statement supposes itself to be an absolute truth, therefore denying any truthfulness that it might contain. In other words, it is a conflict or ambiguity of the law.

As explained in **alloiosis** [009], *Casa Mora* (Mora House) is an unbuilt house that was a research project by Spanish architects Iñaki Ábalos and Juan Herreros, who worked together from 1985 until 2008. This domestic project is a fitting example of antinomy in architecture, as it questions and contradicts two recognized standards and principles applied in most modern houses. Two models define the organization or horizontal distribution of contemporary domestic architecture: the modern open plan and the traditional organization of corridors and rooms with served and servant spaces.

This research experiments with a new model by eliminating transitional spaces between rooms and open floors. The absence of transitional spaces and lack of hierarchy in the distribution of rooms provides room for generic spaces and fluidity replacing traditional domestic schemes. The architects propose an additive system of indoor and outdoor rooms of similar proportions, organized in a 2:1 rectangle and subdivided into five horizontal strips. Thin walls divide the horizontal sectors, creating rooms that host the house's functions, punctuated by small patios. All rooms share a similar surface, and the positions of rooms are interchangeable. The door is the only transitional element separating one space from another.

ÁBALOS & HERREROS, *Casa Mora* (Mora House), 2002–2003, Cádiz, Spain.

Floor plan.

Collaborators: Jacob Hense, Renata Sentkiewicz, Dries Vande Velde, Wouter van Daele.

© Ábalos & Herreros

[Ábalos & Herreros (1985–2008): Iñaki ÁBALOS, Juan HERREROS]

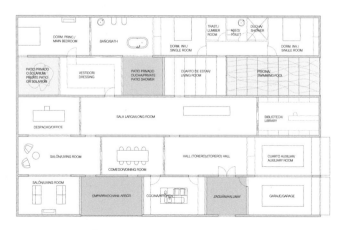

028

G. "expression by the opposite"

Antiphrasis

Irony of one word, often derisively, through obvious contradiction.

He looked like a Vulcan fresh emerged from his forge, a misshapen giant not quite sure of how to maneuver in this bright new world... His real name, the name given to him by his youthful mother before she abandoned him in a Brooklyn orphanage, was Thomas Theodore Puglowski, but his friends all called him Tiny... At least, Tiny supposed, they would if he had any friends...

—Michael McCLELLAND, *Oyster Blues*, 2001.

Contradiction and IRONY [070] define the work of Argentine artist Leandro Erlich. A single change (up is down, inside is out) achieved through simulations and optical effects is the primary strategy he employs in most of his works to question the perception and experience of reality. In 2014 the 21st Century Museum of Contemporary Art in Kanazawa displayed a swimming pool in one of its courtyards as part of the exhibition *Leandro Erlich — The Ordinary?* From the courtyard, the pool appeared to be filled with deep, shimmering water. However, in reality, a layer of water only 10 centimeters deep was suspended over transparent glass.

This art installation is an excellent visual example of **antiphrasis**, which is the use of phrases or words in a way that contrasts their literal meaning, like calling a "dwarf" a "giant," or your worst "enemy" in a debate "my learned friend." Antiphrasis comes from the Greek word *antiphrasis* and means "opposite word." This verbal procedure employs a phrase or word opposite its literal meaning to create an ironic or comic effect, as with Elrich's "fake" pool.

The Spanish group mmmm..., in their work *Divided Street* in Valencia, Spain, employed a strategy similar to Erlich's. The group's artwork divides a pedestrian street by a three-meter transparent plastic wall that still allows people to see what happens on the other side. Passers-by make eye contact as they encounter the same situation on the other side; however, they have to find alternative routes to get to the other side.

mmmm..., *Divided Street*, 2015, Valencia, Spain.
Courtesy of mmmm...

[mmmm...: Alberto ALARCÓN, Emilio ALARCÓN, Ciro MÁRQUEZ, Eva SALMERÓN]

Leandro ERLICH, *Leandro's Pool*, 2014,
Kanazawa, Japan.

Exterior and pool view.

Leandro Erlich — The Ordinary?
Exhibition, May 3 – August 31, 2014.
21st Century Museum of Contemporary Art,
Kanazawa, Japan.
Photo: Keizo Kioku
Courtesy of the Author/21st Century
Museum of Contemporary Art, Kanazawa

METAPHORICAL
& METONYMIC
Substitution

● METAPHORICAL &
METONYMIC Substitution
● Techniques of argument
● AMPLIFICATIO(N)
● Emotional appeals

Operation:
SUBSTITUTION
Relation:
CONTIGUITY

See also
Prosopopopeia [086].

G. "the giving of a face"

Antiprosopopoeia

The representation of persons as inanimate objects.

How, in the name of soldiership and sense,
Should England prosper, when such things, as smooth
And tender as a girl, all essenced o'er
With odors, and as profligate as sweet,
Who sell their laurel for a myrtle wreath,
And love when they should fight; when such as these
Presume to lay their hands upon the ark
Of her magnificent and awful cause?

—William COWPER, *Long Poem The Task: Book II*, The
Time-Piece (excerpts), 1785.

Michael LANDY,
Break Down, (2001),
London, United Kingdom.

Photo: Donald Smith/Artangel
© Michael Landy. Courtesy
of the Artist, Thomas Dane
Gallery, and Artangel

Antiprosopopoeia, etymologically derived from Greek and meaning "the giving of a face," is a color of rhetoric that represents people or parts of a human body as inanimate objects or prosthetic stage property. An example is, "She was a doormat upon which the tread of too many boots had scraped." The name of this figure is the opposite of **prosopopoeia** [086] (a formal term for personification), which occurs when inanimate objects are represented as people or are given human characteristics. Anti-personification can be achieved simply by using a METAPHOR [074] to depict or describe a person as something nonhuman.

British artist Michael Landy spent three years gathering and cataloging all his possessions—including postage stamps, his passport and birth certificate, furniture, books, records, food items, articles of clothing, works of art, and his Saab 900 Turbo 16 S—as the core of his project, *Break Down.* In total, the inventory of his life comprised 7,227 inanimate objects arranged into 10 categories: artwork, clothing, equipment, furniture, kitchen, leisure, motor vehicle, perishables, reading material, and studio material.

A facility was installed specifically for this project and opened to the public in an empty department store on Oxford Street in February 2001. With the help of a team of operatives, Landy systematically took apart, broke down, pulped, and granulated each of his possessions. Two weeks later, everything Landy owned had been destroyed. This provocative reaction to consumerist society represents an excellent expression of visual antiprosopopoeia in which a person (in this case, Michael Landy himself), is defined by his belongings.

Michael LANDY, *Integrated, Dismantling, Sorting and Separation System*, 1998.

© Michael Landy. Courtesy of the Artist and Thomas Dane Gallery

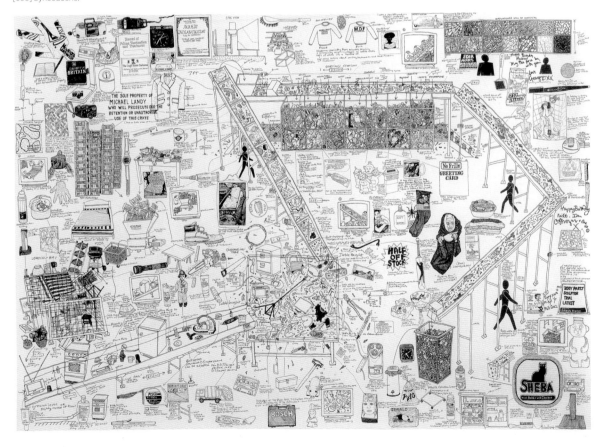

ENALLAGE
● METAPHORICAL &
METONYMIC Substitution
● Ungrammatical, illogical,
or unusual uses of language
● ENALLAGE
● Emotional appeals

Operation:
SUBSTITUTION
Relation:
DIFFERENCE

—Casus pro casu
(L. "one case for
another").

See also
ENALLAGE [054].

G."exchange of case"

Antiptosis

Substituting one case for another.

"I give you this gift with hearty good will, *for* I give this gift to you with hearty good will — the accusative for the dative; he is condemned for murder *for* he is condemned of murther — the dative or accusative for the genitive." A computer virus Cookie Monster's non-negotiable demand, "Me want cookie!," shows that the figure still lives.

—Richard A. LANHAM, *A Handlist of Rhetorical Terms*, 1991.

The action *From the Portfolio of Doggedness* was performed in Vienna in February 1968 by VALIE EXPORT and Peter Weibel. Among other rhetorical devices, it exemplifies **antiptosis**, a syntactic substitution in which one grammatical form (person, case, gender, number, tense) is replaced by another (usually ungrammatical) form. Antiptosis is derived from Greek and means "exchange of case." This color of rhetoric belongs to the family of ENALLAGE [054] and is also known as a figure of exchange.

In this controversial work, EXPORT took Peter Weibel (a fellow artist from Ukraine) for a walk as if he was a dog along the Kärntner Strasse in Vienna, one of the city's central streets and main shopping areas. The work was defined by the Austrian artist as a "sociological and behavioral case study." As Weibel explained, "Here the convention of humanizing animals in cartoons is turned around and transferred into reality: Man is animalized— the critique of society as a state of nature." In this regard, this action is a good example of **antiprosopopoeia** [029] or the representation of personas as animals or inanimate objects.

Peter WEIBEL and VALIE EXPORT, *Aus der Mappe der Hundigkeit* (From the Portfolio of Doggedness), 1968, Kärntnerstrasse, Vienna, Austria.

Documentation of the action *From the Portfolio of Doggedness* carried out in Vienna in February 1968. Black-and-white photographs, vintage prints, (40.3 x 50.3 cm / 50 x 40.3 cm each).
© 2022 Archive Peter Weibel
Courtesy of Peter Weibel

G. "opposition"

Antithesis

Conjoining contrasting ideas.

Contrasted faults through all his manners reign;
Though poor, luxurious; though submissive, vain;
Though grave, yet trifling; zealous, yet untrue;
And e'en in penance, planning sins anew.

—Oliver GOLDSMITH, *The Traveler*, 1868.

Antithesis, derived from the Greek *anti* "against" and *thesis* "a setting, position" literally means "setting opposite." It is a kind of parallelism or parallel structure in which two contrasting ideas are presented in opposition to one another (in words, sentences, or parts of a sentence) to make the principal idea more striking. "If a society cannot help the *many* who are *poor*, it cannot save the *few* who are *rich*" (John F. Kennedy).

Francisco de Goya (1746–1828) painted *La Maja Vestida* (The Clothed Maja) and *La Maja Desnuda* (The Naked Maja) around 1800. The term "maja" refers to women of popular classes notable for their liberalism and beauty. In both paintings, which are displayed together, we can observe the identical format and composition of the same woman reclined "Venus" style. The difference is that she is fully clothed in one image and completely naked in the other.

In his photography, Elliot Erwitt captures how viewers concentrate in a large group (of men) in front of *The Naked Maja*, while a single woman contemplates *The Clothed Maja*. The image plays with contrasts using the imbalance of viewers who congregate in front of one painting and the single viewer in front of the other. Furthermore, this is a matter not only of number but also of gender. Also turning to the IRONY [070] of stereotypes, *The Naked Maja* incites the males' gaze, insinuating that the interest of "men" spectators is focused more on sexual desire than artistic or intellectual matters. In contrast, the "woman" viewer in front of *The Clothed Maja* is assumed to have a higher capacity for comprehension and profundity in art history, as she remains indifferent to the sexuality of the painting.

Walter De Maria (1935–2013), one of the founding fathers of the 1960s Land Art movement, proposed an interior earth sculpture in Munich in 1968. *The Munich Earth Room* consists of covering the inside of a gallery with 250 cubic yards of earth. The earth accumulated in the exposition space pits art against nature, city against country, sophistication against simplicity. Other contrasts include those between the white walls and the dark earth, the regularity of the space and the shapelessness of the material, and the closeness of the artistic atmosphere and the openness of the landscape. Additionally, this work juxtaposes the economic capital of the artistic context against the null value of the earth. *The Munich Earth Room* was the first earth room sculpture executed by the artist. The second was installed at the Hessisches Landesmuseum in Darmstadt, West Germany, in 1974. The first two works no longer exist. The third and last room, *The New York Earth Room* (1977), is the only one that has been conserved to this day.

The same approach of antithetical games continues in *Riverbed* by Olafur Eliasson but from a more modern perspective. In this work, a river invades the rooms of a museum. However, unlike De Maria's proposal, this installation is transitable: viewers can stroll along the riverbed and even smell the different natural materials, opting for experience instead of contemplation. If human actions harass the landscape in the contemporary word, then it is nature that colonizes the artistic space. It transforms the action of walking through a gallery into one of walking along a river, thereby opening up new perceptions for the viewer.

We can observe two fairly similar methods of playing with oppositions of contrasts. Through decontextualization, the architectural space in both examples is occupied with an element of nature that provokes a juxtaposition of opposites, either physically or conceptually. The initial antithesis is that of man versus nature.

Elliott ERWITT, *Prado Museum*,
1995, Madrid, Spain.

Gelatin silver print on paper.
Image: 14.84 x 21.97 in. (37.7 x 55.8 cm).
Support: 19.88 x 23.62 in. (50.5 x 60.5 cm).
© Museo Nacional Centro de Arte Reina Sofía
/Archivo Fotográfico Museo Nacional Centro
de Arte Reina Sofía

Olafur ELIASSON, *Riverbed*, 2014,
Humlebæk, Denmark.

Water, blue basalt, basalt, lava, stone, wood,
steel, foil, hose, pumps, cooling unit.
Installation view: Louisiana Museum of
Modern Art, Humlebæk, Denmark, 2014

Photo: Anders Sune Berg

Courtesy of the Artist;
neugerriemschneider, Berlin; Tanya
Bonakdar Gallery, New York / Los Angeles
© 2014 Olafur Eliasson

Walter DE MARIA (1935–2013),
Munich Earth Room, 1968,
Munich, Germany.

65 cubic yards (50 cubic m.) of dirt
covering an area of 907 sq. ft. (84 sq. m.)
with a depth of 23.625 in. (60 cm).
Heiner Friedrich Gallery, Munich.
Work non-extant.

Photo: Heide Stolz.

© Estate of Walter De Maria, courtesy of
the Walter De Maria Archive

METAPHORICAL
& METONYMIC
Substitution

●METAPHORICAL &
METONYMIC Substitution
●ENARGIA
●Example, allusion, and
citation of authority
●Emotional appeals

Operation:
SUBSTITUTION
Relation:
CONTIGUITY

Antinomasia
— Nominatio
(L. "naming");
Pronominatio;
Surnamer.

See also
METONYMY [075].

G. "use of an epithet or patronymic, instead of a proper name, or the reverse"

Antonomasia

Descriptive phrase for a proper name.

Jerry: The guy who runs the place is a little temperamental, especially about the ordering procedure. He's secretly referred to as the Soup Nazi.

Elaine: Why? What happens if you don't order right?

Jerry: He yells and you don't get your soup.

—*Seinfeld*, "The Soup Nazi," November 1995.

Antonomasia is a color of rhetoric in which a descriptive phrase or epithet replaces a proper name (and vice versa), allowing people to recognize the person in question. Antonomasia is regarded as similar to METONYMY [075] in some respects. An example of antonomasia is when Churchill crossed out a cabinet minister's name and inserted "Some funkstick in the Air Ministry." Alternatively, a person can be given a moniker that expresses a quality associated with them. There are many cultural examples of this: Aristotle as "The Philosopher," William Shakespeare as "The Bard," or Michael Jackson as "The King of Pop." Calling a lover "Casanova," an office worker "Dilbert," Bill Clinton "The Comeback Kid," or Horace Rumpole's wife "She Who Must Be Obeyed" are further examples of antonomasia.

A physical example of antonomasia is the four gigantic sculptures depicting the faces of US Presidents George Washington (1732–1799), Thomas Jefferson (1743–1826), Abraham Lincoln (1809–1865), and Theodore Roosevelt (1858–1919). The four Presidents are carved into the southeastern face of *Mount Rushmore* in the Black Hills of South Dakota. As Gutzon Borglum (1867–1941), architect and sculptor of the Memorial, affirmed,

> The purpose of the memorial is to communicate the founding, expansion, preservation, and unification of the United States with colossal statues of Washington, Jefferson, Lincoln, and Roosevelt. These four presidents were selected based on what each symbolized.

Thus, the monument expresses a set of national values through these four presidents. George Washington represents the struggle for independence, Thomas Jefferson the idea of government by the people, Abraham Lincoln the notion of equality and the permanent union of the states, and Theodore Roosevelt the United States' role in world affairs.

As said above, this color is a type of metonymy. In this case, the monument also utilizes **synecdoche** [096] since the heads describe the presidents.

Gutzon BORGLUM (1867–1941),
Mount Rushmore Monument, 1927–1941,
South Dakota, United States.

An engineer works on George Washington's head
at Mount Rushmore, South Dakota. Sculptor Gutzon
Borglum oversaw the carving of the colossal granite
*Mount Rushmore National Monume*nt in the Black
Hills of South Dakota between 1927 and 1941. As well
as George Washington, the monument also features
sculptures of Thomas Jefferson, Abraham Lincoln, and
Theodore Roosevelt.

London, Keystone Archives
© 2022. Photo Art Media/Heritage Images/Scala,
Florence

033

EXAMPLE,
ALLUSION, AND
CITATION OF
AUTHORITY

● Techniques of argument
● Example, allusion, and
citation of authority
● AMPLIFICATIO(N)

Operation:
AMPLIFICATION
Relation:
CONTIGUITY

Alt. sp. Apodeixis;
Experientia.

G. "demonstration, proof"

Apodixis

Confirming a statement by reference to generally accepted principles or experience.

SORIANO &
ASOCIADOS
arquitectos, *The
Museum of all
Museums,* 2011,
Taipei City, Taiwan.

The New Taipei
City Museum of Art
Proposal, Taipei City,
Taiwan. Conceptual
Design. International
Competition, Third Prize
Winning Proposal.
Courtesy of S&Aa

[Soriano & Asociados
arquitectos: Federico
SORIANO and Dolores
PALACIOS]

Was I aware — was I fully aware of the discrepancy
between us? That the age of the husband should
surpass by a few years — even by fifteen or twenty
— the age of the wife, was regarded by the world as
admissible, and, indeed, as even proper, but she had
always entertained the belief that the years of the wife
should never exceed in number those of the husband.

—Edgar Allan POE, "The Spectacles," 1844.

First underground floor.

"*The Museum of all Museums* is shown as isolated
pieces in a garden of bamboo swaying in the air.
The reeds, in his pendulum movement, glimpse
visitors walking towards the buildings. Only a few
emerged of the whole hundred. But once inside, we
are in the museum of all museums."

Second underground floor.

"The Museum consists of two underground levels for
the exhibition spaces and bodies which protrude, the
lobbies, access points and commercial areas. The parking
lots and all the services necessary for the development
of the energetic efficiency of the museum are the
foundations of the complex."

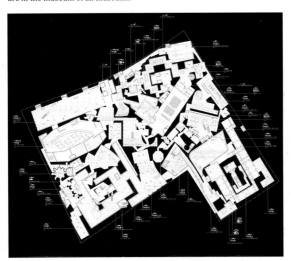

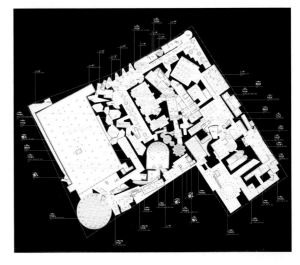

Apodixis (translated as "proof" or "demonstration") uses acknowledged, accepted, and recognized precedents, works, examples, or authors to make an argument more robust and authoritative. Apodixis confirms a statement by referring to common knowledge, universal practices, principles, or experience.

Apodixis (along with **anamnesis** [014], **apomnemonysis** [034], and **epicrisis** [057]) is a figure of ethos because it establishes the ethos (credibility) of the author through logic by utilizing proofs or authorities that are valued by the audience. In this way, apodixis conveys that the speaker or writer is knowledgeable of the topic on which they are speaking or writing. In rhetoric, ethos is seen in the character or emotions of a speaker or writer as they try to persuade an audience. Ethos should not be confused with pathos, which has to do with the emotions the author hopes to induce in the audience.

The New Taipei City Museum of Art by Federico Soriano and Dolores Palacios transposes to architecture the apodixis-based strategy of citing authority figures. A collection of the world's most important art museums comprises this architectural competition entry. One hundred fragments of recognized art galleries from throughout the world are the core of this new art museum in Taipei City. As the architects explain, architecture is understood as the sheer abstraction of a historic landscape. In this case, the direct reference to past matters and the use of fragments of old art museums to form an entirely new proposal exemplifies the use of this rhetorical strategy in architecture.

Collection of generic pieces of plants from the world's museums to be injected into the Taipei City Museum of Art.

"A museum that contains all the museums. All the major museums, a collection of 100 art museums in the world. Architecture as a purified abstraction of historical landscape."

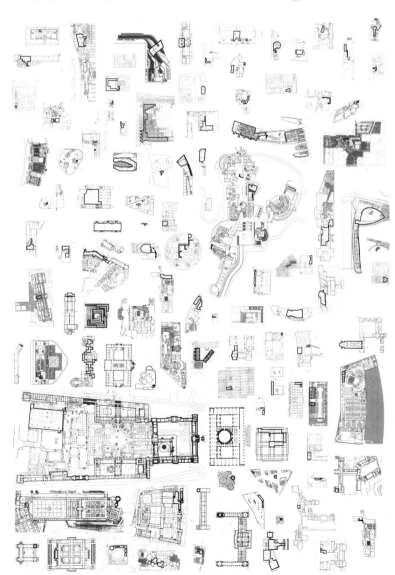

Some of the fragments of the *Museum of all Museums*: The MAXXI or National Museum of the 21st century of Arts Museum, Rome, Zaha Hadid Architects, 1998–2009. Guggenheim Museum, New York, Frank Lloyd Wright, 1959. Denver Art Museum, Denver, Studio Libeskind, 2006. Mercedes-Benz Museum, Stuttgart, UNStudio, 2001–2006. Van Gogh Museum, Amsterdam, Gerrit Rietveld, 1973; Kurokawa, 1999; Hans van Heeswijk Architects, 2015. Ibere Camargo Foundation, Porto Alegre, Alvaro Siza, 2008. Getty Center, Los Angeles, Richard Meier & Partners, 1997. National Gallery of Art, East Building, Washington DC, I. M. Pei, 1978. 21 st Museum of Contemporary Art Kannazawa, Japan, Sanaa, 1999. Prado Museum, Madrid, Juan de Villanueva, 1785; Rafael Moneo, 1998–2007. Museum of Unlimited Growth, Le Corbusier, 1939. Museum of Silkeborg, Jørn Utzon, 1964. Louvre Museum, Paris, Pierre Lescot, 1527; I. M. Pei, 1981. Altes Museum, Berlin, Karl Friedrich Schinkel, 1823–1930. Museo del Tesoro di San Lorenzo, Genova, Franco Albini, 1952–1956.

EXAMPLE,
ALLUSION, AND
CITATION OF
AUTHORITY

● Techniques of argument
● Example, allusion, and
citation of authority
● REPETITIO(N)
● AMPLIFICATIO(N)

Operation:
REPETITION
Relation:
CONTIGUITY

—Commemoratio
(L. "a calling to
mind, mentioning").

G. "recounting, summarizing"

Apomnemonysis

The quotation of an approved authority from memory.

He is well acquainted with my MS., and I just copied
into the middle of the blank sheet the words—
    —Un dessein si funeste,
    S'il n'est digne d'Atrée, est digne de Thyeste.
They are to be found in Crébillon's 'Atrée.

—Edgar Allan POE, "The Purloined Letter," 1844.

Jean TINGUELY (1925–1991),
Homage to New York, 1960,
New York, United States.

Drawing printed on
the brochure for *A Self-
Constructing and Self-
Destroying Work of Art.*

Event in the Abby Aldrich
Rockefeller Sculpture Garden
in 1960. New York, Museum of
Modern Art (MoMA).
Offset, printed in black,
30 x 9.25 in. (76.2 x 23.5 cm).
William C. Seitz Papers, *Art of
Assemblage* 6. The Museum of
Modern Art Archives, NY. Acc. n.:
MA296.
© 2022. Digital image, The
Museum of Modern Art, New
York/Scala, Florence
© Jean Tinguely

Apomnemonysis is an example, allusion, and authority citation (along with **anamnesis** [014], **apodixis** [033], and **epicrisis** [057]) by which established and relevant examples and quotations support an argument or opinion. The word comes from Greek and means "recounting" and "summarizing." (*Commemoratio* —"a calling to mind, mentioning" — is its Latin name.) It works by precisely quoting an approved authority from memory.

The exhibition *Joyous Machines: Michael Landy and Jean Tinguely*, co-curated by renowned British artist Michael Landy and displayed from October 2, 2009, to January 10, 2010, in Tate Liverpool, is an exceptional visual representation of apomnemonysis in iconic language. The show pays homage to Swiss sculptor Jean Tinguely (1925–1991). It celebrates Tinguely's

influence upon Landy's career and shows how both artists' work is connected.

The exhibition devotes special attention to Tinguely's lesser-known early career, tracing a path from his beginnings as an artist in the late 1940s through to his most famous and influential sculpture-happening, *Homage to New York: A Self-Constructing and Self-Destroying Work of Art*, in the Museum of Modern Art. The provocative and innovative artwork was an eight-meter-high self-destroying mechanism that came to life for 27 minutes before catching fire during a performance in the Sculpture Garden of the MoMA on March 17, 1960. Landy created a series of excellent drawings that alluded to Tinguely's work. In the visual and art world, such work is viewed as a quotation of an approved authority, thus reflecting apomnemonysis.

Michael LANDY, *H.2.N.Y. How to Commit Auto-Destructive Suicide at the Sculpture Garden,* 2006, London, United Kingdom.
© Michael Landy. Courtesy of the Artist and Thomas Dane Gallery

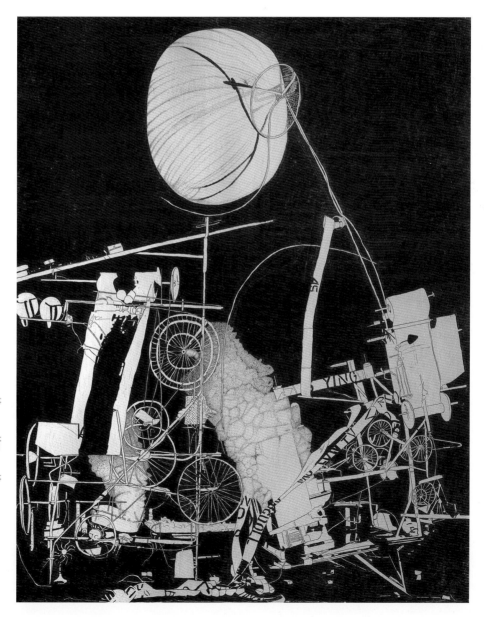

035

AMPLIFICATIO(N)

● Techniques of argument
● AMPLIFICATIO(N)

Operation:
AMPLIFICATION
Relation:
DIFFERENCE

L. "a setting before, to put near"

Appositio

Two juxtaposed nouns, the second elaborating the first.

For *Bridge of Houses see also* Parenthesis [080].

John Fitzgerald Kennedy, a great and good President, the friend of all people of goodwill, a believer in the dignity and equality of all human beings, a fighter for justice, an apostle of peace, has been snatched from our midst by the bullet of an assassin.

—Earl WARREN, "Eulogy for John F. Kennedy," November 24, 1963.

Appositio is a Latin term for *apposition*; its etymology is derived from *ad* "near" and *positio* "placement." This color describes cases in which two descriptive elements—usually noun phrases—are placed adjacent to one another, with one element giving a detailed description or definition of the other. In other words, appositio is the addition of an adjacent, coordinated, explanatory, or descriptive element as in "Henry, King of England" or "Albert Einstein, perhaps the greatest of scientists seemed not to have mastered the physics of hair combing."

During the 1970s, American architect Steven Holl developed two conceptual proposals (never built) on the theme of "Bridges of Houses." One project was for New York and the other for Melbourne. These speculations, highlight three common topics: (1) the combination of different structures and programs to create hybrid forms, (2) the reuse of existing and obsolete urban infrastructures to create a composed history, and (3) the reinforcement of existing urban patterns using new constructions.

According to Bernard Tschumi, "transprogramming" entails combining two or more programs, regardless of their incompatibilities, with their respective spatial configurations. It is a ubiquitous design strategy in architecture, that Steven Holl follows in *Bridge of Houses*, as the project attempts to find urban connections to the relationship between the bridge and domestic programs, between public transit areas and private living areas. In this regard, any combination of different programs within a single spatial configuration

can be understood as an architectural appositio in which "programs" (instead of words) are placed alongside each other with one "function" (the house), to elaborate, clarify, or define the other "program" (the bridge).

The text published in *Pamphlet Architecture* (No. 7) in 1981 describes the New York proposal as follows:

> The site and structural foundation of *The Bridge of Houses* is the existing superstructure of an abandoned elevated rail link in the Chelsea area of New York City. This steel structure is utilized in its straight leg from West 19th Street to West 29th Street parallel to the Hudson River.

> In 1977 West Chelsea began to change from a warehouse district to an art district. *The Bridge of Houses* reflects the new character of the area as a

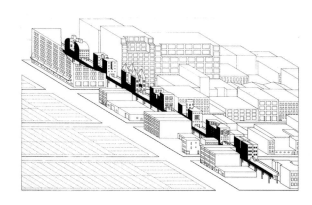

Manhattan Site Plan

Section

[001] Accumulatio; [011] AMPLIFICATIO; [017] Anastrophe;
[025] Antilogy; [035] Appositio; [045] Commoratio;
[047] Congeries; [049] Diallage; [050] Dinumeratio;
[051] Disjunctio; [055] ENARGIA; [056] Epexegesis;
[058] Epitheton; [066] HYPERBATON; Parataxis;
[080] Parenthesis; [082] Ploce; [091] Significatio;
[095] Syncrisis; [100] Topographia; [101] Topothesia.

place of habitation. Re-use rather than demolition of the existing bridge would be a permanent contribution to the character of the city.

This project offers a variety of housing types for the Chelsea area, as well as an elevated public promenade connecting with the Convention Center on its north end. The structural capacity and width of the existing bridge determine the height and width of the houses. Four houses have been developed in detail, emphasizing the intention to provide a collection of housing blocks offering the widest possible range of social-economic coexistence. At one extreme are houses of single-room-occupancy type, offered for the city's homeless; each of these blocks contains twenty studio rooms. At the other extreme are houses of luxury apartments; each of these blocks contains three or four flats. Shops line the public promenade level below the houses.

The *Pamphlet Architecture* series was created to stimulate research; each issue was curated, written, and designed by a single architect.

In speech and writing, appositio often occurs when verbs (particularly verbs of being) in supporting clauses are eliminated to produce shorter descriptive phrases. Therefore, they often function as HYPERBATON [066] or figures of disorder because they can disrupt the flow of a sentence.

Precisely, a departure of the typical architectural order, known as hyperbaton, also happens in *Manhattan Bridge of Houses* since it is an elevated "ornate collection of urban villas." Each house acts as a bridge, thus providing a passageway at the pedestrian level such that the promenade becomes a series of public courtyards.

Steven HOLL, *New York Bridge of Houses*, 1979,
New York, United States.
Oblique projections, site plan, model, elevations,
plans, and sections.
Courtesy of Steven Holl Architects

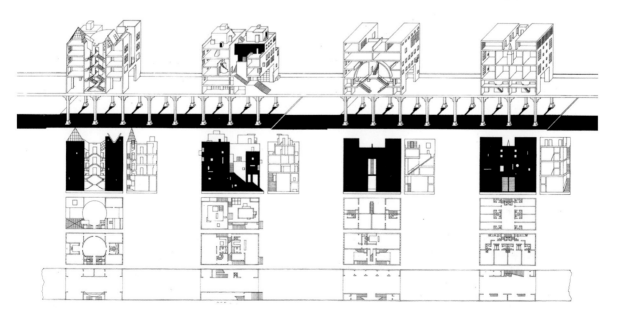

Assonance

Identity or similarity in sound between internal vowels in neighboring words.

if a cheerfulest Elephantangelchild should sit
(holding a red candle over his head
by a finger of trunk, and singing out of a red
book) on a pr*ou*d r*ou*nd cl*ou*d in a wh*i*te h*i*gh n*i*ght

—E. E. CUMMINGS, *Xapie*, "if a cheerfulest Elephantangelchild should sit," 1950.

Assonance is the repetition or resemblance of vowel sounds, preceded and followed by different consonants, in the stressed syllables of adjacent words. Thus Churchill remarked on a "tiny, timid, tentative, tardy" increase in air strength in Britain's rearmament before World War II.

"Time Sections" is part of Daniel Libeskind's renowned *Micromegas Series. The Architecture of End Space*—named after a satirical story by Voltaire. This series is composed of 10 drawings: "The Garden," "Time Sections," "Leakage," "Little Universe," "Arctic Flowers," "The Burrow Laws," "Dance Sounds," "Maldoror's Equation," "Vertical Horizon," and "Dream Calculus." Each drawing is a clear transposition of assonance into architectural language. The line-works of *Micromegas* use only a few similar elements—for example, lines, rectangles, triangles, arches—that are continuously repeated and transformed millions of times to create a small but rich universe.

Libeskind states that

> An architectural drawing is as much a prospective unfolding of future possibilities as it is a recovery of a particular history to whose intentions it testifies and whose limits it always challenges. In any case, a drawing is more than the shadow of an object, more than a pile of lines, more than a resignation to the inertia of convention.

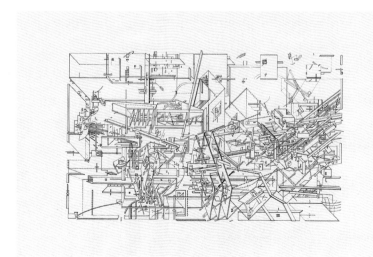

Daniel LIBESKIND, "Time Sections," *Micromegas series. The Architecture of End Space*, 1979.

New York, Museum of Modern Art (MoMA). Silkscreen on paper 26 x 36.125 in. (66 x 91.8 cm). Robert K. and Barbara J. Straus Family Foundation, Inc. 271.1999

© 2022. Digital image, The Museum of Modern Art, New York/Scala, Florence

PUN
- IRONY
- PUN
- AMPLIFICATIO(N)
- Brevity
- Emotional appeals

Operation:
SUBSTITUTION
Relation:
DOUBLE MEANING

— Civill Jest; Merry
Scoffe; Urbanitas
(L. "refinement,
elegance").

See also PUN [088].

G. "wit"

Asteismus

Facetious or mocking answer that plays on a word.

"We will suppose," said the miser, "that his symptoms are such and such; now, doctor, what would you have directed him to take?"

"Take!" said Abernethy, "why, take advice, to be sure."

—Edgar Allan POE, "The Purloined Letter," 1844.

Francis ALŸS, *Turista* (Tourist), 1994, Mexico City, Mexico.

Photographic documentation of an action.

Photo: Enrique Huerta
© Francis Alÿs

[010] Amphibologia; [011] AMPLIFICATIO;
[020] Antanaclasis; [021] Antapodosis;
[028] Antiphrasis; [032] Antonomasia;
[035] Appositio; [037] Asteismus; Augendi Causa;
Brevitas; [052] Ecphonesis; Emphasis; Enantiosis;
[070] IRONY; [071] Isocolon; [074] METAPHOR;
[075] METONYMY; MIMESIS; [081] Paronomasia;
PATHOPOEIA; Peristasis; [088] PUN; [091] Significatio;
[099] Systrophe.

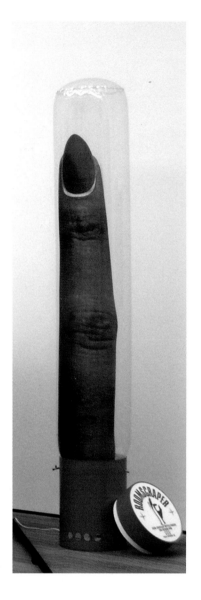

HAUS-RUCKER-CO, *Roomscraper*, 1969.
Structure: base red-colored cardboard drum.
Inflatable pillar with silkscreen of a giant lady-
finger; 15.75 x 82.68 in. (40 x 210 cm).
© Haus-Rucker-Co/Zamp Kelp. Courtesy of
Günter Zamp Kelp

[Haus-Rucker-Co (1967–1992): Laurids
ORTNER, Günther ZAMP KELP, Klaus PINTER,
and Manfred ORTNER]

Asteismus (from the Greek word "city," just as *urbanitas* does from Latin) is a color of rhetoric belonging to the family of PUNS [088], or wordplays, that reflects the quick wit attributed to city-dweller (Lanham 1991, p. 25). Asteismus is exemplified in the following exchange from *The Goon Show*: "Did you put the cat out?" "No, it wasn't on fire." Another example can be found in Fritz Kreisler's famous reply when someone asked him the way to Carnegie Hall: "Practice."

Francis Alÿs's performance *Turista* represents asteismus in the visual world, as the title itself is a play on the Spanish word for "tourist" ("turista"). The fence in front of the Metropolitan Cathedral, located in Downtown Mexico City, is a popular public place where unemployed construction workers, carpenters, plumbers, electricians, house painters, and other workers offer their services. This photograph, which is part of the documentation of the activities of this area, shows the artist alongside these workers, wearing sunglasses, a jacket, and a sign that reads "Turista." As if representing an informal job placement agency in the middle of the plaza, the artist stands among the laborers, offering himself as a tourist under identical conditions.

This simple gesture might be understood in many ways, and it raises various questions about the work of an artist. As Alÿs explained,

> At the time I think it was about questioning or accepting the limits of my condition of outsider, of "gringo." How far can I belong to this place? How much can I judge it? By offering my services as a tourist, I was oscillating between leisure and work, contemplation and interference. I was testing and denouncing my own status. Where am I really standing?

Roomscraper by Viennese group Haus-Rucker-Co ("house movers") is another example of asteismus. In fact, the piece's name is an example of wordplay—as the authors express, "Skyscrapers are scraping the sky. Roomscrapers are scraping living rooms."

Bernard TSCHUMI,
*The Manhattan Transcripts
project,* 1976–1981,
New York, United States.

"Episode 1: The Park,"
1976–1977.

New York, Museum of Modern
Art (MoMA). Gelatin silver
photograph 14 x 18 in. (35.6 x
45.7cm). Purchase and partial
gift of the architect in honor
of Lily Auchincloss. Acc. n.:
3.1995.4.

© 2022. Digital image, The
Museum of Modern Art, New
York/Scala, Florence

G. "unconnected"

Asyndeton

Omission of conjunctions between words, phrases, or clauses.

All is over. Silent, mournful, abandoned, broken,
Czechoslovakia recedes into the darkness.

—Winston CHURCHILL on the Munich
Agreement, 1938.

The Manhattan Transcripts project (1976–1981) by Bernard Tschumi constitutes
an extended theoretical text intended to present an architectural interpretation
of reality. Since some elements are disconnected, these architectural drawings
also provide a visual transposition of the rhetorical device known as **asyndeton**,
in which the conjunctions between words, phrases, or clauses are omitted. An
example of asyndeton in verbal language is the famous phrase uttered by Julius
Ceaser, "Veni, vidi, vici" ("I came, I saw, I conquered"). As Jacques Durand explains,
the visual equivalent of asyndeton is an image that has been fragmented into
parts—for example, into vertical or horizontal strips.

The Manhattan Transcripts involves four city archetypes—the park, street, tower
or skyscraper, and block—and four specific modes of representation—plans,
sections, oblique projections, and perspectives. At the same time, *The Manhattan
Transcripts* simultaneously defines three disjoined levels and sequences of reality:
spaces, events, and movements. Each of these sequences (drawn in frames and
separated into columns and rows) focuses on what happens to the architecture.
Part one ("The Park") begins with a murder in New York's Central Park. A three-
square composition is the specific mode of notation chosen to underscore the

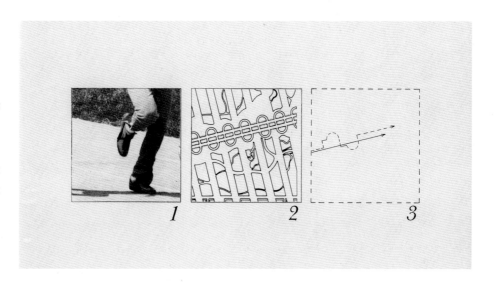

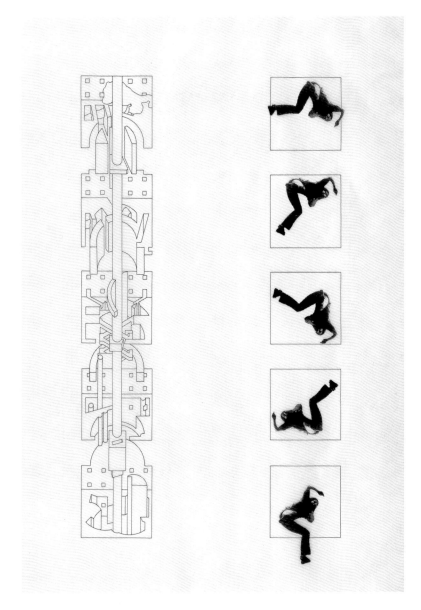

Bernard TSCHUMI, *The Manhattan Transcripts project,* 1976–1981, New York, United States.

"Episode 3: the Tower," 1979.

New York, Museum of Modern Art (MoMA). Ink and photograph reproductions on tracing paper 48 x 24 in. (121.9 x 61 cm). Purchase and partial gift of the architect in honor of Lily Auchincloss 7.1995.9.

© 2022. Digital image, The Museum of Modern Art, New York/Scala, Florence

relationship between an event (photograph), space (plan), and movement (diagram). The movement is annotated through abstractions of news photographs. As Tschumi explains, the photographs show actions, the plans reveal changing architectural manifestations, and the diagrams indicate the protagonists' movements.

A drawing belonging to part three ("The Tower," subtitled "The Fall") addresses the movement of bodies in space by depicting a fall through the floors of a skyscraper. The first column depicts the "space" of the action using oblique projections as the mode of representation. Five duotone photographs illustrate the sequence of "the fall" more objectively than the oblique projections. The vertical discontinuity is more evident in the sequence of events than in the space column. *The Manhattan Transcripts* can be read horizontally (by combining the event, movement, and space) or vertically (by considering the event, movement, and space separately).

Like in verbal language, where conjunctions are eliminated without eliminating grammatical accuracy, *The Manhattan Transcripts* omit some parts of the narrative while representing three levels of reality individually and separately.

G. "increase, amplification"

Auxesis

Words or clauses placed in climactic order.

The school-room was the largest in the house – I could not help thinking, in the world.

—Edgar Allan POE, *William Wilson*, 1839.

Auxesis is a Greek word that means growth, increase, or amplification, as well as a rhetorical term for a gradual increase in the intensity of meaning, with words arranged in ascending order of impact or importance. HYPERBOLE [067] is a subtype of this figure of speech in which a point or its significance is intentionally exaggerated. It may also refer to the use of a heightened word in place of an ordinary one (for example, calling a corporation president a "titan of industry"). Words or clauses placed in climactic order also fall into this category (as in this Jefferson quote, "Give up money, give up fame, give up science, give up the earth itself and all it contains, rather than do an immoral act"). Building a point around a series of comparisons also qualifies as auxesis, as does a general term for AMPLIFICATIO [011] or one of its subdivisions.

Alexandra THELAN, Chee Kit WAN, and Chun KEONG NG,
Superorganism, 2018, Melbourne, Australia.
The Pleasure Palace.

"The Garden of Earthly Delights. A Social Condenser of Contemporary Pleasures," Second-Year Design Studio by María Fullaondo and Joseph Gauci-Seddon, First Semester 2018, Monash Art Design Architecture (MADA), Monash University.
Courtesy of the Authors

A LIVING, BREATHING CITY OF EVER-CHANGING PLEASURES

SUPERORGANISM

An architecture students' hybrid drawing of this "superorganism" or palace of pleasures is a vibrant example of this color of rhetoric. Two points of view (namely, an elevation and a section) illustrate a mega-structure or ship that moves and behaves like an organism. This structure seems to live because of the pleasant activity occurring inside. It represents auxesis through size, the accumulation of fragments of "industrial architecture," and the abundance of actions, characters, and bodies inhabiting the structure, as well as the hanging elements and the mobility of the character of this laboratory.

Between 1956 and 1969, Hans Hollein created a set of photomontages and collages that acted as manifestos of his dissatisfaction with the architectural status quo of the early 1960s. He also used this work to invite speculations about the future of architecture. Hollein's *Copenhagen buried* is another visual representation of auxesis.

Hans HOLLEIN (1934–2014), *Copenhagen buried*, 1969, Copenhagen, Denmark.

Photomontage retouched.

© Private archive Hollein
Courtesy Collection Centre Pompidou, Paris
Musée national d'art moderne/Centre de création industrielle

EMOTIONAL
APPEALS
● Techniques of argument
● REPETITIO(N)
● AMPLIFICATIO(N)
● Emotional appeals

Operation:
AMPLIFICATION
Relation:
DIFFERENCE

—Bomphilogia

G. "booming, buzzing words"

Bomphiologia

Bombastic speech.

"Solus," egregious dog? O viper vile!
The "solus" in the most mervailous face;
The "solus" in thy teeth, and in thy throat,
And in thy hateful lungs, yea, in the maw, perdy,
And, which is worse, within thy nasty mouth!
I do retort the "solus" in thy bowels;
For I can take, and Pistol's cock is up,
And flashing fire will follow.

—William SHAKESPEARE, *Henry V*, (1599).

Bomphiologia (also known as *verborum bombus*, from Greek, literally "booming, buzzing words"), refers to a speech with inflated words, in which the speaker uses pompous and bombastic languages for things of little magnitude.

Un Chien Andalou (An Andalusian Dog) is a 1929 silent short film by the Spanish director Luis Buñuel (1900–1983) and artist Salvador Dalí (1904–1989) that exemplifies bomphiologia in the visual realm. The primary sources of the film's surrealistic images were the dreams of Dalí and Buñuel, and they sought to maintain that dream logic throughout the film. For instance, the events in the film are intentionally disconnected, and no continuity or causation is apparent. Furthermore, the film has no narrative or story: the message is the lack of message.

It is one of the most famous shocking films of the silent era and continues to push the boundaries of violence, even today. It includes an eyeball being slashed by a razor, ants crawling out of a hole in a man's hand, a hand that has been severed, the rotting corpses of two donkeys lying across two pianos, and a couple of young lovers half-buried and seemingly dead on a beach, among other disturbing images.

The images amplify and move the audience's indignation and rage beyond the bombastic imagery of *Un Chien Andalou*. In rhetoric, this strategy is called **cohortatio**. In the Paris premiere, Buñuel and Dalí were prepared for a strong audience reaction. However, the response was the opposite of what they expected—an exasperated Buñuel exclaimed,

> What can I do about the people who adore all that is new, even when it goes against their deepest convictions, or about the insincere, corrupt press,

and the inane herd that saw beauty or poetry in something which was basically no more than a desperate impassioned call for murder?

Un Chien Andalou was several decades ahead of its time.

Luis BUÑUEL (1900–1983) and Salvador DALI (1904–1989), *Un Chien Andalou* (An Andalusian Dog), 1929.
© Heirs of Buñuel. France, Paris, Centre Pompidou - Musée national d'art moderne - Centre de création industrielle
Photo © Centre Pompidou, MNAM-CCI, Dist. RMN-Grand Palais / Georges Meguerditchian

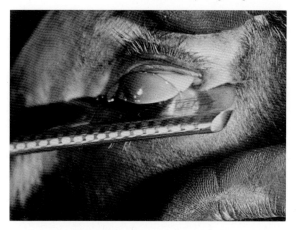

HYPERBATON

● Ungrammatical, illogical, or unusual uses of language
● HYPERBATON
● AMPLIFICATIO(N)
● Emotional appeals

Operation:
REARRANGEMENT
Relation:
DIFFERENCE

—Male colacatum
(L. "badly grouped");
Misplacer.

See also
HYPERBATON [066].

G. "ill-composed"

Cacosyntheton

Awkward transposition of the parts of a sentence.

This is the kind of tedious [sometimes "pedantic"] nonsense up with which I will not put!

—Winston CHURCHILL, "Alleged marginal note," February 27, 1944.

Tom FRIEDMAN, *Untitled*, 1994.
Christie's Images Limited. Gelatin silver print mounted on board, 34.5 x 24.5 in. (87.6 x 62.2 cm).
© 2022. Christie's Images, London/Scala, Florence

Christian SKREIN,
Katharina Sarnitz auf dem Boden der Boutique CM
(Katharina Sarnitz on the floor of the CM Boutique), 1968, Vienna, Austria.
Fashion shot in CM Boutique designed by Hans HOLLEIN, (1966–1967).
Photo: Christian Skrein
© 2022. Photo Austrian Archives/Scala Florence

This 1968 fashion photograph exemplifies a form of HYPERBATON [060] called **cacosyntheton**—a composition or a phrase that is poorly put together, such as when an adjective improperly follows a noun. The image shows Katharina Sarnitz lying like a dead body on the floor of the CM boutique designed by Hans Hollein in Vienna. It is an unusual position for a person, especially if they are a model in a fashion shot. The reflection of the woman's head in the mirror increases the unpleasant effect of this strange vision. In addition, a solitary mannequin completes this intriguing photograph where nothing seems to be in the right place.

Tom Friedman's photography provides an even more vivid example of a change in the order and the natural position of objects (even including a body) in space. A surprising, almost magical effect of a man floating in space is achieved by turning the image.

G. "wit, graceful jest"

Charientismus

Clothing a disagreeable sense with agreeable expressions.

King. Have you heard the argument? Is there no offense in't?

Hamlet. No, no, they do but jest, poison in jest; no offense i' the world.

—William SHAKESPEARE, *Hamlet*, (1600).

In Sylva Rhetoricae, Gideon O. Burton defines **charientismus** as "mollifying harsh words by answering them with a smooth and appeasing mock." Meanwhile, Lanham identifies charientismus as a type of IRONY [070]—for example, clothing a disagreeable sense with agreeable expressions, soothing over a difficulty, or turning aside antagonism with a joke. He provides the following example from Robert Redford about where he lives: "If you stay in Beverly Hills too long, you become a Mercedes."

In a way, the MVRDV's revolutionary vertical pig farm in The Netherlands is a form of charientismus. The vertical farm comprises several 622-meter-high towers, ensuring that all pigs' conditions are equivalent. In this novel environment, pigs have more space than usual, are kept in groups of natural sizes, and have access to better facilities and comfort.

MVRDV, *Pig City*, 2006,
The Netherlands.

Image Credits/Crédits
d'images: Paula van Baak and
Winy Maas, MVRDV harbor.
© MVRDV

[MVRDV founders: Winy MAAS,
Jacob VAN RIJS and Nathalie
DE VRIES]

Operation:
REARRANGEMENT
Relation:
OPOSSITION

—Commutatio

See also
Antimetabole [026].

G. "crossing"

Chiasmus

The ABBA pattern of mirror inversion.

Do I love you because you're beautiful?
Or are you beautiful because I love you?

—Oscar HAMMERSTEIN II and Richard ROGERS,
Do I Love You Because You're Beautiful?, (1957).

Chiasmus, derived from the Greek letter X (chi), is a verbal strategy that balances two or more clauses by reversing their structures. Specifically, the second half of an expression is balanced against the first but with the parts reversed. Thus, chiasmus repeats both ideas and grammatical structures in an inverted order. An example of this device is a crushing comment once made by Samuel Johnson to an aspiring author: "Your manuscript is both good and original, but the part that is good is not original, and the part that is original is not good."

Chiasmus resembles **antimetabole** [026], as both are marked by the inversion of structure. In the simplest sense, the term "chiasmus" applies to almost all such inverted structures. In its strict classical sense, the only function of this device is to reverse the grammatical structure or ideas of sentences; the repetition of words and phrases does not occur.

Prada Transformer by OMA can be considered an architectural chiasmus. The pavilion is a 20-meter-high temporary structure that rotates and combines four cultural events—a fashion exhibition, a film festival, an art exhibition, and a Prada fashion show. Four cranes are used to change the pavilion into

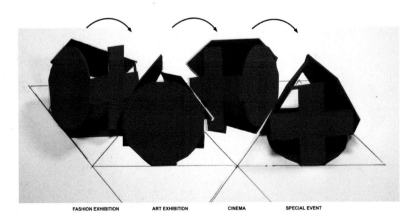

OMA (Rem KOOLHAAS
and Ellen VAN LOON),
Prada Transformer, 2007–
2009, Seoul, South Korea.
© Prada Transformer/OMA
Courtesy of OMA

FASHION EXHIBITION   ART EXHIBITION   CINEMA   SPECIAL EVENT four basic geometric shapes—a circle, a cross, a hexagon, and a rectangle—that lean together and are wrapped in a translucent membrane. Each new facade serves as the setting for its own distinct cultural program. The walls become floors, and the floors become walls as three cranes flip over the pavilion after each event.

Villa Nautilus, Brodsky and Utkins's tribute to the famous submarine in *Twenty Thousand Leagues Under the Sea* by the French writer Jules Verne, is a clear visual example of chiasmus or antimetabole. This underground house for a hermit in the center of a city utilizes repetition in successive clauses. The upper (above-ground) part of the house is repeated in the bottom (below-ground) part. A wardrobe, two chairs, a table, a bookshelf, and even a bottle of wine are duplicated in the vertical section of the refuge. These two areas of the contemporary version of Nemo's home, connected by a spiral staircase, are the same.

[001] Accumulatio;
Aenos; [014] Anamnesis;
[017] Anastrophe; [026] Antimetabole;
[034] Apomnemonysis;
[035] Appositio; [043] Chiasmus;
[046] Conduplicatio; Demonstratio;
[052] Ecphonesis;
Emphasis; [054] ENALLAGE;
[055] ENARGIA; [057] Epicrisis;
[062] Fable; [066] HYPERBATON;
[067] Hyperbole; [069] Image;
[071] Isocolon; [074] METAPHOR;
[075] METONYMY; [078] Palindrome;
PATHOPOEIA; Peristasis;
REPETITIO(N); [091] Significatio;
[101] Topothesia.

BRODSKY & UTKIN, *Villa Nautilus. A Bastion of Resistance*, 1985.

[Brodsky & Utkin: Alexander BRODSKY and Ilya UTKIN]

G. "ladder"

Climax

Mounting by degrees through linked words or phrases, usually of increasing weight and in parallel construction.

of this wine may be verified that merry induction, that good wine makes good blood, good blood causeth good humours, good humours cause good thoughts, good thoughts bring forth good works, good works carry a man to heaven, ergo good wine carry man to heaven.

—James HOWELL, *Family Letters*, (1645–1650).

Generally, **climax** (also known as *anabasis, ascensus,* or the *marching figure*) refers to the arrangement of words, phrases, or clauses in order of increasing importance, often in parallel structure. A famous line from the *Adventures of Superman Television Series* is an example of this color of rhetoric: "Look! Up in the sky! It's a bird! It's a plane! It's Superman!" Climax, or **gradatio**, is sometimes achieved through **anadiplosis**—the repetition of the last word of one line or clause to begin the next.

Tango (1981), an animated short film by Polish director Zbigniew Rybczyński, is an excellent visual transposition of climax (among other figures of rhetoric). During the 55th ceremony of the Annual Academy Awards (1983), *Tango* was announced as the winner in the category of Best Animated Short Film. It is an unusual film that is joyful to the point of delirium. It defies the viewer's expectations and transforms the cinematic linear narrative. For example, there is no written text or dialogue, no voiceover, no main character, no single focus. There is no argument or causal development. Nothing is explained. Little makes sense.

There is a setting: a room with three doors, a window, a bed, a bookshelf, and a table where, entirely unexpectedly, a group of characters enter successively and perform a single repeated action in a loop. Few stage elements are needed to contextualize the actors' performances. The first element that becomes visible is a ball that sneaks out the window. The ball introduces a second character: the boy who owns the ball and does not hesitate to enter the room through the window to recover it. After this, one person after another (36 people in total) enters the small space and assumes a single, specific role. Each performance is repeated. Some of the activities performed are eating, sleeping, dressing, crying, fixing a light bulb, doing a headstand, and cleaning the floor. All the characters behave as if no one else is there, while the viewer is a privileged observer who sees everything. The lack of a written or verbal narrative contrasts with the accumulation of visual information and sound. A tango is heard, and synchronized sound effects are repeated. For eight minutes, everything happens.

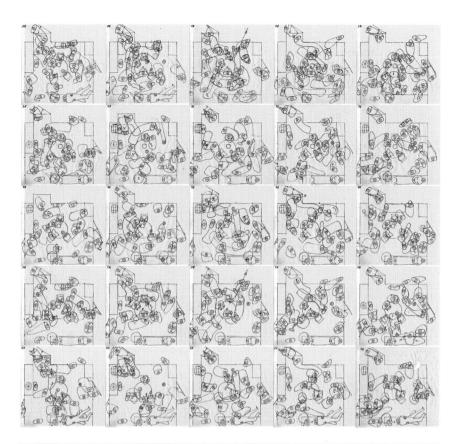

"Thirty-six characters from different stages of life — representations of different times — interact in one room, moving in loops, observed by a static camera. I had to draw and paint about 16.000 cell-mattes, and make several hundred thousand exposures on an optical printer. It took a full seven months, sixteen hours per day, to make the piece. The miracle is that the negative got through the process with only minor damage, and I made less than one hundred mathematical mistakes out of several hundred thousand possibilities. In the final result, there are plenty of flaws ® black lines are visible around humans, jitters caused by the instability of film material resulting from film perforation and elasticity of celluloid, changes of colour caused by the fluctuation in colour temperature of the projector bulb and, inevitably, dirt, grain and scratches."
(Zbig Rybczyński)

Zbigniew RYBCZYŃSKI, *Tango*, 1980, Poland.

Live Action Animation, 35 mm color, 08: 10.' Music: Janusz Hajdun.

Courtesy of Zbigniew Rybczyński

045

L. "lingering"

Commoratio

Emphasizing a strong point by repeating several times in different words.

This parrot is no more. It has ceased to be. It's expired and gone to see its maker! This is a late parrot. It's a stiff! Bereft of life! It rests in peace! If you hadn't nailed it to the perch it would be pushing up the daisies! It's run down the curtain and joined the choir invisible! This is an ex-parrot!

—MONTY PYTHON, *The Dead Parrot Sketch*, 1969.

In rhetoric, repeating a point several times using different words is known as **commoratio** (the term comes from Latin and means "lingering"). Henry Peacham gives the following example of this device: "expelled, thrust out, banished, and cast away from the city." Commoratio is similar to **synonymia** [098] or **communio**. Whereas **anaphora** [016], **epistrophe**, **epanalepsis**, and **antimetabole** [026] repeat the same word or words (in different ways) for emphasis, commoratio repeats the same idea using different words or phrases.

Juan de Sande's artwork depicting several wigs represents commoratio in visual language. In this work, 90 black-and-white photographs of wigs emphasize the same notion. It is helpful to clarify that although all objects are wigs (at least 14 different wigs can be distinguished), each mannequin head is photographed from a different point of view, making every component or part of this grid unique. In this sense, commoratio is very similar to another figure called **epimone**, in which the same idea is repeated using the same words or phrases. Epimone literally means "to remain on a point."

Examples of commoratio seen in architecture can be found in the drawings or counter-constructions developed between 1917 and 1923 by Theo van Doesburg (1887–1931) as materializations of the ideas

and concepts of the De Stijl. As the MoMA explains, Theo van Doesburg understood modern architecture and modern painting as complementary, arguing that the two had something essential in common: the flat plane. He believed that painting could be a laboratory for testing architectural ideas.

In 1924, van Doesburg published "Towards a Plastic Architecture," the most serious and coherent attempt to formulate and give syntax to modern architecture. As demonstrations of this new architecture and manifestations of the new style, Theo van Doesburg and Cornelis van Eesteren (1897–1988) designed a series of private houses and generated a series of theoretical drawings. These drawings use oblique projections (specifically, plan obliques) as the system of representation. Some of the plan-obliques were produced at the same time as the houses and followed the same vocabulary and language. However, they were intended not to be a projection of a specific building but abstract explorations of spatial relationships. The signs of functional architecture, such as doors, windows, stairs, walls, floors, and roofs, are absent from these drawings. Moreover, there is no directional clue allowing the front to be distinguished from the back. Instead, the structure floats freely in space and time.

[010] Amphibologia; [011] AMPLIFICATIO;
[015] Anantapodoton;
[018] ANATOMY; [021] Antapodosis;
[033] Apodixis; [034] Apomnemonysis;
[038] Asyndeton; Augendi Causa;
Chronographia; [045] Commoratio;
[046] Conduplicatio; Demonstratio;
[049] Diallage; [050] Dinumeratio;
[052] Ecphonesis; [053] Ellipsis;
Emphasis; Exemplum; [071] Isocolon;
[074] METAPHOR; [075] METONYMY;
Progressio; REPETITIO(N);
[090] Scesis onomaton;
[091] Significatio; [092] Simile;
[096] Synecdoche; [098] Synonymia;
Tautology; [[101] Topothesia.

Theo VAN DOESBURG (1887–1931)
and Cornelis VAN EESTEREN
(1897–1988), *Counter-Construction
(Maison d'Artiste)*, 1923.

Collection Het Nieuwe Instituut, donation
Van Moorsel/ DOES, ab5130
Courtesy of Het Nieuwe Instituut

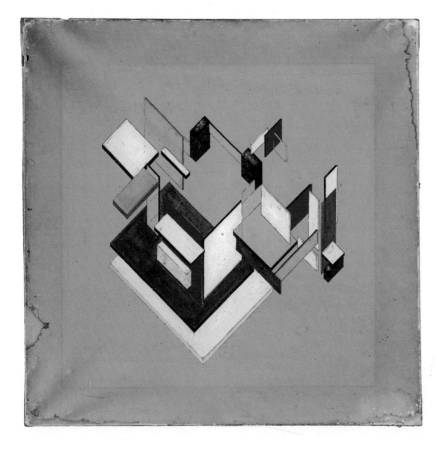

Theo VAN DOESBURG (1887–1931)
and Cornelis VAN EESTEREN
(1897–1988), *Counter-Construction
(Maison Particulière)*, 1923.

Collection Het Nieuwe Instituut/ EEST, 3.209
Courtesy of Het Nieuwe Instituut

[001] Accumulatio; [008] Alliteration;[009] Alloiosis; [011] AMPLIFICATIO;
[013] Analogy; [016] Anaphora; [018] ANATOMY; [021] Antapodosis;
[025] Antilogy; [029] Antiprosopopoeia; [036] Assonance; Augendi Causa;
[045] Commoratio; [047] Congeries; Consonance; Diaeresis; [051] Disjunctio;
Distribution; [052] Ecphonesis; Emphasis; [058] Epitheton; [067] Hyperbole;
[071] Isocolon; [074] METAPHOR; [075] METONYMY; MIMESIS; Parataxis;
PATHOPOEIA; Peristasis; [083] Polyptoton; Progressio; REPETITIO(N);
[090] Scesis onomaton; [091] Significatio; [092] Simile; [096] Synecdoche;
[098] Synonymia; Tautology.

Juan DE SANDE, *Untitled* (Wigs),
2015–2016.
Courtesy of Juan de Sande

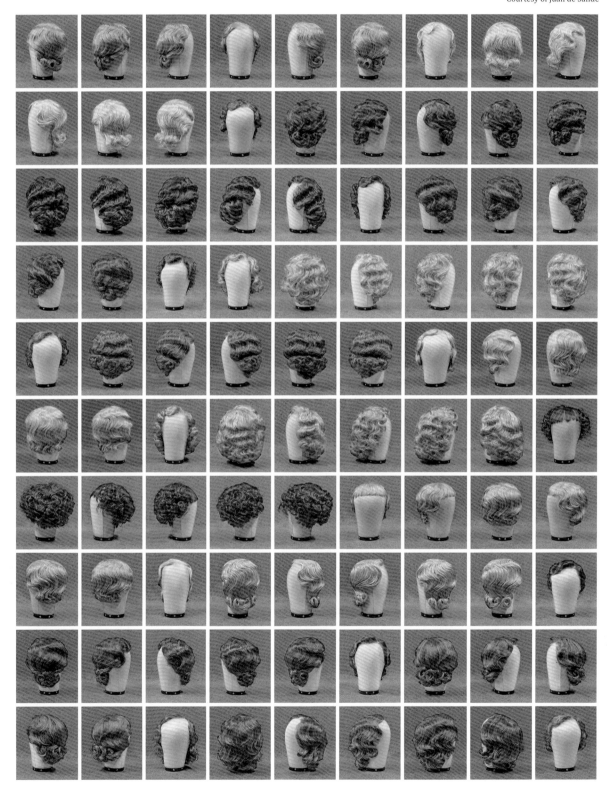

L. "doubling, repetition"

Conduplicatio

Repetition of a word or words in succeeding clauses.

The inherent vice of capitalism is the unequal sharing of blessings; the inherent virtue of socialism is the equal sharing of miseries.

—Winston CHURCHILL, October 22, 1945.

Conduplicatio is a rhetorical color characterized by the repetition of one or more words in successive clauses. This device is used for two purposes: (1) for amplification or emphasis (for example, "You are promoting riots, Gracchus, yes, civil and internal riots") or (2) to express emotion (for example, "you were not moved when his mother embraced your knees? You were not moved?").

In 2018, Olafur Eliasson presented *The unspeakable openness of things*, his first solo exhibition in Beijing. In this show, each space conjured a discrete environment dedicated to a specific natural phenomenon. The massive orange centerpiece light installation with the same name as the exhibition was created especially for the site and referenced the orange air pollution alert for Beijing and other cities. The large-scale room comprised a giant ring of light, that cast a warmly saturated orange light upon the space. As in some of Eliasson's other art pieces, a mirror surface placed on the room's ceiling defined and determined the spatial experience. On this occasion, the complete ring was built because of the reflection on the top. All elements, including the visitors of the installation, were duplicated and repeated optically.

Olafur ELIASSON, *The unspeakable openness of things*, 2018, Beijing, China.

Foil mirror, mono-frequency lamps, aluminium, paint (black, white). Installation view: Red Brick Art Museum, Beijing.
Photo: Xing Yu, 2018.
Courtesy of the Artist; neugerriemschneider, Berlin; Tanya Bonakdar Gallery, New York / Los Angeles
© 2018 Olafur Eliasson

G. "heap, pile, collection"

Congeries

Word heaps.

Apart from better sanitation and medicine and education and irrigation and public health and roads and a freshwater system and baths and public order, what have the Romans done for us?

—MONTY PYTHON, *Life Of Brian*, 1979.

Congeries is the accumulation of words, statements, or phrases that essentially say the same thing. Congeries is simply the Latin term for *synathroesmus* ("collection" or "union"), and it is a form of amplification similar to **accumulatio** [001]. The words or phrases that are piled up may or may not differ in meaning to produce a similar emotional effect. In *The Garden of Eloquence* (1577), Henry Peacham defines this deviation as "a multiplication or heaping together of many words signifying diverse things of like nature." Congeries is also defined as the combination of **synonymia** [098] and accumulatio, as it forms a group of words (usually adjectives) to modify or describe a subject in one expression.

Spanish artist Daniel Canogar transposed this strategy of accumulation of things and objects in the large photographic murals in his *Other Geologies* series with the intention of questioning social issues such as mass consumption and visual excess. All the pieces of *Other Geologies* pile up and collect discarded objects and technological material—such as toys, computers, videotapes, and mattresses—found in different junkyards and street markets. Naked bodies seem to drown in the jumble of waste that appears to be a death trap. These human figures can also be understood as another waste material. In this sense, *Other Geologies* is a form of **antiprosopopoeia** [029] or antipersonification —the representation of persons as things or inanimate objects.

Daniel CANOGAR,
Other Geologies III, 2011.
Photo Kodak Endura assembled
on aluminum frame. 59 x 98.4 in.
(150 x 250 cm).
Courtesy of Daniel Canogar

G. "making straight, setting right"

Correctio

Correction of a word or phrase used previously.

REPETITIO(N)
● Techniques of argument
● REPETITIO(N)

Operation:
REPETITION
Relation:
DIFFERENCE

—Diorismus
(G. "distinction,
definition");
Epanorthosis
(G."settingstraight");
Epidiorthosis;
Epitimesis
(G. "censure,
criticism").

See also Metanoia
(G. "change of
mind or heart;
correction"); alt. sp.
Metania — Penitent.

Caius Caesar, a young man, or rather almost a boy ... collected a very stout army of the invincible class of veterans, and lavished his patrimony—though I have not used the proper phrase; for he did not lavish it, he invested it in the salvation of the State.

—CICERO, *Philippicae*, 44–43 BC.

Correctio (etymologically from Latin, signifying "correction," or "amendment," and from Greek "making straight," or "setting right,") is a kind of redefinition that occurs when one corrects or makes an amendment to a word or phrase that was just employed. The revision could be more appropriate, or it could further specify the original word's meaning, often by overtly stating what something is or is not. Peacham postulates two kinds of correctio. The first is correcting the word before it is uttered: "We have brought here before you, Judges... not a thief but a violent robber, not an adulterer, but a breaker of all chastity" (Cicero against Verres). The second is correcting the word after is uttered: "You brother, no, no brother, yet the son (Yet not the son, I will not call him son) of him I was about to call his father" (W. Shakespeare, *As You Like It*). Correctio, especially *dicti correctio* (diction correction), prevails when one word is replaced with a more appropriate word. An example is provided by Terence's Menedemus in *Heauton Timorumenos*: "I have an only son, a mere lad. Ah, what do I say? Have ...? Son? No, I had a son, Chremes; whether I have one now I can't tell." Cicero in the *Philippics* (*Philippicae)* uses this device talking about Caesar.

The sport of skiing is the protagonist of this example of correctio selected from the visual handbook, *How to Ski by the French Method. Emile Allais' Technique.* The most effective strategy for explaining an idea is to describe any possible errors committed alongside the successes. In the image, the ideal body positions for two different slopes are defined using photographs of

Pierre BOUCHER (1908–2000), *How to Ski by the French Method,* 1947, Paris, France.

Technique.

From *Émile Allais, How to Ski by the French Method* (Flèche Publishers: Paris, 1947), 25, photographs and design by Pierre Boucher, translated by Agustin Edwards.

the skiers. In the top picture, the optimal positions for the two situations are defined; however, the author decides to add some information on what not to do. Simultaneously, the incorrect body position is described at the bottom of the composition and is corrected visually by superimposing the figure of the correct position of the skier in the foreground with more intensity.

Correctios are also found in many paintings. The most famous "corrections" are visible in Diego Velazquez's paintings. In fine art, these corrections are called "pentimenti." The word "pentimento" (plural *pentimenti*) is derived from the Italian "pentirsi," which means to repent or change one's mind. Pentimento is a change made by the artist during the process of painting. These changes are usually hidden beneath a subsequent paint layer. In some instances, they become visible because the paint layer above has become transparent over time, as in the horse's hind legs of the equestrian portrait of Philip IV by Diego Velázquez. Pentimenti can also be detected using infra-red reflectograms and X-rays. They are interesting because they show the development of the artist's design. They can also be used to attribute paintings to particular artists.

Diego VELAZQUEZ (1599–1660),
Philip IV on Horseback, 1635.
Oil in canvas; 119.29 x 124.8 in.
(303 x 317 cm).
© Archivo Fotográfico Museo Nacional del Prado

Operation:
ADDITION
Relation:
DIFFERENCE

—Consummatio
(L. "summing up").

G. "interchange"

Diallage

Bringing several arguments to establish a single point.

If now, in addition to all these things, you have properly reflected upon the odd disorder of the chamber, we have gone so far as to combine the ideas of an agility astounding, a strength superhuman, a ferocity brutal, a butchery without motive, a *grotesquerie* in horror absolutely alien from humanity, and a voice foreign in tone to the ears of men of many nations, and devoid of all distinct or intelligible syllabification. What result, then, has ensued?

—Edgar Allan POE, *The Murders in the Rue Morgue*, 1841.

Diallage is a rhetorical figure by which different arguments (each having been considered fully in its own terms) are brought together to bear on a single point, as in "John says we need to go South. Jane wants to go West. What is important is that we can't stay here." The term diallage is derived from the classical Greek word for "interchange." The Latin term is *consummatio* and means "summing up." Diallage is a figure of summary and a technique of argument.

This drawing by Sophie Davis titled *Super Flatness* is a visual diallage summarizing all the arguments considered in her research on "Flatness." The research sought to devise a concept and process by which one can design for the urban (not the singular) consciousness. "Flatness" finds whatever is ingrained in "place" and harnesses this to supersede the need for "placemaking" techniques, or quick fixes, that are currently used in urban scenarios to enhance a "place's" identity.

Davis created a series of prototypes to investigate how to express (draw and disseminate) Flatness. The investigation revealed some techniques for manipulating and hybridizing space, movement, and time (regarding active use and engagement), both visually and conceptually. The three colors in this drawing are a combination of three hybrid drawings that exemplify these concepts through the notions of "community" (red), "necessity" (blue), and "pace" (green).

Essentially, Flatness focuses on "tactics of thought" or spatialised (and occupied) conversations as strategies to prepare the audience for the future of "place" and its inherent identity.

Flatness proposes change by creating makeshift operations and making "place" through makeshift(ing), both visually and conceptually, temporary or diagrammatic approaches to makeshift interventions.

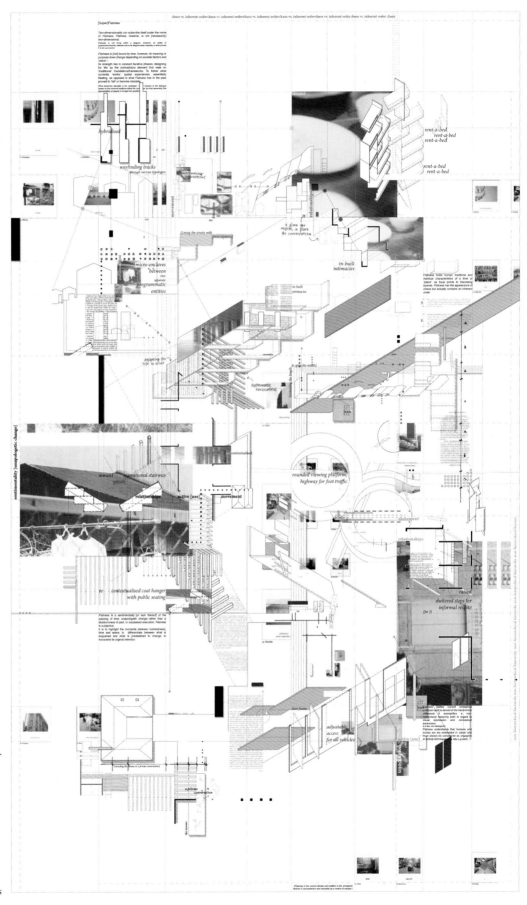

Sophie DAVIS,
Super Flatness, 2019,
Melbourne, Australia.

*Discontinuous
Theater*, summary
drawing.

"Rear Window" Master
Advanced Design Studio
and Studies Unit by
María Fullaondo, First
Semester 2019, Monash
Art Design Architecture
(MADA), Monash
University.

Courtesy of Sophie Davis

G. "enumeration"

Dinumeratio

Dividing a subject into subheadings; amplifying a general fact or idea by giving all of its details.

AMPLIFICATIO(N)
● Techniques of argument
● AMPLIFICATIO(N)

Operation:
ADDITION
Relation:
DIFFERENCE

—Denumeratio (L. "enumeration"); Enumeratio.

1. Diaeresis (G. "dividing, division")
—Eutrepismus
(G. "preparation");
Ordinatio (L. "setting in order, regulating").

See also Digestion; Distribution.

2. Anacephalaeosis
(G. "summary");
Anamnesis [014].
A summary or recapitulation, intended to refresh the hearer's memory.

But, I think that any ontological history of our selves ha[s] to analyze three set[s] of relations: our relations to truth; our relations to obligation; our relations to ourselves and to the others.

—Michel FOUCAULT, "The Culture of the Self," 1983.

Meagan VELLEMAN, *Adaptive Freeform*, 2020, Melbourne, Australia.

Generative design process: crono-analogies.

"Children & Elders' Games" Advanced Design Studio and "Open Secrets" Studies Unit by Ciro Márquez and María Fullaondo, Monash Art Design Architecture (MADA), Monash University.

Courtesy of Meagan Velleman

Dinumeratio, also known as *denumeratio, enumeratio, eutrepismus*, or *ordinatio*, is a rhetorical strategy for listing or detailing the parts of something. It is a type of amplification or division in which a subject is further distributed into its components or parts.

Meagan Velleman's design process, approach, and proposal *Adaptive Freeform*, (developed in the Advanced Master Design Studio "Children and Elders' Games" at Monash University) is a graphic and architectural transposition of this rhetorical device. By the middle of the 16th century, concerns about the conduct and education of children converged with interest in how they play. In 1560 Pieter Bruegel the Elder (ca. 1525–1569) painted *Children's Games*, an oil-on-panel depicting more than 200 children playing over 80 different games. Using this painting as a conceptual background, "Children and Elders' Games" studio explored contemporary forms of playing and reflected on the notion of "playground" in society. The studio

questioned the forms of leisure segregated by age along three dimensions: the user (children and elders in collusion), the program (traditional and contemporary games), and the space (vertical, horizontal, and oblique playgrounds).

This small sample of drawings (that make up the complete proposal of Meagan Velleman) lists all the details and constituent parts of the final playscape. Each piece also describes the generative design process step-by-step. Systematic and meticulous explorations and analyses of a set of games allowed similar and varied geometries to be extracted. Furthermore, the game analyses were interpreted, processed, and translated into architectural elements. Various notions and elements such as rotation, scale, grid, anchor, fold, and boundary were explored and used to formulate adaptable and transformable playscapes. Grids and rotational systems also generated an adaptable architecture for playscapes on multiple levels.

Meagan VELLEMAN, *Adaptive Freeform*, 2020, Melbourne, Australia.

Generative design process: generated grids and floor plans.

"Children & Elders' Games" Advanced Design Studio and "Open Secrets" Studies Unit by Ciro Márquez and María Fullaondo, Monash Art Design Architecture (MADA), Monash University.

Courtesy of Meagan Velleman

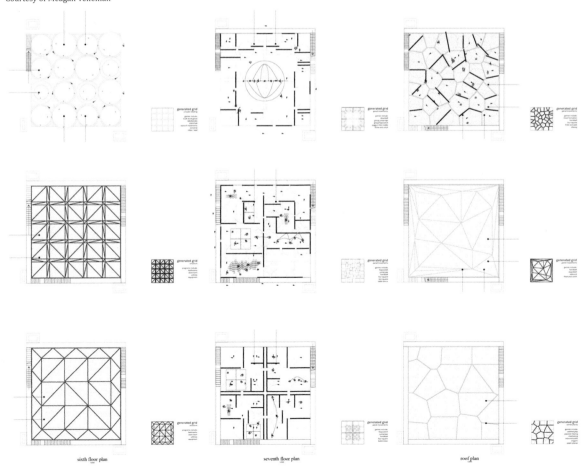

sixth floor plan   seventh floor plan   roof plan

L. "separation"

Disjunctio

Use different verbs to express similar ideas in successive clauses.

By the Roman people, Numantia was destroyed, Carthage razed, Corinth demolished, Fregellae overthrown.

— The Ad Herennium

Richard Serra's *Verblist* lies halfway between visual and verbal language. As Serra famously said, "Drawing is a verb," highlighting the role of the actions in artistic creation and merging both languages conceptually in one sentence. *Verblist* is an expression of the rhetorical figure called **disjunction**, which involves using different verbs to express similar ideas in successive clauses. This color of rhetoric is related to **hypozeuxis** in that every clause in a sentence has its own subject and verb.

Using a pencil, Richard Serra lists on two sheets of paper the infinitives of 84 verbs, such as to roll, to crease, to fold, to store, and 24 possible contexts—for example, of gravity, entropy, and nature—in four columns of text. Serra compiled what he called "actions to relate to oneself, material, place, and process" and employed it as a kind of guide for his subsequent practice in multiple mediums.

Richard SERRA, *Verblist,*
1967–1968.

New York, Museum of Modern Art (MoMA). Graphite on two sheets of paper, (each) 10 x 8.5 in. (25.4 x 21.6 cm). Gift of the artist in honor of Wynn Kramarsky. Acc. n.: 843.2011.a-b.

© 2022. Digital image, The Museum of Modern Art, New York/Scala, Florence
© Richard Serra

#1. To stretch (77) Cause something to become longer or wider by pulling it.
#3. To remove (17) Take (something) away or off from the position occupied.
#4. To cut (14) Make an opening, incision, or wound in (something) with a sharp-edged tool or object.
#5. To spread (40) TO extend a surface area, width, or length.
#6. To droop (26) Bend or hang downwards limply.
#7. To cover (60) Put something on top of or in front of (something) in order to protect or conceal it.
#8. To twist (7) Form into a bent, curling, or distorted shape.
#9. To enclose (56) Surround or close off on all sides.
#10. To flow (27) Move steadily and continuously in a current or stream.
#11. To spill (25) Cause or allow (liquid) to flow over the edge of its container, especially unintentionally.
#12. To spray (80) Apply (liquid) to someone or something in the form of tiny drops.
#13. To simplify (18) Make (something) simpler or easier to do understand.
#14. To discard (51) Get rid of (someone or something) as no longer useful or desirable.
#15. To bounce (78) Move quickly up, back, or away from a surface after hitting it.
#16. To drop (16) Let or make something fall vertically.
#17. To support (37) Bear all or part of the weight of.
#18. To bundle (45) Tie or roll up (a number of things) together as though into a parcel.
#20. To smear (34) Coat or mark (something) messily or carelessly with a greasy or sticky substance.
#21. To surround (57) Be all around someone or something.
#22. To scatter (48) Throw in various random directions.
#23. To expand (72) Become or make larger or more extensive.
#24. To hang (41) Suspend or be suspended from above with the lower part dangling free.
#26. To arrange (49) Put (things) in a neat, attractive, or required order.
#25. To systematize (81) Arrange according to an organized system.
#27. To fold (3) Bend (something flexible and relatively flat) over on itself so that one part of it covers another.
#28. To store (4) Keep or accumulate (something) for future use.
#29. To force (83) Make a way through or into by physical strength.
#30. To grasp (43) Seize and hold firmly.
#31. To lift (29) Raise to a higher position or level.
#32. To hinge (70) Attach or join with or as if with a hinge.
#33. To gather (47) Come together, assemble or accumulate.
#34. To splash (23) Cause (liquid) to strike or fall on something in irregular drops.
#35. To mark (71) Make a visible impression or stain on something.
#36. To collect (42) Bring or gather together (a number of things).
#37. To impress (31) Make (someone) feel admiration and respect.
#38. To erase (79) Rub out or remove (writing or marks). Remove all traces of.
#39. To curve (28) Form or cause to form a curve.
#40. To roll (1) Move in a particular direction by turning over and over an axis.

Saskia DAALE-SETIADY, *The Factory of Culture,* 2020, Melbourne, Australia.

Inventory of material culture: Nouns (Items of a 21st Century 'Basic B$%*h') + Verbs.

"World Memory. Isles for Culture Consumption" Second-Year Design Studio by María Fullaondo, Monash Art Design Architecture (MADA), Monash University.

Courtesy of Saskia Daale-Setiady

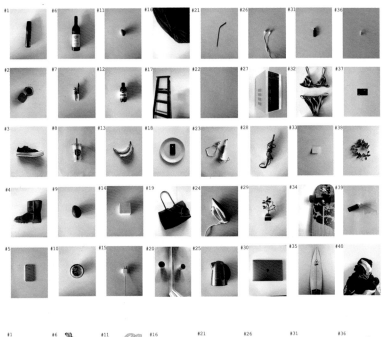

#1. A lotion containing chemicals that react with the skin to produce and artificial suntan.
#2. A cosmetic preparation spread over the face and left for some time to delay or lessen the effects of ageing.
#3. A cosmetic for darkening and thickening the eyelashes.
#4. A covering for the hand worn for protection against the cold or dirt.
#5. A written or printed work consisting of pages glued or sewn together along one side and bound in covers.
#6. A colourless, transparent, odourless, liquid wand is the basis of the fluids of living organisms.
#7. A drug or medicine for relieving pain.
#8. An East-Asian drink of tea containing grains of tapioca and often blended with sweetener and flavorings, served cold with a straw.
#9. A pale yellow edible fatty substance made by churning cream and used as a spread or in cooking.
#10. A thick paste or spread made from ground chickpeas and sesame seeds, olive oil, lemon and garlic.
#11. A domestic fowl kept for its eggs or meat, especially a young one.
#12. A lightly sparkling beverage made by fermenting black or green tea and sugar with a culture of various bacteria and yeasts.
#13. An attractively arranged bunch of flowers, especially one presented as a gift or carried at a ceremony.
#14. A white crystalline substance which gives seawater its characteristic taste and is used for seasoning.
#15. The imparting or exchanging of information by speaking, writing, or using some other medium.
#16. A long upholstered piece of furniture for several people to sit on.
#17. A flat length of wood or rigid material, attached to a wall or forming part of a piece of furniture, that provides storage or a display.
#18. A seat without a back or arms, typically resting on three or four legs on a single pedestal.
#20. A surface, typically of glass coated with a metal amalgam, which reflects a clear image.
#21. A stringed musical instrument, with a fretted fingerboard, typically incurved sides, and six or twelve strings.
#22. A mechanical device for measuring time, indicating hours, minutes and sometimes seconds by hands on a round dial.
#23. A small brush with a long handle, used for cleaning the teeth.
#24. An electrical tool with two metal or ceramic parts that you heat and use to make your hair straight.
#26. An electrical device worn on the ear to listen to music and radio
#25. A machine or percolator for making coffee.
#27. An enclosed compartment, usually part of a cooker, for cooking and heating food.
#28. A handheld implement, typically an electrical one, with a heated flat steel nase, used to smooth clothes.
#29. A domestic or tamed animal kept for companionship.
#30. A large enclosed shopping area from which traffic is excluded.
#31. A building or room containing collections of books, periodicals and sometimes films and recorded music for use of borrowing.
#32. A photo-sharing application for computers and mobile phones.
#33. The name of a social media service for sending pictures and messages that delete after opening.
#34. A long, narrow shaped board used in the sport of riding a wave towards the shore (surfing).

To spread   To flow   To bounce   To smear   To systematize   To grasp   To mark   To roll

#35. A short narrow board with two small wheels fixed to the bottom of either end which a person can ride, propelling themselves with one foot.
#36. An act of teleporting (transport across space and distance instantly).
#37. A series of connected railway carriages or wagons moved by locomotive or by integral motors.
#38. A music festival/ gathering held in the springtime in the 'Coachella valley', California.
#39. A pebbly or sandy shore, especially by the sea between high and low water marks.
#40. A large natural elevation of the earth's surface rising abruptly from the surrounding level.

Despite the list's ambiguity, all verbs relate to the actions generally applied during the artistic process. The verbs in the list describe the processes of giving form to something or changing something. The idea underlying this artwork comes from an observation Richard Serra made while working in his studio. The process was central at the beginning of Richard Serra's career:

> When I first started, what was very, very important to me was dealing with the nature of process. So what I had done is I'd written a verb list: to roll, to fold, to cut, to dangle, to twist…and I really just worked out pieces in relation to the verb list physically in a space.

The following two works are the first exercise of a second-year design studio called *World Memory*. Students created an inventory of culture consumption by combining "nouns" (or things that humans make and use to consume culture) and "verbs" (or actions expressing the act of consuming culture). Each noun was linked to an action chosen from Richard Serra's *Verblist*. The verbs' visual expressions were displayed through paintings, prints, and details from traditional Japanese art called "Ukiyo-e." Meanwhile, the nouns were represented by everyday objects.

Junhao CHEN, *The Factory of Culture: Conceptualising JAPAN,* 2020, Melbourne, Australia.

Inventory of material culture and tactical proposals.

"World Memory. Isles for Culture Consumption" Second-Year Design Studio by María Fullaondo, Monash Art Design Architecture (MADA), Monash University.

Courtesy of Junhao Chen

EMOTIONAL
APPEALS
● METAPHORICAL &
METONYMIC Substitution
● AMPLIFICATIO(N)
● Brevity
● Emotional appeals

Operation:
SUBSTITUTION
Relation:
SIMILARITY

Ecphonema —
Epecphonesis;
Epiphonesis
(G. "acclamation");
Exclamatio; Outcrie.

See also
Apostrophe;
Paenismus.

G. "exclamatio"

Ecphonesis

Exclamation expressing emotion.

O lamentable estate! O cursed misery!
O wicked impudency! O joy incomparable!
O rare and singular beauty!

—Henry PEACHAM, *The Garden of Eloquence*, 1593.

Ecphonesis, etymologically from Greek, literally means "a voice out by crying." It expresses emotions with pathetic or emotional exclamations (commonly known as rhetorical exclamations).

In October 1960, Yves Klein (1928–1962) asked photographers Harry Shunk and Janos Kender to take a series of pictures documenting a jump from a second-floor window. This second leap (the artist claimed to have executed the first jump earlier in the year) was made from the rooftop of his art dealer's house in the Paris suburb of Fontenay-aux-Roses. Two negatives—one showing Klein leaping and the other depicting the surrounding scene—were printed together to create a seamless "documentary" photograph. To complete the illusion that he was capable of flight, Klein distributed a fake broadsheet at Parisian newsstands commemorating the event with an ecphonesis in the title: "A man in space! The painter of space leaps into the void!"

Yves KLEIN (1928–1962), *Le Saut dans le Vide* (Leap into the Void), 1960, Paris, France.

Artistic action by Yves Klein, photographed by Harry Shunk (1924–2006) and Janos Kender (1937–2009), 1960. New York, Metropolitan Museum of Art. Gelatin silver print. 10.19 x 7.87 in. (25.9 x 20 cm). Purchase, The Horace W. Goldsmith Foundation Gift, through Joyce and Robert Menschel, 1992 (1992.5112). Yves Klein's performance (c) ADAGP, Photograph: Shunk-Kender © J. Paul Getty Trust. Getty Research Institute, Los Angeles (2014.R.20).

© 2022 Image copyright The Metropolitan Museum of Art/Art Resource/Scala, Florence
© The Estate of Yves Klein c/o VEGAP 2021

OMISSION
● METAPHORICAL &
METONYMIC Substitution
● Techniques of argument
● AMPLIFICATIO(N)
● Omission

Operation:
OMISSION
Relation:
SIMILARITY

Eclipsis —
Brachylogia (G.
"brevity in speech
or writting"); Default.

For *Casa Mora see
also* Alloiosis [009];
Antinomy [027].

G. "defect; omission"

Ellipsis

Omission of a word or short phrase easily supplied (understood in context).

"Did he ... peacefully?" she asked.
"Oh, quite peacefully, ma'am," said Eliza. "You couldn't tell when the breath went out of him. He had a beautiful death, God be praised."
"And everything ... ?"
"Father O'Rourke was in with him a Tuesday and anointed him and prepared him and all."

—James JOYCE, *Dubliners*, 1917.

In rhetoric, **ellipsis** (etymologically from the ancient Greek word *élleipsis*, literally meaning "omission") refers to the omission of an expected word or short phrase that might be needed to complete a sentence but not necessarily required to convey its meaning. "The average person thinks he isn't." In this quote by Father Larry Lorenzoni, the term "average" is omitted but understood after "isn't." According to ifioque.com, a successful occurrence of an ellipsis usually necessitates three conditions. First, the ellipsis relies on cognizance of the audience, as the reader or listener must consciously recognize and fill in the missing unit. Second, the missing words must be predictable; the

effect may be a moment of emphasis on the omission. Third, brevity, verve, and elegance should be achieved by the omission.

A visual example of this rhetorical device is this plan of *Casa Mora* (Mora House) by Iñaki Ábalos and Juan Herreros. This research project has already been analyzed as the transposition of two figures: **alloiosis** [009] and **antinomy** [027]. This example of ellipsis works because the plan removes all the elements and shows just the furniture. In this way, the drawing highlights the lack of hierarchy in the rooms. The various pieces of furniture—the bathtub, dining table, office table, toilet, desk, chairs, bathroom and

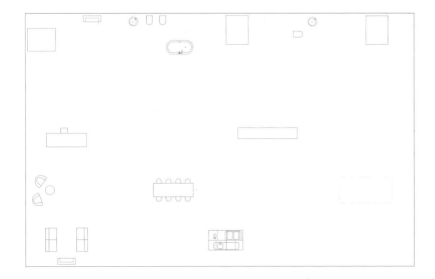

ÁBALOS & HERREROS, *Casa Mora*
(Mora House), 2002–2003, Cádiz,
Spain.

Collaborators: Jacob Hense,
Renata Sentkiewicz, Dries Vande Velde,
Wouter van Daele.

© Ábalos & Herreros

[Ábalos & Herreros (1985–2008):
Iñaki ÁBALOS, Juan HERREROS]

kitchen sinks, cookware, couches, armchairs, tables, and beds—are used to identify each housing space.

In this sense, the plan is also an example of METONYMY [075], as various objects take the place of other objects to which they are closely related. In the furniture plan, the main piece of furniture names and replaces the rooms of the house.

Ludwig Mies van der Rohe (1886–1969) created numerous montages and collages between 1910 and 1965 that define his understanding of architecture. Mies van der Rohe's large collage of the unrealized *Museum for a Small City* is an excellent example of visual ellipsis. The definition of the interior space and description of the project depicted in this spatial composition is built with just five elements and very few visual strategies.

Each of the elements in the photomontage synthesizes some of the main ideas of the project. All walls, floors, ceilings, windows, and columns are removed from the composition.

Three works of art—namely, Picasso's *Guernica* and two figurative sculptures by Aristide Maillol (1861–1944), *Night* and *Young Girl Reclining*—that might have been part of the collection are positioned freely in the open space and govern the foreground of the composition. In the background, two rectangular photographs of nature suggest the outdoor spaces or courtyards as planes of green and water. Both images are cut into two pieces separated by a narrow vertical gap that indicates the positions of the columns (the presence of the absence). Finally, the composition, size, and placement of the photographs insinuate this museum's perspective.

Ludwig MIES VAN DER ROHE (1886–1969),
Museum for a Small City, 1942.

Interior perspective.

New York, Museum of Modern Art (MoMA). Cut-out photographs and photographic reproductions of Maillol, *Night,* 1905 and *Young Girl Reclining,* c. 1912; and of Picasso, *Guernica,* 1937, on illustration board, 30 x 40 in. (76.2 x 101.6 cm). Mies van der Rohe Archive, gift of the architect. Acc. n.: 724.1963

© 2022. Digital image, The Museum of Modern Art, New York/Scala, Florence
© Ludwig Mies Van Der Rohe

Operation:
SUBSTITUTION
Relation:
DIFFERENCE

—Exchange.

See also
Alleotheta [007];
Anthimeria [023];
Anthypallage [024];
Antiptosis [030];
Hypallage [065].

G. "interchange"

ENALLAGE

General term for substitution of one case, person, gender, number, tense, mood, part of speech, for another.

Being now awake, I'll queen it no inch farther,
But milk my ewes, and weep.

—William SHAKESPEARE, *The Winter's Tale*, 1623.

ENALLAGE (called "exchange" by George Puttenham) is the general category of a group of several rhetorical devices, including **alleotheta** [007], **anthimeria** [023], **anthypallage** [024], **antiptosis** [030], and **hypallage** [065]. Specifically, enallage (derived from Greek signifying "commutation," "change," or "exchange") is a form of wordplay that occurs when a part of speech or a particular modification is exchanged for another. Generally, enallage involves the substitution of one tense, number, or person for another. Sometimes a particular case, gender, or mood is exchanged for another (Lanham 1991, p. 40).

Heinrich F. Plett describes enallage as a figure of syntactic substitution in which a grammatical form (person, case, gender, number, or tense) is replaced with a deviant or ungrammatical one. The substitution of person ("I takes my Friday with me") (Daniel Defoe, *Robison Crusoe*) or the replacement of number ("Equality of domestic power/Breed scrupulous faction") (W. Shakespeare, *Anthony and Cleopatra*) are examples from literature. When employed with functional intentionality, enallage is a rhetorical figure.

Sister Miriam Joseph cites the following Shakespearean examples of enallages: "Is she as tall as me?" (*Anthony and Cleopatra,*) and "And hang more praise upon deceased I" (*Sonnet* 72). She also cites the following instance in which a singular verb is replaced with a plural subject: "Is there not wars? Is there not employment?" (*2 Henry IV*).

According to Heinrich Bullinger, enallage is a figure of grammar consisting of an exchange of words or the substitution of one word for another. It differs from METONYMY [074] which consists of the exchange of one noun for another noun. Enallage involves exchanging one part of speech for another (anthimeria); one tense, mood, person, or number for another; or one case for another (antiptosis). However, the definition of enallage does not include the exchange of one noun for another noun (metonymy).

As explained in the alleotheta entry, using one grammatical form in place of another in verbal language does not imply a change in meaning. However, in iconic language, changing a visual element, such as material, size, scale, function, program, context, site, or user, does imply a significant change regarding the piece's meaning. This strategy is present in many art and spatial works. In this regard (and from a general point of view), any decontextualization can be understood as a form of enallage relatively close to metonymy.

DILLER SCOFIDIO + RENFRO, *Blur Building*,
2002, Swiss Expo 2002, Yverdon-les-Bains,
Switzerland.

May 15, 2002–October 20, 2002; Commission
1998. Partners: Elizabeth Diller and Ricardo
Scofidio. Project Directors: Dirk Hebel and Eric
Bunge. Design Team: Charles Renfro, Reto Geiser,
David Huang, Karin Ocker, Andreas Quadenau,
Deane Simpson, and Lyn Rice.

Photo (general view): Beat Widmer
Courtesy of Diller Scofidio + Renfro

[DS + R: Elizabeth DILLER, Ricardo SCOFIDIO,
Charles RENFRO]

[007] Alleotheta; [010] Amphibologia; [011] AMPLIFICATIO;
[023] Anthimeria; [024] Anthypallage; [030] Antiptosis;
Augendi Causa; Demonstratio; Emphasis; [054] ENALLAGE;
[058] Epitheton; [064] Horismus; [065] Hypallage;
[067] Hyperbole; [070] IRONY; [074] METAPHOR;
[075] METONYMY; [079] PARADOX; PATHOPOEIA; [091] Significatio;
[100] Topographia.

The Blur Building by Diller Scofidio + Renfro, originally produced for the Swiss Expo 2002, is an excellent architectural translation of enallage. This exposition pavilion is a building made of fog (water), an obviously unusual material for architecture.

> *The Blur Building* is an architecture of atmosphere—a fog mass resulting from natural and manmade forces. Water is pumped from Lake Neuchâtel, filtered, and shot as a fine mist through 35,000 high-pressure nozzles. A smart weather system reads the shifting climatic conditions of temperature, humidity, wind speed and direction and regulates water pressure at a variety of zones (Diller Scofidio + Renfro).

Therefore, this work constitutes a case of visual enallage, as it involves the replacement of an ordinary architectural material with an infrequently used one.

Water is not only the primary (unusual) material of the building; it is also the pavilion site. Furthermore, the architects (ironically) explain that "Water is also a culinary pleasure. The public can drink the building."

The 1972 unrealized project *Big Piano*, designed by the Austrian group Haus-Rucker-Co for the biennial "Documenta" art exhibition in Kassel, shares many characteristics with the *Blur Building*. *Big Piano* is an urban musical instrument shaped like a staircase leading to a viewing platform for 50 people. It is 70 feet (21 meters) high and has 90 steps braced on a steel-pipe scaffold. At the top, an artificial balloon-like cloud appears several times a day, hiding the platform. The stairs were designed to produce different amplified sounds when stepped on—sounds that follow chromatic scales. Visitors move up and down and make random tone sequences that are audible in the city center.

HAUS-RUCKER-CO, *Big Piano*, 1972, Documenta 5, Kassel, Germany.

© Haus-Rucker-Co/Zamp Kelp. Courtesy of Günter Zamp Kelp

[Haus-Rucker-Co (1967–1992): Laurids ORTNER, Günther ZAMP KELP, Klaus PINTER, and Manfred ORTNER]

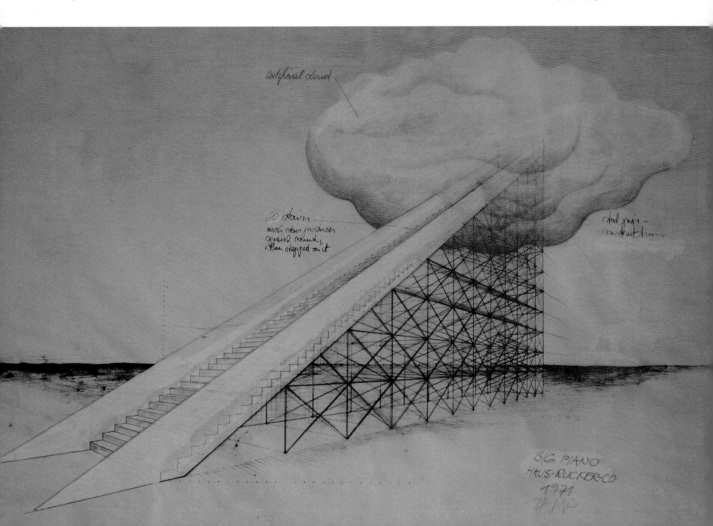

055

● ENARGIA
● Techniques of argument
● AMPLIFICATIO(N)

Operation:
AMPLIFICATION
Relation:
DIFFERENCE

—Energia; Ecphrais
(G. "description").

See also
Anatomy [018];
Pragmatographia [085];
Topographia [100];
Topothesia [101].

G. "vividness, distinctness"

ENARGIA

A general term for visually powerful, vivid description.

In our kitchen, he would bolt his orange juice (squeezed on one of those ribbed glass sombreros and then poured off through a strainer) and grab a bite of toast (the toaster a simple tin box, a kind of little hut with slit and slanted sides, that rested over a gas burner and browned one side of the bread, in stripes, at a time), and then he would dash, so hurriedly that his necktie flew back over his shoulder, down through our yard, past the grapevines hung with buzzing Japanese-beetle traps, to the yellow brick building, with its tall smokestack and wide playing fields, where he taught.

—John UPDIKE, "My Father on the Verge of Disgrace," *Licks of Love: Short Stories and a Sequel*, 2000.

ENARGIA is a generic term expressing any visually powerful or vivid description that recreates something or someone. *Demonstratio, dyatyposis, hypotyposis,* are synonyms.

As Balasz Takac describes, the 19th century was marked by (among many other things) the emergence of a significant number of art movements that changed the ways humanity perceived the role of art and artists in society. Realism appeared in the 1840s as a reaction to Romanticism. This particular stylistic persuasion was expressed through literature and painting, aiming to portray contemporary issues objectively, without any idealization and without any of the unnecessary drama and pathos typical of the Romantics. In this regard, in 1866, the lead painter behind the Realist movement, Gustave Courbet (1819–1877), created the provocative painting *L'Origine du monde* (The Origin of the World). The painting portrays a woman's thighs, torso, part of one breast, and (the center of attention) her genitals. This controversial painting constitutes an excellent example of enargia.

Courbet is probably the first artist to depict female genitalia in such blatant fashion devoid of any particular religious or mythological context. *The Origin of the World* is controversial for two reasons: first, because it presented a bold description of something that was considered taboo and, second, because of the subversive title.

Another example of enargia is Anna Chan's second-year project, *Sweetx Prototyping Factory*—an architectural space that generates a "collective identity." Two superimposed drawings—a section and a plan—summarize this open, spacious, vibrant confectionery prototyping facility. The factory aims to merge design, product development, and representation. The factory, which resembles an ice-cream cone, produces a material culture related to the consumption of confectionery goods for the population of Megasaki City (e.g., delivery vehicles, dining tables, and sweets parlors). The stimulating factory encourages visitors to socialize and interact and form a collective identity related to the previous inventories. Concepts that remain constant throughout the semi-open, semi-underground structure are hierarchy and attachment.

Gustave COURBET (1819–1877), *L'Origine du monde*
(The Origin of the World), 1866.

Oil on canvas, 18.11 x 21.65 in. (46 x 55 cm). Paris,
Musee d'Orsay.

©2022. DeAgostini Picture Library/Scala, Florence

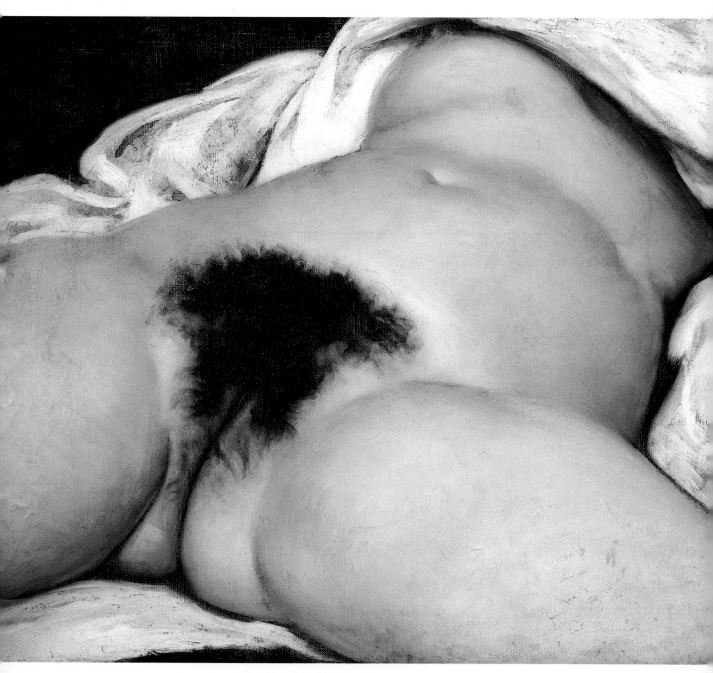

Anna CHAN, *Sweetx Prototyping Factory*, 2020, Melbourne, Australia.

Superimposed hybrids drawings and tactical proposals.

"World Memory. Isles for Culture Consumption" Second-Year Design Studio by María Fullaondo, Monash Art Design Architecture (MADA), Monash University.

Courtesy of Anna Chan

[001] Accumulatio; Aenos; [006] Allegory; [009] Alloiosis; [010] Amphibologia; [011] AMPLIFICATIO; [014] Anamnesis; [018] ANATOMY; [031] Antithesis; Augendi Causa; [039] Auxesis; [040] Bomphiologia; Cacemphaton; [044] Climax; [045] Commoratio; [047] Congeries; Demonstratio; Diaeresis; [049] Diallage; [050] Dinumeratio; [051] Disjunctio; [052] Ecphonesis; [054] ENALLAGE; [055] ENARGIA; [060] Exergasia; [062] Fable; [066] HYPERBATON; [067] Hyperbole; [069] Image; [071] Isocolon; [074] METAPHOR; [075] METONYMY; [079] PARADOX; PATHOPOEIA; Peristasis; [087] Proverb; [091] Significatio; [092] Simile; [096] Synecdoche; [097] Synoeciosis; [098] Synonymia; [101] Topothesia.

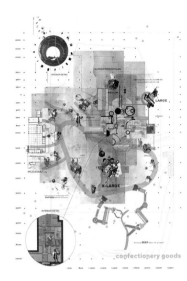

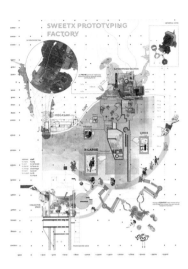

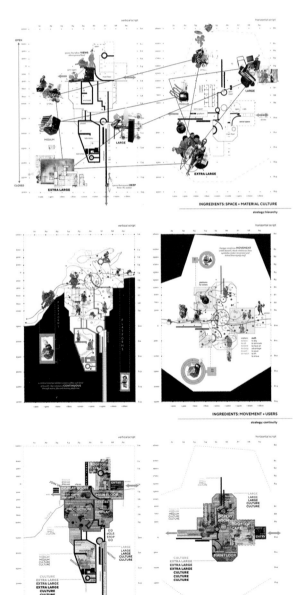

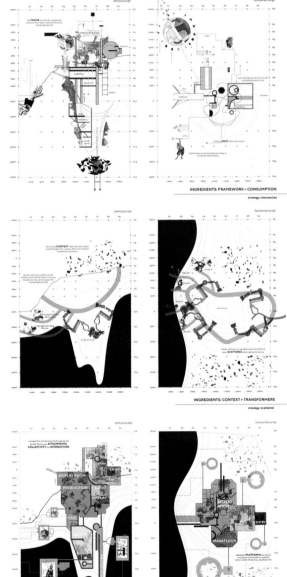

G. "explanation"

Epexegesis

Adding words or phrases to further clarify or specify a statement already made.

For I know that in me (that is, in my flesh) dwelleth no good thing.

—ROMANS 7:18

Epexegesis (derived from Greek with a literal meaning of "additional words") involves subjoining a word, phrase, clause, or passage to explain more fully the meaning of an indefinite or obscure expression. In other words, it is the immediate restatement of an idea in a more precise or in-depth way.

In 1997, John Baldessari (1931–2020) provided his contribution to that year's Venice Biennale, a body of work titled *The Goya Series*. This work was inspired by famous Spanish painter Francisco de Goya's (1746–1828) posthumously penned series,

The Disasters of War (1810–1820). *The Goya Series* marked Baldessari's return to examining the dialogue between imagery and text. The artwork included diptychs composed of black-and-white photographs of various objects, and one or more words on the canvas. In this regard, the series exemplifies epexegesis by adding words or phrases to clarify the meanings of the images. However, it is unclear whether Baldessari includes words to clarify the meaning of the image or whether the photograph specifies the words.

John BALDESSARI (1931–2020), *Goya Series*, "And," 1997.

Ink jet and synthetic polymer paint on canvas, 75 x 60 in. (190.5 x 152.4 cm). Mr. and Mrs. Thomas H. Lee Fund. Acc. n.: 151.1998 © 2022. Digital image, The Museum of Modern Art, New York/Scala, Florence © John Baldessari (1997). Courtesy Estate of John Baldessari © (2022) Courtesy Sprüth Magers

Goya Series, "No One Knows Why," 1997.

Ink jet and enamel paint on canvas, 75 x 60 in. (190.5 x 152.4 cm).
© John Baldessari (1997). Courtesy Estate of John Baldessari © (2022). Courtesy Sprüth Magers

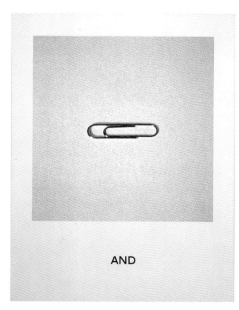

AND

NO ONE KNOWS WHY

G. "judgment"
Epicrisis

The speaker quotes a passage and comments on it.

EXAMPLE,
ALLUSION, AND
CITATION OF
AUTHORITY

● Techniques of argument
● Example, allusion, and
   citation of authority
● AMPLIFICATIO(N)
● Emotional appeals

Operation:
REPETITION
Relation:
SIMILARITY

—Adjudicatio
(L. "judgment").

> When I warned them that Britain would fight on alone, whatever they did, their generals told their Prime Minister and his divided Cabinet. "In three weeks England will have her neck wrong like a chicken." Some chicken! Some neck!
>
> —Winston CHURCHILL, speech to Canadian Parliament Ottawa, December 30, 1941.

Kazimir MALEVICH
(1878–1935), *Arkhitekton
Alpha* (Alpha Architecton),
1923.

Reconstruction by
Poul Pedersen, 1978.

Photo © Centre Pompidou,
MNAM-CCI, Dist. RMN-Grand
Palais / Jacques Faujour

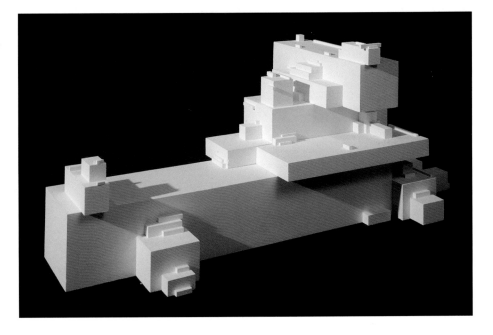

In 1919, Kazimir Malevich (1878–1935) declared that the ultimate form was "architectural Suprematism." Moreover, Suprematism was "the only possible system in an era of new architecture." From 1923 to 1930, Malevich produced a group of three-dimensional assemblages of abstract forms called "*Arkhitektons*" or "architectons." Malevich's constructions are plaster blocks made up of several rectangular blocks juxtaposed with one another. As socks-studio.com states,

> No function is shown or translated into form, the final shape being the pure result of assembling abstract masses in vertical or horizontal. With their

spatialization of abstraction and their formal non-objectivity, the arkhitektons embody Malevich's effort to translate the suprematist principles of composition to three-dimensional forms and architecture.

Kazimir Malevich's influence on the early work of Zaha Hadid (1950–2016) is noticeable in works such as *Malevich's Tektonik*, presented at the Architectural Association in London. In this work, Hadid placed Malevich's sculpture *Architekton Alpha* (1920) in an urban context such that it became a piece of architecture. Therefore, this strategy is an architectural

Zaha HADID (1950–2016),
Malevich's Tektonik,
1976–1977, London,
United Kingdom.

Painting, part of her fourth-year
project at the Architectural
Association.
© Zaha Hadid Foundation

For my graduation project from
the AA, I wanted to explore
the "mutation" factor for the
program requirements of a hotel
on the Hungerford Bridge over
the Thames. The horizontal
tektonik conforms to and makes
use of the apparently random
composition of Suprematist
forms to meet the demands of
the programme and the site.
The bridge links the nineteenth
century side of the river with the
South Bank, which is dominated
by the Brutalist forms to meet
the demands of the programme
and the site.
The structure's fourteen
levels systematically adhere
to the tektonik, turning all
conceivable constraints into
new possibilities for space.
The project has particular
resonance with my later
projects: first, in the Great
Utopia show at the Guggenheim,
in which I was able to realize
some of these tektoniks in
concrete form, and second,
in the Habitable Bridge
project, which considered the
possibilities of a mixed-use
development over the Thames
(Zaha Hadid).

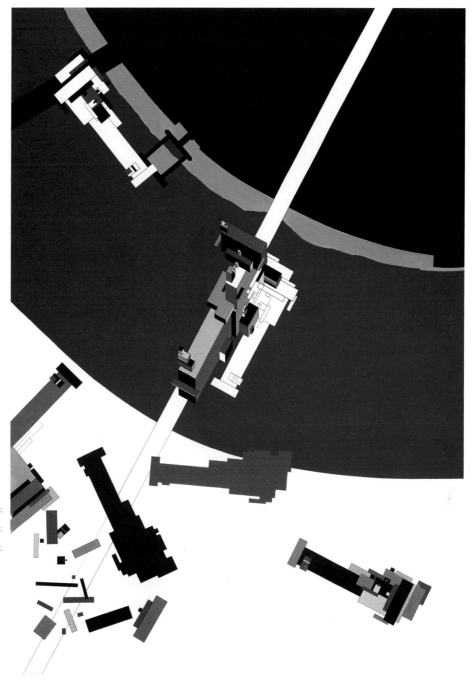

equivalent of **epicrisis**, in which the speaker or writer quotes a passage and then comments on it. The project imposed a series of horizontal layers on London's Hungerford Bridge on the Thames.

Hadid would continue researching ideas about juxtaposition and superimposition in her fifth-year thesis, *The Museum of the 19th Century* (1977–1978).

> The continuous line with many trajectories on the same surface evolved in my drawings and paintings at this time; I was using different perspectives to develop distortion (Zaha Hadid).

On the occasion of Malevich's major exhibition at the Tate Modern in 2014, Hadid explained,

> The 1970s were a critical time of investigation. Although architects had little work, we were very productive with drawings. One result of my interest in Malevich was my decision to employ painting as a design tool. I found the traditional system of architectural drawing to be limiting and was searching for a new means of representation. Studying Malevich allowed me to develop abstraction as an investigative principle.

G. "attributed"

Epitheton

Qualifying the subject with an appropriate adjective.

God! he said quietly. Isn't the sea what Algy calls it: **a great sweet mother?** The **snot-green** sea. The **scrotum-tightening** sea! I must teach you. You must read them in the original. Thalatta! Thalatta! She is our great sweet mother...

—James JOYCE, *Ulysses*, 1920.

Hans HOLLEIN (1934–2014), *Architecture Pills*: "Non-physical Environment," 1967.

Pill on paper, 8.27 x 6.30 in. (21 x 16 cm).
Photo: Roland Kraus
© Private archive Hollein

Hans Hollein
non-physical environment

Hollein 1967

Epitheton is a descriptive rhetorical device that describes a place, a thing, or a person to help make its characteristics more prominent than they really are. It is also known as a "by-name" or "descriptive title." Epithets are often used to describe characters, objects, ideas, and settings more vividly and understandably, thereby giving richer meanings to the original concept.

Hans Hollein (1934–2014) provided a new meaning to architecture, demanding an interdisciplinary form of work and extending the boundaries of the discipline. In 1967 he declared that "Everything is Architecture," and, one year later that "Architects have to stop thinking in terms of buildings only." Hollein developed the notion of "environment" (*Umwelt*) and devised several systems for altering perception as his controversial works exemplify. "Non-physical Environment" belongs to his series of *Architecture Pills,* where a pill is considered architecture just as any building is. Pills are capable of altering the perception of reality and space, producing emotional and physical impressions. *Non-physical Environmental* expresses and synthesizes Hollein's position using a two-word phrase (an epitheton). The notion of "environment" is further described and qualified by the adjective "non-physical."

Carrie Mae WEEMS, *Colored People series*:
"Blue Black Boy," 1990.

Gelatin silver photographs toned blue; overmat,
wood frame, Plexiglass with applied lettering.
16.875 x 16.875 in.
(42.86 x 42.86 cm). Framed, each.
Virginia Museum of Fine Arts,
Richmond. Purchased with funds from
the Polaroid Foundation

The incorporation of verbal language characterizes the work of American artist Carrie Mae Weems. Its use explains some of the strategies for manipulation and variation of discourse in visual artworks.

Overlaps in drawing and visual works, before the advent of digital tools, have been—and remain—one of the most widespread techniques for achieving specific results (for example, to clarify or emphasize an idea). "Blue Black Boy" from the *Colored People Series,* created between 1989 and 1990, provides many indications of visual and verbal language properties and includes two different visual epithetons. In general, the iconic language is more polysemic, more open to interpretation, and (in a sense) less accurate than verbal language. A reading of the series title, *Colored People,* indicates at least two direct meanings or interpretations of a two-word phrase. On the one hand, the adjective "colored" refers to the Black race, but it can also mean people of any color.

In principle, the visual signs facilitate the transmission or communication of sensory data, such as color, texture, and shape, while the verbal signs add to the precision of conceptual information. Paradoxically, the opposite occurs in this series, as sensory or visual information (such as color as expressed by the verbal sign, "colored") is ambiguous from the start without resorting to any form of procedure. In contrast, owing to the multiple possible readings of "colored," the photograph requires the viewer to apply some processes or additional resource. All the photographs in the series are in black and white and show black boys and girls. The images have been superimposed with a translucent color tint (in this case, blue) as a color filter.

A word appears under each of the three photos, and, together, the words describe what the photographs show: "Blue Black Boy." Again, an epitheton defines the noun "boy." The three images' meanings match the textual information, but these meanings are emphasized by superimposing and repeating the same message twice.

Operation:
OMISSION
Relation:
SIMILARITY

—Interrogatio;
Questioner.

Related to Epiplexis
(G. "rebucke");
Hypophora;
Ratiocinatio
(L. "calm reasoning;
reasoning by asking
questions").

G. "a questioning"

Erotesis

A "rhetorical question," one that implies an answer but does not give or lead us to expect one.

Hath not a Jew eyes?
Hath not a Jew hands, organs, dimensions,
senses, affections, passions?
If you prick us, do we not bleed, if you tickle us,
do we not laugh?
If you poison us, do we not die?

—William SHAKESPEARE, *The Merchant of Venice*, (1598).

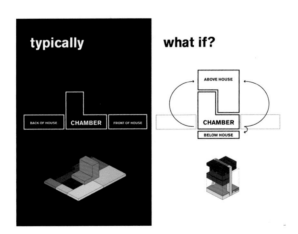

OMA + REX (Rem KOOLHAAS
and Joshua RAMUS),
The Dee and Charles Wyly Theater,
2009, Dallas, United States.
Image courtesy of OMA

This diagram of the *Dee and Charles Wyly Theater* employs a rhetorical question or **erotesis** to explain the essence of this project, which defies conventional theater design. The compact, vertical orientation of the *Dee and Charles Wyly Theater*, with its 12 stories, allows support spaces to be stacked above and beneath the auditorium rather than being wrapped around it. As the architects described,

> Instead of circling front-of-house and back-of-house functions around the auditorium and fly tower, the *Wyly Theater* stacks these facilities below-house and above-house. This strategy transforms the building into one big "theater machine." At the push of a button, the theater can be transformed into a wide array of configurations—including proscenium, thrust, and flat floor—freeing directors and scenic designers to choose the stage-audience configuration that fulfills their artistic desires.

REPETITIO(N)
● Techniques of argument
● REPETITIO(N)
● AMPLIFICATIO(N)
● Emotional appeals

Operation:
REPETITION
Relation:
DIFFERENCE

Exargasia—
Epexergasia;
Expolitio (L.
"polishing, adorning,
embellishing");
Gorgious.

Joseph KOSUTH, *One and Three Chairs*, 1965.

New York, Museum of Modern Art (MoMA). Wooden folding chair, photographic copy of a chair, and photographic enlargement of a dictionary definition of a chair; chair, 32.38 x 14.88 x 20.88 in. (82 x 37.8 x 53 cm); photo panel, 36 x 24.13 in. (91.5 x 61.1 cm); text panel, 24 x 24.13 in. (61 x 61.3 cm). Larry Aldrich Foundation Fund. 393.1970.a-c

© 2022. Digital image, The Museum of Modern Art, New York/Scala, Florence © Joseph Kosuth

G. "working out, treatment"

Exergasia

Repeating the same thought in many figures.

Now is the time to rise from the dark and desolate valley of segregation to the sunlit path of racial justice.
Now is the time to open the doors of opportunity to all of God's children.
Now is the time to lift our nation from the quicksands of racial injustice to the solid rock of brotherhood.

—Martin LUTHER KING Jr., "I Have a Dream" Speech, August 28, 1963.

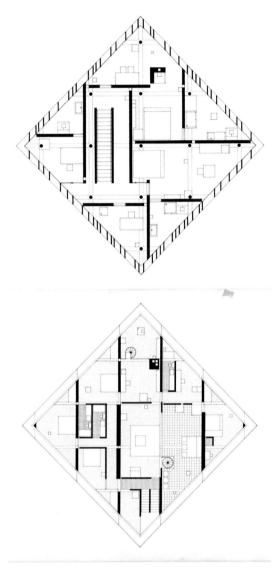

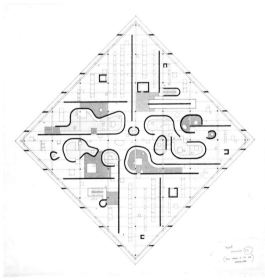

Exergasia (also called *epexergasia*) is a series of sentences or phrases with the same meaning or implying the same thing. An example is the following description of a beautiful woman: "She hath a winning countenance, a sparkling eye, an amiable presence, a cheerful aspect." The Latin term for exergasia is *expolitio*, meaning "a polishing up." By such repetition, the meaning is embellished and strengthened as opposed to being merely explained or interpreted in subsequent repetitions. Exergasia occurs in the form of repetition to further illustrate what has been said. In other words, it is used to make a point and emphasize an important idea.

American artist Joseph Kosuth researched the linguistic character of visual phenomena. One of his best-known works, *One and Three Chairs*, created in 1965, permits an understanding of the sign concept. A sign is an object, phenomenon, or material action that represents or replaces another, either by nature or convention. As explained before, every sign consists of three inseparable parts: the signifier, the signified, and the referent. Kosuth's installation consists of three objects: a chair; a black-and-white photograph of a chair; and a panel with the written definition of the word "chair," as listed in an English dictionary. In some ways, both the artwork and the piece's title express some language-related concepts. The work shows a "chair" as an object visually represented by three different signs, three signifiers that correspond to the same referent: a chair. The first signifier is the visual sign (a black-and-white photograph of a chair), the second is the verbal sign (the dictionary definition of the word "chair"), and the third is the object sign (a wooden folding chair).

Exergasia involves repeating the same thought, idea, or subject in different words so that the concept is better explained and developed. Therefore, it resembles **synonymia** [098] or **scesis onomaton** [090] but differs in that it does not merely repeat synonymous words—it uses synonymous expressions or senses instead.

In this regard, the three projects —*Diamond House A, Diamond House B,* and *Diamond Museum C*— part of a six-year investigation by American architect and educator John Hejduk (1929–2000), can be understood as exergesia or scesis onomaton equivalents. According to the architect, the three projects are "explorations of the formal and architectural implications of the diamond canvases of Mondrian for architects of today." Each project focuses on the same topic (diamond configuration) using different elements such as columns (House A), planes (House B), and biomorphic shapes (Museum C).

John HEJDUK (1929–2000), *Diamond Series:*
"House A, House B, Museum C," 1963–1967.
"House A" Plan, Ink with graphite on cardboard, 30.31 x 30.31 in. (77 x 77 cm). DR 1998:0060:003:002
"House B" Plan, Ink with graphite on cardboard, 20 x 30 in. (50.9 x 76.3 cm). DR1998:0061 :002:003
"Museum C" Plan, Ink on translucent paper, 35.43 x 35.62 in. (90 x 90.5 cm). DR1998:0062:006
John Hejduk fonds Canadian Centre for Architecture © CCA

For *Diamond Series*, *see also* Scesis onomaton [090].

Operation:
OMISSION
Relation:
SIMILARITY

—Apophasis
(G. "denial");
Speedie Dispatcher.

G. "proof by elimination"

Expeditio

Rejection of all but one of various alternatives.

There is no remedy for love, none you can drink or eat, no song you can sing, nothing but kisses and embraces and the coming together with naked bodies.

—LONGUS, *Daphnis and Chloe,*
(Second or third century AD).

Throwing Three Balls in the Air to Get a Straight Line (Best of Thirty-Six Attempts) by conceptual artist John Baldessari (1931–2020) is a visual form of **expeditio**. It also represents Baldessari's interest in language and games as structures generated by chance. The lithograph title (almost a description) matches this rhetorical figure's definition: the rejection of all but one instance from a set of alternatives. While Baldessari threw three balls at once 36 times (the number of exposures on a standard 35 mm film roll) trying to line them up in midair, his then-wife Carol Wixom operated the camera. He rejected 24 attempts and chose the 12 shots he considered the best.

John BALDESSARI (1931–2020),
Throwing Three Balls in the Air to Get a Straight Line (Best of Thirty-Six Attempts), 1973.

Offset lithograph in 12 parts.
(Each image) 7 x 10.24 in. (17.8 × 26 cm).
(Each sheet) 9.48 x 12.75 in. (24.1 × 32.4 cm).
Edition of 2,000.
© John Baldessari 1973. Courtesy Estate of John Baldessari © 2022.
Courtesy Sprüth Magers

Operation:
SUBSTITUTION
Relation:
SIMILARITY

—Apologue
(G. "account, story,
fable").

See also Aenos
(G. "tale, story
[esp. with a moral],
fable"); Exemplum
(L. "pattern, model");
Progymnasmata
(G. "preliminary
exercises");
Simile [092].

[001] Accumulatio; [003] Adianoeta;
[006] Allegory; [011] AMPLIFICATIO;
[014] Anamnesis; [031] ANTITHESIS;
Apophasis; [040] Bomphiologia;
[067] HYPERBOLE; [070] IRONY;
[074] METAPHOR; [075] METONOMY;
[079] PARADOX; [087] Proverb;
[091] Significatio; [092] Simile; [097]
Synoeciosis.

Francis ALŸS in
collaboration with
Cuauhtémoc MEDINA and
Rafael ORTEGA, *Cuando la
Fé Mueve Montañas* (When
Faith Moves Mountains),
2002, Lima, Peru.

Photographic
documentation of an
action.

Color photograph, 10.875 x
13.875 in. (27.6 x 35.2 cm).
Gift of The Speyer Family
Foundation; Kathy and
Richard S. Fuld, Jr.; Marie-
Josee and Henry R. Kravis;
Patricia Phelps de Cisneros;
Anna Marie and Robert F.
Shapiro; The Julia Stoschek
Foundation; Duesseldorf; and
Committee on Media Funds.
Acc. n.: 208.2007.34. New
York, Museum of Modern Art
(MoMA).

© 2022. Digital image, The
Museum of Modern Art, New
York/Scala, Florence
Courtesy of the Artist

L. *fabula*, "discourse, narrative, story"

Fable

A short allegorical story that conveys a lesson or moral.

Truly I tell you, if you have faith as small as a
mustard seed, you can say to this mountain,
"Move from here to there," and it will move.
Nothing will be impossible for you.

—MATTHEW 17:14-20.

In this project titled *When Faith Moves Mountains*, Francis Alÿs plays with a saying of
biblical tradition, "When faith moves mountains." This famous sentence is a synthesis of a
teaching of Jesus recounted in the gospel according to St. Matthew. The narration looks at
the image of a mountain, which is always enormous in comparison to the mustard seed. The
disproportion between the two elements symbolizes how little gross effort can be if it is not
accompanied by grace, trust, and confidence. Paradoxically, the principle that drove *When
Faith Moves Mountains* was "maximum effort, minimal result." The most apparently minimal
change was affected, and only through the most massive collective efforts. However, the
message is still very positive; it is a project in which one resigns in the present to invest in a
future promise.

METAPHORICAL &
METONYMIC Substitution

● METAPHORICAL &
METONYMIC Substitution
● Techniques of argument
● AMPLIFICATIO(N)
● Emotional appeals

Operation:
SUBSTITUTION
Relation:
CONTIGUITY

—Proposopopeia [086].

L. "invention"

Fictio

Attributing rational actions and speech to non-rational creatures.

With how sad steps, ô Moore, thou climb'st the skies,
    How silently, and with how wanne a face,
    What, may it be that even in heav'nly place
That busie archer his sharpe arrowes tries?
Sure, if that long with Love acquainted eyes
    Can judge of Love, thou feel'st a Lover's case;
    I reade it in thy lookes, thy languisht grace,
To me that feele the like, thy state descries.

—Philip SIDNEY, *Astrophil and Stella*, (1580s).

The rhetorical strategy of **fictio** is noticeable in these two snapshots of Samantha Romana's *Garden of Contemporary Pleasures*. The snapshots express the pleasure of being able to teleport via an archway or door to another place or country ("Anywhere Doors. East–West") and the pleasure of being able to transform the body to any shape or size when needed ("The Resizers. Space"). Both details of the garden emphasize the relationships between context and the main activity of the garden (pleasures) using the rhetorical strategy of attributing rational actions and speech (for example, travel, door access, body culture) to non-rational creatures (camels and boars).

Samantha ROMANA, *The Garden of Earthly Delights*, 2017, Melbourne, Australia.

Snapshots.

"The Garden of Earthly Delights. A Social Condenser of Contemporary Pleasures," Second-Year Design Studio by María Fullaondo and Joseph Gauci-Seddon, First Semester 2017, Monash Art Design Architecture (MADA), Monash University.

Courtesy of Samantha Romana

G. "marking out by boundaries, limitation"

Horismus

A definition by opposites. Brief description often antithetical.

PROPERTY IS THEFT! That is the war-cry of '93!
That is the signal of revolutions!

—Pierre-Joseph PROUDHON, *What is Property?*, 1840.

HAUS-RUCKER-CO, *Rooftop Garden.*
Oasis in the Urban Grid, 1971,
New York, United Sates.
© Haus-Rucker-Co/Zamp Kelp, Klaus Pinter.
Courtesy of Günter Zamp Kelp

[Haus-Rucker-Co (1967–1992):
Laurids ORTNER, Günther ZAMP KELP,
Klaus PINTER, and Manfred ORTNER]

Horismus is a rhetorical color involving the provision of a clear and concise definition of a subject's attributes. Several pieces of Haus-Rucker-Co, such as the collage *Oasis in the Urban Grid*, provide a clear and brief definition (often antithetical) addressing questions of environmentalism, the relationship between the natural landscape and artificial environment, and the space occupied by nature in the city. This collage suggests a space capsule with its microclimate in Manhattan. The rooftop garden conquest the summit of a New York City building. It is an oasis in the urban environment that attempts to transform the current situation of nature as a mere fragment in our building environment. This project aimed to raise awareness of our current landscape culture.

ENALLAGE
● METAPHORICAL &
METONYMIC Substitution
● Ungrammatical, illogical,
or unusual uses of language
● ENALLAGE
● HYPERBATON
● Techniques of argument
● AMPLIFICATIO(N)
● Emotional appeals

Operation:
SUBSTITUTION
Relation:
DIFFERENCE

See also
ENALLAGE [054].

G. "interchange, exchange"

Hypallage

Awkward or humorous changing of agreement or application of words.

I see a voice. Now will I to the chink,
To spy and I can hear my Thisby's face.

—William SHAKESPEARE, *A Midsummer Night's Dream,* (1596).

Untitled, 1950–1990,
Tbilisi, Georgia.
Photo: Unknown

Tony RAY-JONES, *Glyndebourne*, 1967
(printed later).
Gelatin silver print; 8 x 12.125 in.
(20.32 x 30.8 cm).
San Francisco Museum of Modern Art,
Purchase through a gift of the Black Dog
Private Foundation
© Estate of Tony Ray-Jones
photo: courtesy of SFMOMA

This terrific Tony Ray-Jones photograph depicting a couple having tea in the middle of the countryside is an example of a type of ENALLAGE [054] called **hypallage**. (The term comes from Greek and means "interchange, exchange.") In this image, the usual indoor and private context of having a cup of tea has been replaced by a green meadow with sheep and cows. The couple seems to enjoy their teatime nonetheless. As Tschumi explains, along with reciprocity and conflict, indifference is one possible relationship between activities and spaces. This photograph demonstrates an indifferent relationship.

This photograph of a woman on some street in Tbilisi (Georgia) talking on the phone through a window and watching closely by what could be her daughter is another magnificent example of this rhetorical figure.

G. "transposed"

HYPERBATON

Operation:
REARRANGEMENT
Relation:
IDENTITY

—Transcensio
(L. "climbing over");
Trangressio
(L. "going across");
Transiectio
(L. "passing over");
Trespasser.

See also

A generic figure of various forms of departure from ordinary word order.

Object there was none. Passion there was none. I loved the old man.

—Edgar Allan POE, "The Tell-Tale Heart," 1843.

SITE, *Proposal for Waterwall: Building Facade and Canal Inversion,* 1975, The Stuky Mills, Giudecca Island, Venice, Italy.

Model showing water as the facade and facade as the piazza.

1975 Venice Biennale, International Art Exhibition "From Nature to Art, from Art to Nature."
Courtesy of James Wines

[SITE: James WINES, Denise Mc LEE, Stomu MIYAZAKI, Sara STRACEY, Koshua WEINSTEIN]

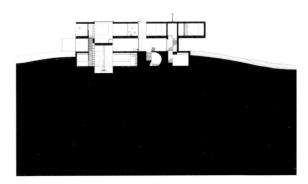

OMA (Rem KOOLHAAS), *Maison à Bordeaux* (House in Bordeaux), 1994–1998, Bordeaux, France.
Photo: Hans Werlemann
© OMA

SITE's exhibition proposal for Molino Stucky on Giudecca Island is a distinct example of HYPERBATON in architecture, as the project inverts the normal relationship between building and canal surfaces. The facade becomes the canal, and the canal becomes the facade. This inversion is achieved by extending the front promenade to act as a horizontal replica of the facade and then installing a vertical glass wall. A hydraulic sprinkler system, suspended on a steel space frame, allows a continuous cascade of water to flow over the glass. The shimmering, transparent water wall stands out in marked contrast to the monumentality and ornate decoration of the traditional facades found in Venice.

Leutschenbach School by Christian Kerez moves away from the standard order of architectural elements and spaces, particularly regarding the placement of a gymnasium on top of a school building. As the architects describe, the spaciousness of the site was preserved by reducing all rooms to the lowest common denominator and stacking them atop one another, with public functions accommodated in mezzanines. The classrooms are housed in a three-story steel-framed structure, and the gymnasium (of approximately the same height) is surrounded by a continuous frame structure resembling that of the classroom block. The result is not merely a gymnasium on top of a school building but a structure of references that are repeated on multiple levels. On the ground floor, the building is contracted into a minimal core area.

The Bordeaux House by OMA represents another form of hyperbaton in architecture. The house was designed to resolve the functional, physical, and psychological requirements of the owner (who was confined to a wheelchair due to an automotive accident) and his family. Koolhaas opted for a three-floor house instead of a one-floor house (the usual solution for a disabled person). The architect proposed a house—or, rather, three houses stacked on top of each other, with each floor representing its own world. All floors are joined by an elevator that serves as a common axis. The house revolves around the elevator, designed as a mobile platform that completes and generates most of the spaces. The movement of the elevator continually changes the architecture of the house. In this way, a machine is its heart.

Christian KEREZ, *Leutschenbach School*, 2009, Zürich, Switzerland.
© Christian Kerez

Operation:
SUBSTITUTION
Relation:
SIMILARITY

—Exuperatio; Loud
Lyer (Puttenham's
second term);
Overreacher;
Superlatio.

G. "excess, exaggeration"

Hyperbole

Exaggerated or extravagant terms and not intended to be understood literally; self-conscious exaggeration.

For instance of a lion;
He roared so loud, and looked so wondrous grim,
His very shadow durst not follow him.

—Alexander POPE, "Peri Bathous, Or the Art
of Sinking in Poetry," 1728.

HAUS-RUCKER-CO, *14-metre inflatable index finger,* 1971, motorway to Nuremberg Airport, Nuremberg, Germany.

Symposion Urbanum Nürnberg, 1971

© Haus-Rucker-Co/Zamp Kelp, Laurids Ortner, Manfred Ortner. Courtesy of Günter Zamp Kelp

[Haus-Rucker-Co (1967–1992): Laurids ORTNER, Günther ZAMP KELP, Klaus PINTER, and Manfred ORTNER]

Hans HOLLEIN (1934–2014), *Urban Renewal in New York*, 1964, New York, United States.

Aerial perspective.

New York, Museum of Modern Art (MoMA). Cut-and-pasted photograph on a photograph, composition: 7.5 x 9.5 in. (19 x 24.1 cm). Philip Johnson Fund. Acc. n.: 433.1967. © 2022. Digital image, The Museum of Modern Art, New York/Scala, Florence

Hyperbole is a well-known color of rhetoric consisting of exaggerated statements that express strong feelings or produce a powerful impression; such statements are not intended to be taken literally. Haus-Rucker's 14-meter inflatable index finger by the motorway to Nuremberg Airport also transgresses the norms of physical reality, in this case by increasing, among other things, the natural size of an index finger.

Urban Renewal: New York is one of Hans Hollein's (1934–2014) photomontages produced in the 1960s, in which hyperbole is used as the primary creative strategy. These collages decontextualize everyday objects and machine technology to generate imaginary proposals for buildings, landscapes, and cities. The exaggeration of a cigarette, sparkplug, boxcar, or aircraft carrier and their insertion in a new context transforms the original object's meaning. These visual manifestos confirm Hollein's statement that "Everything is Architecture."

As Craig Buckley explains in *Graphic Assembly*, the transformation of these objects does not alter their form; the perception of change arises solely from objects' displacement into a new context. Central to these montages was the capacity of such displacement to manipulate the perception of scale. In this aerial view of New York, the drive shaft of a machine engine was pasted into the financial district of Lower Manhattan, echoing the violent insertion of much urban renewal while visually suggesting the island's conversion into a massive ship.

HYPERBATON

●Ungrammatical, illogical, or
unusual uses of language
●HYPERBATON
●AMPLIFICATIO(N)
●Emotional appeals

Operation:
REARRANGEMENT
Relation:
DIFFERENCE

—Preposterous.

See also
HYPERBATON [066].

G. "the latter [put as] the former"

Hysteron Proteron

Syntax or sense out of normal logical or temporal order.

Th' Antoniad, the Egyptian admiral,
With all their sixty, fly and turn the rudder.

—William SHAKESPEARE, *Antony and Cleopatra*, (1606).

Yoana DOLEVA,
Contemporary Proverbs,
"To sit through an evacuation.
Horse droppings are not figs,"
2019, Melbourne, Australia.

"Rear Window" Master Advanced
Design Studio and Studies Unit by
María Fullaondo, First Semester
2019, Monash Art Design
Architecture (MADA), Monash
University.
Courtesy of Yoana Doleva

Horse droppings are not figs

"The Generic city has easy phone numbers, not the resistant ten-figure frontal lobe crunchers of the traditional city but smoother versions"

A generic city caters to the every growing necessities of its weakening users. The city does not educate to equip users with autonomy but perpetuates their ignorance. Ignorance is beyond bliss; it is complementary. All space is smooth space, with minimal effort and no risk of compromise.

Hans HOLLEIN (1934–2014), *Just landed. Hans Hollein in his mobile office*, 1969, Austria.

The photo was made during the shooting of "Das österreichische Portrait / Folge 19: Hans Hollein" (The Austrian Portrait / no. 19: Hans Hollein). Produced by Telefilm. Broadcasted on December 12, 1969, Österreichischer Rundfunk ORF (Austrian Broadcasting Corporation ORF). Installation PVC-foil, pneumatic, electric blower (or vacuum cleaner), typewriter (Hermes Baby), telephone, drawing board, pencil, rubber, thumbtacks, floor piece synthetic turf 225 x ø 120 cm.

Photograph © Private archive Hollein Courtesy of Generali Foundation Collection – Permanent Loan to the Museum der Moderne Salzburg

Hysteron proteron and *hysterologia* are similar rhetorical figures—specifically, they are forms of HYPERBATON [066] consisting of a departure from the ordinary, logical, or temporal order of words. Yoana Doleva's contemporary proverb "To sit through an evacuation" conceptually works with figures of PARADOX [079], but the visual expression of this saying opts to use **hyperboles** [067] and hyperbatons. The temporal richness and diversity of fragments in the photomontage are interesting, as they combine and represent different media and times. Doleva uses two main fragments to generate this vision. The painting *The Venus of Urbino* (also known as *Reclining Venus*), created in 1534 by Italian painter Titian (1506–1576), is combined with the *Pruitt-Igoe Housing* project (1950–1973) in the US city of St. Louis, designed by Minoru Yamasaki (1912–1986). The proverb portrays Venus reclined on the world-famous image of the demolition of this housing project.

In the TV series "The Austrian Portrait," aired on Austrian television on December 12, 1969, the architect Hans Hollein (1934–2014) presented his *Mobile Office*, also called the "Transportable Studio in a Suitcase." It is a pneumatic room adapted to human dimensions and equipped with a telephone, typewriter, and a drafting board. In this way, *The Mobile Office* is conceived as a transportable architectural studio in a suitcase. Flanked by airplanes and cameramen, the photograph documenting the action shows Hollein laid on a meadow of what seems an aerodrome as a demonstration of his "invention" —the workplace in the age of communications — provokes some surprise by its foreboding character. Specifically, the logical order of certain architectural elements and social stereotypes are questioned. Mobile, transportable, pneumatic, transparent, individual, public, minimal are some of the unusual characteristics of this architectural office, which transgress the logical forms of designing and conceiving a place to work. In "Everything Is Architecture"— Hollein's manifesto of 1966–1967—the architect wrote, "Early examples of the extension of architecture through communications media are telephone booths —buildings of minimal size but directly incorporating the global environment."

Operation:
SUBSTITUTION
Relation:
SIMILARITY

L. *imago*, "imitation, copy, likeness"

Image

A thing that represents something else; a symbol, emblem, representation.

Peter Wegner's *Lever Labyrinth* exhibition at Lever House (1952) in midtown Manhattan during summer 2005 exemplifies this trope. This public installation, that was part of the Lever House Summer exhibition series, reinterprets the green hedges of a 16th-century garden maze. *Lever Labyrinth* was situated within the larger labyrinth of the city and occupied the interior space of the iconic modernist skyscraper, the Lever House by Skidmore, Owings & Merrill (SOM). This indoor miniature city evokes the Manhattan skyline, as it is a miniature image of New York.

> Like the city, *Lever Labyrinth* comes and goes, twists and turns, dead ends, begins again. Its questions are direct even if its answers are elusive: Where am I? What's around the corner? What's real? What matters? What does it mean? Am I trapped or free, lost or found? (Peter Wegner)

The work is made from 2.4 million sheets of recycled and recyclable paper in various shades of green structured across 50 steel modules of seven paper stacks each. *Lever Labyrinth* is constructed of paper, an everyday material in office buildings and homes but is a highly unusual construction material. In that sense, the exhibition also exemplifies figures such as ENALLAGE [054] and METONYMY [075]. It is interesting that Wegner's use of paper ignores its bi-dimensionality. By stacking the paper, the author transforms its properties and enhances the sculptural mass of its slender third dimension. As Wegner states:

> In this sculpture, the questions are mediated by paper. It's just ordinary paper, not a fine art material. We usually think of paper as nothing but surface, a two-dimensional plane. But paper has a third dimension—the edge. Those edges add up. The sheets become a stack, the stacks become a wall, and the walls become a maze. The various greens of the paper are inspired by the hedges of a garden maze. *Lever Labyrinth* is nature, abstracted and reconstituted: Paper—formerly pulp, formerly trees.

Peter WEGNER, *Lever Labyrinth,* 2005, New York, United States.

Exhibition at Lever House, New York, 390 Park Avenue, New York, NY, May 9, 2005– September 4, 2005.

Courtesy of Peter Wegner

G. "affectation of ignorance"

IRONY

1. Implying a meaning opposite to the literal meaning.
2. Speaking in derison or mockery.

(1) *Mr. Bennet*: "I admire all my three sons-in-law highly. Wickham, perhaps, is my favourite."

—Jane AUSTEN, *Pride and Prejudice*, 1813.

(2) It was said by a French king, to one that praid his reward, showing how he had been cut in the face at a certain battle fought in his service: ye may see, quoth the king, what it is to run away and look backwards.

—George PUTTENHAM, *The Arte of English Poesie*, (1589).

IRONY (also known as *illusio, dissimulatio, ironia, simulatio,* or the *dry mock*; etymologically from the Greek word meaning "dissimulation" or "feigned ignorance") is a rhetorical technique by which the surface meaning of a phrase is different from the underlying, intended meaning. Alternatively, irony can be defined as a form of speech in which the speaker's words directly contradict what they intend the listener to understand them to mean.

Irony can be divided into three categories: verbal irony, dramatic irony, and situational irony. Verbal irony occurs when a speaker uses masked words to express something contrary to their intended meaning. For instance, one might say, "Oh, what a happy day," when it has been raining all day. Dramatic irony usually appears in movies and literary works. It is presented as a situation in which the audience knows something that a character does not. Finally, situational irony involves situations in which the manifested outcome contrasts with the expected outcome based on how events naturally unfold. A fire station catching on fire is an example of situational irony.

Rem Koolhaas' 1972 Architectural Association thesis titled *Exodus, or The Voluntary Prisoners of Architecture* exemplifies the use of irony in architecture. This project is full of rhetorical figures in terms of their conception and development. For example, the project's title, which alludes to Cold War West Berlin, might be understood as an **oxymoron** [077] since it links two words with contradictory impressions—"prisoner" and "voluntary." In this regard, *Exodus* could have illustrated many tropes in this book in addition to irony such as **allegory** [010], **antithesis** [031], **Hyperbole** [067], or PARADOX [079]. However, it has been placed as an example of this device because irony is one of the most important and best-known figures of rhetoric.

Koolhaas proposes a restricted enclave encircled by a forbidding wall, a prison in the middle of London, and one in which people sought refuge voluntarily. Here, the wall becomes a condition of freedom via self-imprisonment. The voluntarily segregated people seek shelter within the walls of a prison of metropolitan scale. In other words, the irony of this project focuses on how Koolhaas turned the scheme of a prison into

Rem KOOLHAAS, Madelon VRIESENDORP, Elia and
Zoe ZENGHELIS, *Exodus, or The Voluntary Prisoners of
Architecture,* 1972, London, United Kingdom.

The Strip, aerial perspective (project, 1972).

New York, Museum of Modern Art (MoMA). Cut-and-pasted paper
with watercolor, ink, gouache, and color pencil on gelatin silver
photograph (aerial view of London), 16 x 19.875 in. (40.6 x 50.5
cm). Patricia Phelps de Cisneros Purchase Fund, Takeo Ohbayashi
Purchase Fund, and Susan de Menil Purchase Fund. 362.1996

© 2022. Digital image, The Museum of Modern Art, New York/Scala,
Florence
© OMA AMO (Rem Koolhaas)

a desirable habitat using a radical mirror inversion of significance and attraction. He proclaims that

> division, isolation, inequality, aggression, destruction, all the negative aspects of the Wall, could be the ingredients of a new phenomenon: architectural warfare against undesirable conditions, in this case, London.

Another noteworthy aspect of the project is the combined use of verbal and visual languages to articulate the proposal. Initially, this project was Koolhaas, Madelon Vriesendorp, and Elia and Zoe Zenghelis's entry in the competition *The City as Meaningful Environment*, organized by Italian journal *Casabella* in 1972. The project consists of a series of collages of Koolhaas's diploma project at the Architectural Association and various items from outside the architectural field, such as images of newspapers, photographs of artwork, and pictures of amorous scenes. The project also included a short text describing the various architectural elements and their functions. Koolhaas very often augments his projects with a strong narrative in the form of a text, a story, or a **fable** [062] to substantiate and complete the visual and graphic content of the proposal.

Once, a city was divided in two parts. One part became the Good Half, the other part the Bad Half. The inhabitants of the Bad Half began to flock to the good part of the divided city, rapidly swelling into an urban exodus. If this situation had been allowed to continue forever, the population of the Good Half would have doubled, while the Bad Half would have turned into a ghost town (Rem Koolhaas).

As in Koolhaas's thesis, verbal irony provides some added meanings to a situation. Ironical statements and situations in literature develop readers' interest. It makes a work of literature more intriguing and forces readers to use their imagination and comprehend the author's underlying meanings.

Diller Scofidio's *Overexposed* (1995) is the second work chosen to illustrate irony in the visual and spatial world. *Overexposed* is a 24-minute continuous video that pans across and up and down the surface of SOM's building (former Pepsi-Cola Corporation Headquarters) at 500 Park Avenue in New York. Paradoxically, the project questions the role of glass in Modernist architecture using one of the signature curtain wall buildings of the 20th century designed by SOM's Gordon Bunshaft and Natalie de Blois.

DILLER SCOFIDIO, *Overexposed*,
1995, The Getty Center, Los Angeles,
United States.
Courtesy of Diller Scofidio + Renfro

[DS + R: Elizabeth DILLER, Ricardo SCOFIDIO, Charles RENFRO]

BALANCE
● Techniques of argument
● REPETITIO(N)
● AMPLIFICATIO(N)
● Balance
● Omission

Operation:
REPETITION
Relation:
SIMILARITY

—Compar
(L. "like, equal");
Even (Puttenham's
term for Parison);
Parimembre;
Parison (G. "evenly
balanced").

G. "of equal members or clauses"

Isocolon

Phrases of approximately equal length and corresponding structure.

Pity is the feeling which arrests the mind in the presence of whatsoever is grave and constant in human sufferings and unites it with the sufferer. Terror is the feeling which arrests the mind in the presence of whatsoever is grave and constant in human sufferings and unites it with the secret cause.

—James JOYCE, *A Portrait of the Artist as a Young Man*, 1916.

There are two basic visual schemes to compare: juxtaposition and superimposition. In *City Metaphors*, O. M. Ungers (1926–2007) uses a specific type of juxtaposed comparison called small multiples to establish a triple analogy between an organism, a city, and a mechanism. This type of juxtaposition compares many elements or multiples arranged in a rectangular grid. Thus, it is a visual equivalent of **isocolon**—a succession of sentences, phrases, and clauses of grammatically equal length. In isocolon, a sentence has a parallel structure, and similar grammatical forms are repeated.

Examples of this device can fall under any of the following types. *Bicolon* comprises two grammatically equivalent structures, such as in Harley Davidson's slogan: "American by Birth. Rebel by Choice." When there are three grammatically equivalent structures, the phrase is called a *tricolon*. An example of this is "That government of the people, by the people, and for the people shall not perish from the earth" (Abraham Lincoln). A *tetracolon*, (also known as a quatrain, occurs when four parallel grammatical structures are written in succession—for example,

I'll give my jewels for a set of beads, /My gorgeous palace for a hermitage, /My gay apparel for an almsman's gown, /My figured goblets for a dish of wood (W. Shakespeare, *Richard II*).

City Metaphors can be understood as four sentences of equal length that describe four city systems or structures: street, sewer, subway, and power systems. As in isocolon, each analogy has a parallel structure, and the elements are repeated. Each "sentence" comprises the same elements: an organism, a city, and a mechanism.

In Ungers's triple analogy, the multiples are placed next to each other. A specific distance separates them based on a set of rules. Also, the size and proportion of the human, Manhattan, and the machine are equal or similar, and the separation or distance facilitates comparisons between the elements. The multiples are always separated by the same distance. Since the shapes of the compared elements—Manhattan, man, and car—are different, the separation or distance between components is similar.

Oswald Mathias UNGERS (1926–2007),
City Metaphors, 1976.

A triple analogy: an organism (a human being), a
city (Manhattan), and a mechanism (a car).

Courtesy of Ungers Archiv für
Architekturwissenschaft (UAA)

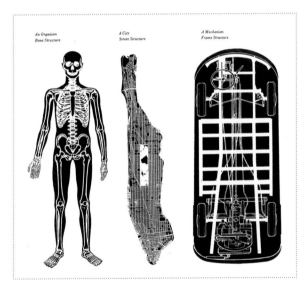

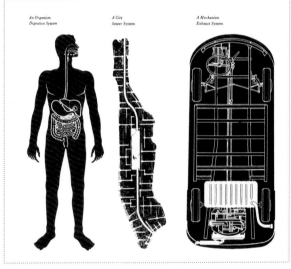

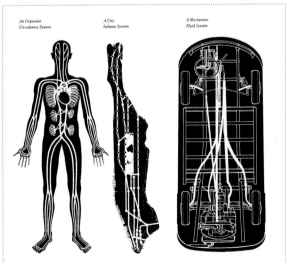

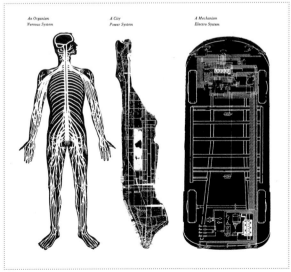

Operation:
OMISSION
Relation:
CONTRADICTION

—Antenantiosis
(Positive statement
made in a negative
form); Moderatour.

See also
Meiosis [080].

Related to
Tapinosis.

Opposite to
Hyperbole [067].

G. "plainness, simplicity"

Litotes

Denial of the contrary; understatement that intensifies.

I am no prophet — and here's no great matter;
I have seen the moment of my greatness flicker,
And I have seen the eternal Footman hold my coat, and snicker,
And in short, I was afraid.

—T. S. ELLIOT, *The Love Song of J. Alfred Prufrock*, 1915.

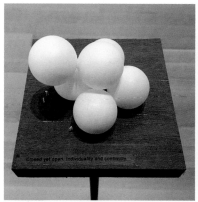  

Sou FUJIMOTO Architects,
Architecture Is Everywhere, 2015–2016,
Chicago, United States.
Chicago Architecture Biennial 2015,
October 3, 2015 – January 3, 2016.
Installation views of the exhibition
Surrounds: 11 Installations,
MOMA, October 21, 2019 – January 5, 2020.

In verbal language, **litotes** is a deviation featuring a phrase that utilizes negative wording or terms to express something positive, such as when a politician once said to his charlatan subordinate, "A period of silence from you would now be not unwelcome." In litotes, "more is understood than is said." Another example is saying, "He is not the wisest man in the world" to indicate that "He is a fool" (Peacham).

[Litotes continues in the next entry]

Operation:
OMISSION
Relation:
DOUBLE MEANING

—Diminutio
(L. "decrease,
lessening");
Disabler; Extenuatio;
Imminutio
(L. "lessening,
weakening").

See also
Litotes [079].

Related to Tapinosis.

G. "lessening"

Meiosis

To belittle, often through a trope of one word; use a degrading epithet.

I am a very foolish fond old man,
Fourscore and upward, not an hour more or less;
And, to deal plainly,
I fear I am not in my perfect mind…

—William SHAKESPEARE, *King Lear,* (1606).

Litotes [072] sometimes overlaps with another rhetorical device, **meiosis**. The word "meiosis" originates from the Greek word meaning "to diminish" or "to make smaller," and it can be defined as a witty understatement that belittles or dismisses something or somebody, particularly by using terms that indicate that something is less important than it should be. In literature, however, meiosis describes understatements used to highlight a point, explain a situation, or understate a response to enhance the effect of a dramatic moment. When using meiosis in speech, the speaker might use phrases to express that something is much less critical than it really is. When used as a literary device, meiosis captures the attention of the reader. It can also subtly highlight a point. In meiosis, and understatement is fully intentional, as in the use of "Childish carriage" to describe a "Rolls Royce," or Oscar Wilde's description of an English country gentleman fox-hunting as "the unspeakable in full pursuit of the uneatable."

Litotes and meiosis are intentional understatements that intensify. A visual equivalent of these rhetorical devices is the exhibition *Architecture is Everywhere* by Japanese architect Sou Fujimoto. The installation was created for the Chicago Architecture Biennial 2015. The exhibition consists of everyday items used to construct miniature architectural models. The scale and surprising appropriation of everyday objects—for example, potato chips, ping-pong balls, an ashtray, matchboxes, sponges, staples, and sticky notes—create surreal situations that generate new meanings. Fujimoto seeks "a different understanding of nature," and the installation represents the Japanese firm's philosophy that "architecture is first found and then made."

American artist Fred Sandback (1943–2003) worked with elastic cord and acrylic yarn to delineate and frame different spaces, creating volumetric forms using the most minimal means possible.

Fred SANDBACK (1943–2003), *Untitled* (Two-part Vertical Construction, from Ten Vertical Constructions), 1977–1979, Beacon, United Sates.
Rust-red acrylic yarn
Situational: spatial relationships established by the artist; overall dimensions vary with each installation. Collection Dia Art Foundation, New York. Installation view Dia: Beacon
Photo: Bill Jacobson, courtesy Fred Sandback Archive and Dia Art Foundation. Art by Fred Sandback © Fred 2022 Sandback Archive

Sandback's sculptures outline planes and volumes in space. Though he employed metal wire and elastic cord early in his career, he soon dispensed with mass and weight by using acrylic yarn to create works that address their physical surroundings—the "pedestrian space," as Sandback called it—of everyday life. By stretching lengths of yarn horizontally, vertically, and diagonally at different scales and in varied configurations, the artist developed a body of work that elaborated on the phenomenological experience of space and volume with unwavering consistency and ingenuity (David Zwirner Press Release on Fred Sandback).

Another example of litotes and meiosis is Friedman's self-portrait, produced in 1998 (one of his most elementary pieces). The work is a full-body photograph of the artist. A module is extracted digitally: a one-pixel-thick column disintegrates into a bitmap or "raster" image. A column of pixels is repeated via a horizontal juxtaposition, generating a linear structure that creates the final image. The result is an abstract image that evokes a landscape in motion. However, the proportion and colored shapes reveal the anthropomorphic source of the work and the process that generated it.

No distinction is made between litotes and meiosis in these spatial and visual examples. All the works of art are thought or created using an opposing technique to exaggerate (**hyperbole** [067]). Fujimoto plays with the scale of the elements to change their meaning by changing their size. In this way, unexpected materials—specifically, small everyday objects—are transformed into architecture. Meanwhile, Friedman repeats a single column of pixels to generate a new form of portrait. Contrarily, Sandback works with minimal and linear elements to outline planes and volumes, thus creating new architectural spaces and transforming the spaces within spaces.

Tom FRIEDMAN, *Untitled* (Self portrait), 1998.

Chromogenic print. Frame: 25 x 46.75 in. (63.5 x 118.7 cm). Purchase, Jennifer and Joseph Duke Gift, 1999 (1999.230). New York, Metropolitan Museum of Art.

© 2022. The Metropolitan Museum of Art/Art Resource/Scala, Florence

074

METAPHORICAL
& METONYMIC
Substitution

- METAPHORICAL &
METONYMIC Substitution
- IRONY
- PARADOX
- ENARGIA
- PUN
- Ungrammatical, illogical,
or unusual uses of language
- ENALLAGE
- HYPERBATON
- Techniques of argument
- Example, allusion, and
citation of authority
- REPETITIO(N)
- AMPLIFICATIO(N)
- ANTITHESIS
- Brevity
- Balance
- Omission
- Emotional appeals

Operation:
SUBSTITUTION
Relation:
SIMILARITY

G. "transference"
METAPHOR

075

METAPHORICAL
& METONYMIC
Substitution

● METAPHORICAL &
METONYMIC Substitution
● IRONY
● PARADOX
● ENARGIA
● PUN
● Ungrammatical, illogical,
or unusual uses of language
● ENALLAGE
● HYPERBATON
● Techniques of argument
● Example, allusion, and
citation of authority
● REPETITIO(N)
● AMPLIFICATIO(N)
● ANTITHESIS
● Brevity
● Balance
● Omission
● Emotional appeals

Operation:
SUBSTITUTION
Relation:
CONTIGUITY

—Denominatio;
Hypallage (2);
Misnamer;
Transmutation;
Transnominatio.

G. "change of name"

METONYMY

The replacement of one word for another that has a spatial, temporal, or causal contiguity with the first.

The party preserved a dignified homogeneity, and assumed to itself the function of representing the staid nobility of the countryside—East Egg condescending to West Egg, and carefully on guard against its spectroscopic gayety.
—F. SCOTT FITZGERALD, *The Great Gatsby*, 1925.

[010] Amphibologia;
[011] AMPLIFICATIO;
[014] Anamnesis;
[016] Anaphora;
[032] Antonomasia;
Augendi Causa;
Chorographia;
[046] Conduplicatio;
Demonstratio;
[049] Diallage;
[052] Ecphonesis;
Emphasis;
[060] Exergasia;
[066] HYPERBATON;
[067] Hyperbole;
[069]Image;[070]IRONY;
[071]Isocolon;Metalepsis;
[075] METONYMY;
PATHOPOEIA;
[083] Polyptoton;
[085] Pragmatographia;
REPETITIO(N);
[091] Significatio;
[096] Synecdoche;
[100] Topographia.

METONYMY is the replacement of one word for another, where the two words have some relationship (spatial, temporal, or causal contiguity). There are several different types of metonymy: effect for cause/cause for effect, physical for moral, matter for object, container for content, abstract for concrete, author for work, place of origin for object, etc.

Many theorists consider metonymy as being as central as the METAPHOR [070]. Most rhetorical devices can generally be understood as metonymies or metaphors. Both are tropes that substitute one word for another based on contiguity relationships (in metonymy) or similarity (in metaphor). In this regard, contiguity covers similar relationships; on the contrary, similarity does not include all contiguous relationships. Hence, it seems that more figures of rhetoric can be placed under the umbrella of metonymy.

Metonymy plays a crucial role in the conception of the *Tourisms: SuitCase Studies* exhibition by Diller Scofidio.

One of the most popular forms of tourism in the U.S. is travel to the national past. With such a short history, the American public savors every detail, particularly with the aura of a place—to stand on the site where the general fell, to occupy the space of the boyhood bed of the 16th president. Fifty identical Samsonite suitcases transport the contents of the exhibition and double as display cases for these contents. Each suitcase is a case study of a particular tourist attraction in each of the fifty states in the U.S. Each looks critically at official and unofficial images and texts. Only two types of sites are studied: famous beds and famous battlefields, two sites in which

DILLER SCOFIDIO, *Tourisms: SuitCase Studies*, 1991, Walker Art Center, Minneapolis, United States.

Exhibition view of the Samsonite suitcases installed at Walker Art Center (May 3, 1991–June 30, 1991). The show was the fifth in the series "Architecture Tomorrow" organized by the Walker Art Center and traveled to four others museums of the country: Wexner Art Center, the List Center for the Visual Arts, the FRAC Basse-Normandie, and the Whitney Museum of Art.

Photo: Michael Mora
Courtesy of Diller Scofidio + Renfro

[DS + R: Elizabeth DILLER, Ricardo SCOFIDIO, Charles RENFRO]

the subtlety of tourism's construction of aura most strongly feeds the hunger for the real, no matter the degree of artifice required to produce it…

[E]ach of fifty suitcases contains a postcard (picture on one side, message on the reverse seen in mirror image) and related materials about a specific tourist attraction in each of the fifty states. The tourist sites are either bedrooms or battlefields. Hanging from the lower half of each suitcase is a rubberoid sheet with printed statements about travel taken from a variety of literary sources. The number of tourist dollars spent in each state appears below the quotations (Diller & Scofidio, 1991).

At the very least, *Tourisms: SuitCase Studies* expresses the following metonymies or substitutions by contiguity: bed/bedroom and battlefield for tourist attraction, bed/bedroom and battlefield for site, suitcase for tourism, suitcase for travel, suitcase for bed/bedroom, suitcase for battlefield, suitcase for states of the United States of America, bed/bedroom for president states of the United States of America, suitcase for installation, suitcase for memories, and suitcase for tourism earnings.

Operation:
SUBSTITUTION
Relation:
SIMILARITY

— Newnamer;
Nominatio
(L. "naming");
Nominis fictio
(L. "feigning of a
name"); Procreatio.

G. "the making of words"

Onomatopoeia

Use or invention of words that sound like their meaning.

The murmur of innumerable bees, the wind "soughing" (*sooing, sowing, suffing*, according to taste or tree) in the trees.

— Richard A. LANHAM, *A Handlist of Rhetorical Terms*, 1991.

Onomatopoeia refers to a word (or words) that phonetically mimics the sound of the thing it describes. For example, the words we use to describe the noises that animals make are all onomatopoetic, such as a dog's "bark," a cat's "meow," or a cow's "moo." Although onomatopoeic words are considered verbal signs, there is a slight but detectible connection between the signifiers and the objects to which they refer. They are signs that mimic the sound of something to signify it. Interestingly, onomatopoetic words differ from one language to another, as the words must fit into the broader linguistic system. For example, while a pig says "oink" in English, it says "buu" in Japanese, "grunz" in German, "knor" in Dutch, and so on.

The artwork *Bus* displayed on this page can be considered a physical equivalent of onomatopoeia since it is halfway between iconic and verbal language. The art group mmmm… created this permanent bus stop in Baltimore by playing with the appearance of the word "BUS" and the shape of the letters B, U, and S. Each wood-and-steel sculpture/letter stands 14 feet tall and seven feet wide (around four by two meters). The letters are big enough to accommodate several people and protect them from rain, sun, wind, and inclement weather. They allow people to assume different sitting and standing postures while waiting for the bus. The "S" allows people to lie back while they wait, and the "B" provides shelter. *Bus* is not just a bus stop; it is a place to enjoy, interact, and meet while waiting for the bus. It is a leisure space in the middle of the busy city, a fun place for waiting for a bus.

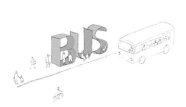

mmmm…, *BUS*, 2014,
Baltimore, United States.
Courtesy of mmmm…

[mmmm…: Alberto ALARCÓN,
Emilio ALARCÓN, Ciro MÁRQUEZ,
Eva SALMERÓN]

PARADOX
● METAPHORICAL &
METONYMIC Substitution
● IRONY
● PARADOX
● Brevity
● Balance
● Emotional appeals

Operation:
ADDITION
Relation:
CONTRADICTION

See also
PARADOX [079];
Synoeciosis [097].

L. "a witty, paradoxical saying," lit. "pointedly foolish"

Oxymoron

A combination of two contradictory terms. A condensed paradox.

Here's much to do with hate but more with
love.
Why then. O brawling love! O loving hate,
O anything of nothing first created!
O heavy lightness, serious vanity,
Misshapen chaos of well-seeming forms!
Feather of lead, bright smoke, cold fire,
sick health!
Still-waking sleep, that is not what it is!
This love feel I, that feel no love in this.
Dost thou not laugh?

—William SHAKESPEARE, *Romeo and Juliet*, (1596).

The word oxymoron is of Greek origin, combining the word *oxy* (sharp) and *moron* (dull, stupid, foolish). Thus, an **oxymoron** not only names a contradiction, but it is an oxymoron itself. It may be used to achieve a desired rhetorical effect, as in "working vacation" and "uninvited guest." It may also result from conceptual sloppiness, as in "extremely average," "original copy," or "same difference." Oxymorons remain unnoticed when the meanings of the contradictory parts are not distinguished, as in "spendthrift," "virtual reality," and "artificial intelligence" (Klaus Krippendorff, "Design Research, an Oxymoron?").

Examples of oxymorons can be found in casual conversations and in literature. Many examples of this color of rhetoric arise in everyday expressions, such as "act natural," "fast asleep," "civil war," "jumbo shrimp," "pretty ugly." Oxymorons can also imply IRONY [070], such as in the expressions "academic administration," "business ethics," "airline food," "apartment living," or "military intelligence."

The difference between an oxymoron and a PARADOX [079] is that a paradox can include full sentences or groups of sentences. An oxymoron, on the other hand, is a combination of two contradictory

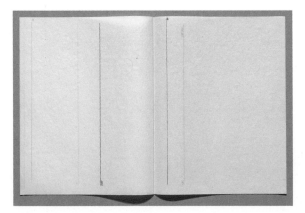

John CAGE (1912–1992), *4' 33" (In Proportional Notation),* 1952-unfolded.
Ink on paper, page (each): 11 x 8.50 in. (27.9 x 21.6 cm). Sheet (each, unfolded): 11 x 16.94 in. (27.9 x 43.1 cm). Acquired through the generosity of Henry Kravis in honor of Marie-Josee Kravis. Acc. n.: 1636.2012.
© 2022. Digital image, The Museum of Modern Art, New York/Scala, Florence

"4'33" (In Proportional Notation) is one of three versions of the score for Cage's "silent piece," a musical composition first performed by the pianist David Tudor on August 29, 1952, in Maverick Concert Hall, Woodstock, New York, as part of a recital of contemporary piano music. While the lost original score used conventional musical notation to signify three periods of silence, this version is composed of a series of vertical lines that visually represent the duration of four minutes and thirty-three seconds of silence" (MoMA).

or opposite words. A paradox seems to contradict the general truth while containing an implied truth. Meanwhile, an oxymoron produces a dramatic effect but does not make literal sense.

This device has been used brilliantly in art and architecture, even changing the very notion of what music is. In 1952, American experimental composer John Cage (1912–1992) composed *4'33"*, a three-movement composition for any instrument or combination. The score instructs the performer(s) not to play their instrument(s) for the duration of the piece, which consists of three movements. The title refers to the total length (in minutes and seconds) of the first public performance. The premiere was given by the American pianist David Tudor (1926–1996) as part of a recital of contemporary piano music. Tudor sat quietly at his piano, opening and closing the keyboard lid to mark the progression of the three movements. Although it is commonly perceived as "four minutes thirty-three seconds of silence," the piece consists of the sounds of the environment that the listeners hear while it is "performed," what Cage called "the absence of intended sounds." Cage once recounted that "you could hear the wind stirring outside during the first movement. During the second, raindrops began pattering the roof, and during the third people themselves made all kinds of interesting sounds as they talked or walked out."

Jana STERBAK, *Distraction*
(Hairshirt), 1992.
Color photograph, 19.3 x 14.2 in.
(49 × 36 cm).
© Jana Sterbak

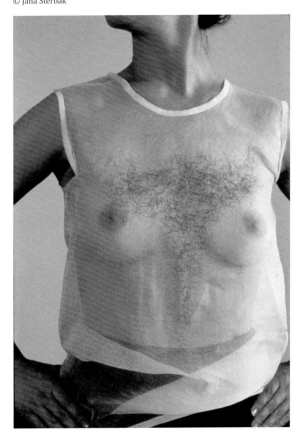

This piece becomes for Cage the essence of his idea that any sounds may constitute music. He considers all the sounds around audiences as music. *4'33"* also exemplifies Cage's interest in using chance as a compositional strategy.

Distraction or *Hairshirt* by artist Jana Sterbak exemplifies the oxymoron in the visual world. Sterbak was born in Prague (1955) and moved to Canada with her parents in 1968. She is interested, above all, in the human body, and she creates conceptual objects to be worn and allow the wearer to experience both bodily and out-of-body freedom. *Hairshirt*, a shirt designed to be worn by a woman, is covered in hair, thus imitating the male torso.

The series of *Teatri Impossibili* (Impossible Theaters), designed in 1968 by the architectural group Archizoom Associatti demands the disappearance of the professional actor. Instead, the public plays the leading role as the only active component in the scene. As in the work of Cage and Sterback, this conceptual architectural project contradicts the classical and ordinary meanings and experiences of the elements of the scene and theater—for example, the actors, the audience, and the stage.

In the first "Teatro d'Incontro Ideologico (Theater of Ideological Meeting)," two sectors are divided by a curtain without a stage. When the curtain opens, the two areas remain separate. At the same time, the public becomes both the actor and viewer. Two megaphones allow communication between opposite sectors. The gap prevents the changing of areas to eliminate the risk of confrontation between the two "sides."

"Teatro Privato del Potere (Private Theater of Power)" consists of a colossal chair or the "chair of power," whose dimensions are out of scale. A straight staircase allows one to get up the throne of power. Once on the chair, it is possible to look at a small mirror hanging by the ceiling.

A large, opaque, black box dominates the scene of the "Teatro della Forma Premeditated (Theater of the Predetermined Form)." The audience sits on regular chairs arranged as a banquet around the black box with an opening hidden by a curtain. The volume and arrangement of the space disable the communication between the public. Most of the audience members cannot see the play or action occurring throughout the theater.

The fourth "Teatro Segreto in Ambiente Domestico (Secret Theater in Domestic Space with Metal Gazebo)" recreates a typical "room" in which the public can play a (pre)determined role using a variety of props such as hats, sunglasses, and beards.

ARCHIZOOM Associati, *Teatri Impossibile (pour* Pianesta *Fresco n°2)* (Impossible Theaters), 1968.

Teatro d'incontro ideologico con baratro murato.
Teatro privato del potere con dilatazione dimensional.
Teatro delle forma premeditata in ambiente unico.
Teatro segreton in ambiente domestico con gazebo metal.

© Centre Pompidou, MNAM-CCI, Dist. RMN-Grand Palais / Philippe Migeat © Andrea Branzi

[Archizoom Associatti (1966–1974):
Andrea BRANZI, Gilberto CORRETTI,
Paolo DEGANELLO, Massimo MOROZZI,
Dario BARTOLINI, Lucia BARTOLINI]

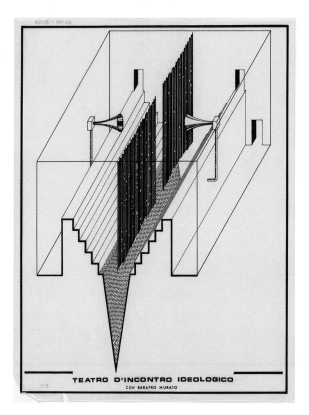

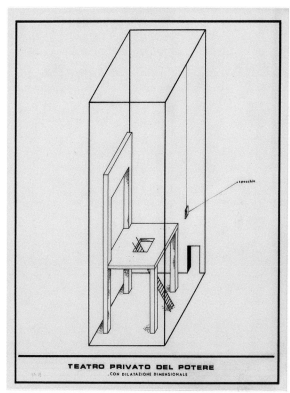

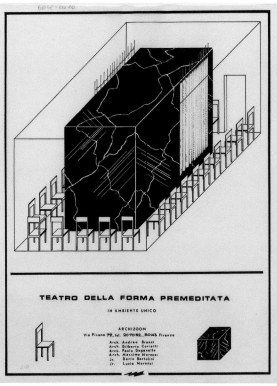

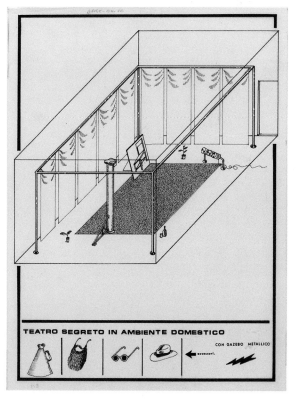

078

PUN
● PUN
● REPETITIO(N)
● Brevity
● Balance
● Omission

Operation:
REARRANGEMENT
Relation:
DOUBLE MEANING

See also
Chiasmus [043].

G. "running back again"

Palindrome

Words, phrases, or sentences that make sense read backwards as well as forwards.

T. Eliot, top bard, notes putrid tang
emanating, is sad. I'd assign it a name: gnat
dirt upset on drab pot-toilet.

—Charles OSBORNE, *W. H. The Life of a Poet*, 1979.

Ashkhen MANUKYAN, *Sound of Spaces Game,*
2020, Melbourne, Australia.

"Children & Elders' Games" Advanced Design Studio and
"Open Secrets" Studies Unit by Ciro Márquez and María
Fullaondo, Monash Art Design Architecture (MADA),
Monash University.

Courtesy of Ashkhen Manukyan

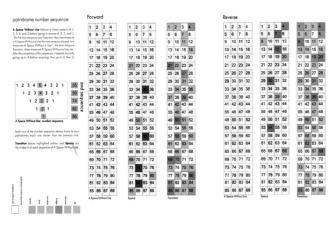

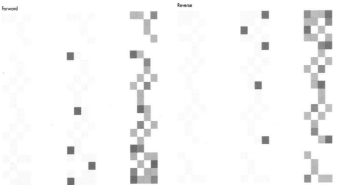

The term **palindrome** is derived from two Greek words, *palin*, which means "again," and *dromos*, which means "way" or "direction." It is defined as a number, word, sentence, symbol, or even a sign that can be read forward and backward with the same effect and meaning. Examples of palindromes are "Able was I ere I saw Elba" and "Madam, I'm Adam." A palindrome seems to represent an extremely compressed version of a **chiasmus** [043].

In the middle of the 17th century, Ben Jonson was the first writer to introduce this term in English.

Sound of Spaces Game, an architectural project by Ashkhen Manukyan, uses the principles of combinatorics and this rhetorical mechanism (specifically, a palindrome number sequence) to generate an experimental playground. The experimental writing by Georges Perec titled *Species of Spaces and Other Pieces* also informs this project conceptually.

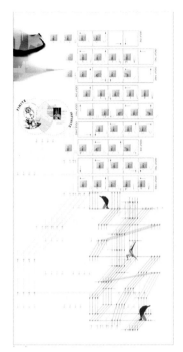
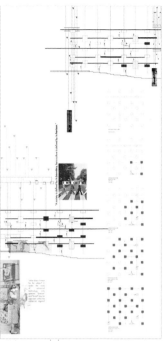

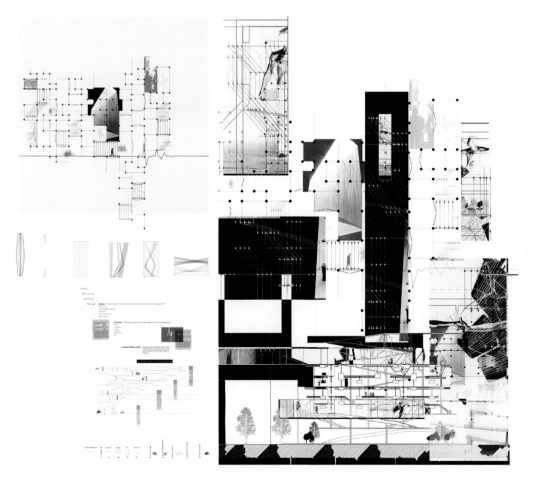

G. "contrary to opinion or expectation"

PARADOX

A seemingly self-contradictory statement, which yet is shown to be (sometimes in a surprising way) true.

We all know that Art is not truth. Art is a lie that makes us realize truth, at least the truth that is given us to understand.

— Pablo PICASSO, "Picasso Speaks: A Statement by the Artist," interview with Marius de Zayas, *The Arts*, (1923).

A PARADOX is an apparently contradictory statement that contains some truth. The word "paradox" is derived from the Greek *paradoxon*, which means "against opinion" or "contrary to expectation." This deviation usually has two parallel elements that appear logically inconsistent, yet they contain a truth. For example, the Socratic paradox of "No one does wrong willingly, but is unwillingly that all who do wrong do wrong."

The paradox expressed in *Housing for Homeless*, a project developed in 1985 in Wes Jones's architectural office, proposes a residential building comprising a stack of vehicles for the homeless to live in. In this case, the seemingly self-contradictory statement acts on two levels. First, there is a conceptual contradiction in creating a house for people who, by definition, live on the streets. On the other hand, cars, vans, or small vehicles are occasionally used and inhabited by the homeless. Reflecting on these circumstances, Jones proposes a multi-floor housing block. The housing units consist of vertically and horizontally stacked cars, thus eliminating or transforming the nature and essence of this type of object.

Another demonstration of this color of rhetoric in art is *Paradox of Praxis 1* by Belgian-born Francis Alÿs (as the title itself expresses). This piece of art is a record of an action carried out under the rubric of "sometimes making something leads to nothing." For more than nine hours, Alÿs pushed a block of ice through the streets of Mexico City until it completely melted. This action was the synthesis of several themes explored by Alÿs during the mid-1990s and a decisive moment in his attempt to reflect on the underlying logic of the peripheral economies of the South. The performance highlights the massive disproportion between effort and results in much of Latin American life through a paradox. Alÿs alluded to the seemingly unproductive hardship involved in the daily survival tactics of most people in the region. At the same time, *Paradox of Praxis 1* emphasizes the dissolution of the sculptural object and the rejection of the physicality of sculpture by enacting the physical disintegration of the ice cube through its circulation.

Francis Alÿs is trained as an architect and has lived and worked in Mexico for over 30 years. His interest in architecture and the city is explicit in this performance. The action also offers a series of views into the physical conditions of the city, its buildings and urban structures, facades, colors, materials, pavements, dirt, and traffic. The artwork is also used to provide a photographic view of daily life of Mexico City.

JONES Partners: Architecture (Wes JONES),
Housing for Homeless, 1985.
Courtesy of Jones Partners: Architecture

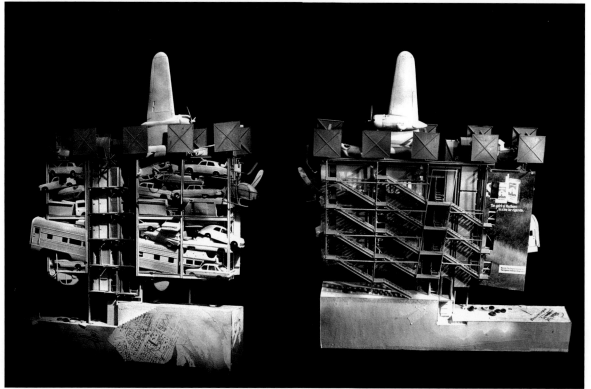

Francis ALŸS, *Paradox of Praxis 1* (Sometimes doing something leads to nothing), 1997, Mexico City, Mexico.

Photographic and video documentation of an action.

Photo: Enrique Huerta
Courtesy of the Artist

G. "insertion"

Parenthesis

A word, phrase, or sentence inserted as an aside in a sentence complete in itself.

It is now necessary to warn you that your concern for the reader must be pure: you must sympathize with the reader's plight (most readers are in trouble about half the time) but never seek to know the reader's wants. Your whole duty as a writer is to please and satisfy yourself…

—William STRUNK Jr. and E. B. WHITE,
The Elements of Style, 1918.

The word "parenthesis" comes from the Greek word meaning "to place" or "alongside." **Parentheses** contain qualifying or explanatory sentence, clause, or word inserted into a paragraph or speech. However, deleting a parenthetical statement does not grammatically affect the text.

The visual handbook *How to Ski by the French Method. Emile Allais' Technique* is a remarkable visual document created by French designer and illustrator Pierre Boucher (1908–2000). Though it was published in 1947, all the graphic aspects, strategies, and resources that it uses to define this sport are appropriate and adequate for our times. In this double-page spread, the action is divided into five steps, presented in a nearly perfect elevation as if it were a row of five perfectly synchronized skiers.

Pierre BOUCHER
(1908–2000), *How to Ski by the French Method*, 1947, Paris, France.

Christianias.

From *Émile Allais, How to Ski by the French Method* (Flèche Publishers: Paris, 1947), 54–55, photographs and design by Pierre Boucher, translated by Agustin Edwards.

In written language, we often insert clarifying information that interrupts the normal syntactic flow within parentheses. This interruption complements and specifies the information of a specific statement. The ski lesson of these pages shows various superimposed graphic parentheses. The positions of the various parts of the skier's body on a slight slope are shown with a series of graphic elements that work as a visual form of parenthesis. Different arrow types, arcs, and lines of text are used as explanatory notes. Among these secondary elements, the red superimposed complementary arrows provide the most clarification.

The Melbourne Bridge project by Steven Holl was presented to a competition organized by the city of Melbourne. It was developed at the same time as *The Bridge of Houses* in New York (**Appositio** [035]). Holl's proposal connects a vast urban area of train lines to the city grid and the Yarra River. The connection consists of seven different building bridges, or "urban arms" as Holl calls them. Each bridge above the train lanes is a continuation of the existing streets and laneways of the Melbourne grid and has a specific name: Bridge of Pools and Baths, Cultural Bridge, Bridge of Piazzas, Bridge of Ancient/Modern Columns, Bridge of International Trade, Bridge of Odd Flowers, and Bridge of Houses.

A different housing typology is inserted on each bridge to act the same way parentheses do with words. In the Melbourne project, all the housing typologies are developed from a rectangular floor plan with a central courtyard. However, each building bridge adopts a unique character based on the future inhabitant of the structure: House of the Decider, House of the Doubter, House for a Man Without Opinions, The Riddle, Dream House, Four Tower House, and Matter and Memory.

Steven HOLL, *Melbourne Bridge of Houses*, 1979, Melbourne, Australia.

Oblique projections, plans, and sections.

Melbourne Competition (seven bridges). Readaptation of a vast area of train lanes that disconnected the urban grid with the Yarra River.

Courtesy of Steven Holl Architects

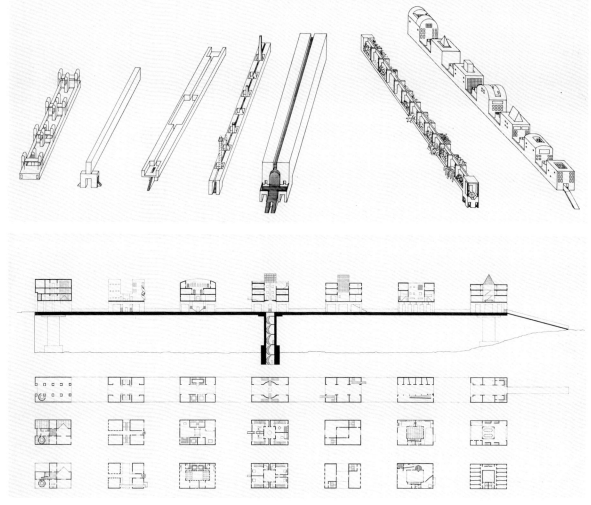

For *Bridge of Houses*, see also Appositio [035].

G. "play upon words which sound alike"

Paronomasia

Playing on the sounds and meanings of words.

If you spot kay
Tell him he may
See you in tea
Tell him from me.

—James JOYCE, *Ulysses*, 1920.

PUN
● METAPHORICAL &
METONYMIC Substitution
● PUN
● Techniques of argument
● REPETITIO(N)
● AMPLIFICATIO(N)

Operation:
SUBSTITUTION
Relation:
DOUBLE MEANING

—Adnominatio
(L. "two words of
different meaning
but similar sound
brought together");
PUN; Skesis.

See also PUN [088].

Paronomasia is a type of wordplay involving words with similar sounds but more than one meaning (punning). It is related to **adnominatio** and **polyptoton** [083], while it is unlike **antanaclasis** [020], in which the words being punned sound similar, but not identical. William Shakespeare was notorious for the use of PUNS [088] in his plays. In the following quote from *Romeo and Juliet*, the words "soul" and "sole" sound alike but have different meanings, thus creating humor: "You have dancing shoes with nimble soles; I have a soul of lead…So stakes me to the ground I cannot move." Another example comes from *Richard III*: "Now is the winter of our discontent / Made glorious summer by this sun of York…"

There are five types of typographic paronomasia. Homophonic paronomasia uses words that sound the same but have different meanings, such as "Pour out corruption's slag from every pore." Homographic paronomasia comprises words that are spelled the same but have different meanings, such as "David doesn't feel well today" and "My uncle is digging a new well." Homonymic paronomasia contains words that include both homographs and homophones. Instances of compound paronomasia contain two or more puns in one sentence. Finally, in recursive paronomasia, the second part of a pun depends upon the meaning of the first.

The photomontage *Olly and Dolly sisters* by Moholy Nagy (1895–1946) is a visual depiction of paronomasia. The same shape—a black circle—appears three times and has three different meanings in this work. The head of one of the sisters and dancers, Olly, is represented by a black circle. Another circle of the same size and color is used to express the other sister, Dolly. Dolly is also represented by the head, one single element expressing the whole. In this sense, this work is also an example of a color of rhetoric called **synecdoche** [096], which involves representing a whole by naming one part (or vice versa). Finally, the third big circle serves as the support on which one of the sisters sits.

László MOHOLY-NAGY (1895–1946), *Das Tanzerpaar Olly & Dolly sisters* (The Dancers Olly & Dolly sisters), 1925.

Gelatin silver print, photomontage (photography). 14.75 × 10. 81 in. (37.5 × 27.5 cm). Photo (C) Centre Pompidou, MNAM-CCI, Dist. RMN-Grand Palais / Jacques Faujour

REPETITO(N)
● METAPHORICAL &
METONYMIC Substitution
● PUN
● Techniques of argument
● REPETITIO(N)

Operation:
REPETITION
Relation:
DOUBLE MEANING

—Conexio
(L. "binding
together, close
union"); Copulatio
(L. "coupling,
joining"); Diaphora
(G. "dislocation,
difference,
disagreement");
Doubler; Epanodos
(G. "return;
recapitulation,
fuller statement
of a point"); Swift
Repeate; Traductio
(L. "leading along;
a transferring or
metonymy; repetition
of a word").

See also
Antanaclasis [020];
Epiploce.

G. "plaiting"

Ploce

Repetition of a word or a name with a new signification after the intervention of another word or words.

We'll be over, we're coming over,
And we won't come back till it's over
Over there.

—George M. COHAN, "Over There," 1917.

Ploce is a rhetorical term that describes the repetition of a word or name, often with a different sense, after the intervention of one or more other words. Peacham confined the term ploce to the repetition of a proper name, while **diaphora** denotes the repetition of ordinary words.

The Kuleshov effect is a film-editing technique that serves as a perfect example of ploce in film. As a teacher at Moscow Film School, the Russian director Lev Kuleshov (1899–1970) conducted an experiment to demonstrate how a viewer's interpretation of the same image can be influenced through juxtaposition with a second image. He edited a close-up of an expressionless man (*Tsarist* silent film actor Ivan Mosjoukine) and juxtaposed it with three alternate ending shots: a dead child in a coffin, a bowl of soup, and a woman lying on a divan. Then, the director showed the three miniature films to three separate audiences and asked viewers to interpret what the man was thinking. Viewers who saw the image of the dead child believed the man's expression indicated sadness. When followed by a plate of soup, they felt the man's expression indicated hunger. Finally, when paired with the image of the reclining woman, audiences assumed the man was expressing lust. However, the man's expression was identical in all three miniature films. Thus, the audiences' interpretations depended entirely on the image that followed. In other words, meaning was added to the same image based on the context of the scene.

The Kuleshov experiment was revolutionary for its time, as the first to demonstrate the importance of the juxtaposition of shots or images. The context also determines the meaning, as demonstrated by this Reiser + Umemoto diagram on the perception of scale. In this example, the same form is perceived as being different sizes depending on the context.

Lev KULESHOV (1899–1970), "Diagram of the Kuleshov Effect," (1921).

The Kuleshov Effect was a film experiment and cognitive event conducted by Soviet filmmaker Lev Kuleshov. It explored how audiences derive more meaning from the interaction of two sequential shots than from a single shot in isolation.

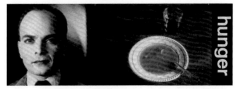

REISER + UMEMOTO, "Diagram on
perception of Scale," 2006.

Reiser + Umemoto, *Atlas of Novel
Tectonics*, (Princeton Architectural
Press: 2006), 119–121.

Courtesy of Reiser + Umemoto

[Reiser + Umemoto: Jesse REISER and
Nanako UMEMOTO]

The Human Scale

At the scale of clothing and furniture, the form appears natural.

Beyond the Scale of Furniture but Smaller than a House

At this intermediate scale (that of the interior), the form
is indeterminately furniture and partition.

Larger than a Building and Smaller than a City

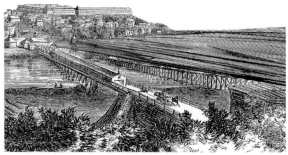

At this scale the form, while alien as a building type, begins to become
coextensive with urban networks, the natural/artificial geography of the city.

Larger than a House and Smaller than a Building

The form approaches the scale of a small landscape feature but
runs the risk of being mimetic. At this scale domestic networks
may interact with the form in a non-normative way.

At the Scale of the Landscape, the Form Appears Natural Again

At this scale both the form and the network have slipped back into
conventional relationships: folds appear in cloth and rock alike.

REPETITIO(N)

● Techniques of argument
● REPETITIO(N)
● AMPLIFICATIO(N)

Operation:
REPETITION
Relation:
SIMILARITY

Polyptiton—
Adnominatio;
Paregmenon
(G. "led aside,
disgression");
Traductio
(L. "leading along;
a transferring
or metonymy;
repetition of a
word").

G. "employment of the same word in various cases"

Polyptoton

Repetition of words from the same root but with different endings.

Let me not to the marriage of true minds
Admit impediments. Love is not love
Which **alters** when it **alteration** finds,
Or bends with the **remover** to **remove**...

—William SHAKESPEARE, *Sonnet 116*, (1609).

The repetition of the same root word is called **polyptoton**. Each time, a slightly different word is used, as in this quote by Cynthia Ozick: "To imagine the unimaginable is the highest use of the imagination."

In 1973 and 1976, Allan Wexler proposed an architectural polyptoton by transforming and varying the facade of the World Trade Center every night using only the light switches and window shades. As the author explains,

> Each evening the cleaning person consults a calendar positioned at each window of the building to determine if a light is to be left on or a window shade adjusted. ON/OFF—the binary system in operation. The illusion is that World Trade Center's facade is sliced, dissected, rearranged, or transformed into other facades. The Empire State Building or Notre Dame can be displaced to lower Manhattan.

Allan WEXLER, *Proposal for the Manhattan Skyline, World Trade Center*, 1973, 1976, New York, United States.
© Allan Wexler

G. "bound together"

Polysyndeton

Use of a conjunction between each clause.

There were frowzy fields, and cow-houses, and dunghills, and dustheaps, and ditches, and gardens, and summer-houses, and carpet-beating grounds, at the very door of the Railway. Little tumuli of oyster shells in the oyster season, and of lobster shells in the lobster season, and of broken crockery and faded cabbage leaves in all seasons, encroached upon its high places

—Charles DICKENS, *Dombey and Son*, 1848.

Polysyndeton means "bound together" and involves the use of conjunctions like "and," "or," "but," and "of" to join successive phrases or clauses. The device joins words, phrases, and clauses to bring continuity to a sentence and rhythm to the text by repeating conjunctions in quick succession, thus emphasizing the ideas connected by the conjunctions.

In the visual and spatial world, *Coffee Seeks its Own Level* by American interdisciplinary artist Allan Wexler illustrates this rhetorical figure. Wexler's work is inspired by the basic scientific principle "water seeks its own level." Four cups of coffee are linked together. If one person alone lifts his cup, coffee overflows from the other three cups. All four people need to coordinate their actions and lift simultaneously to prevent the coffee from overflowing.

Allan WEXLER, *Coffee Seeks its Own Level*, 1990.
© Allan Wexler

ENARGIA

● ENARGIA
● Techniques of argument
● AMPLIFICATIO(N)

Operation:
AMPLIFICATION
Relation:
DIFFERENCE

—Counterfait Action;
Descriptio.

See also
ENARGIA [055].

G. "description of an action, affair"

Pragmatographia

Vivid description of an action or event.

I am a rogue if I were not a half-sword with a dozen of them two hours together. I have 'scaped by miracle. I am eight times thrust through the doublet, four through the hose; my buckler cut through and through; my sword hacked like a handsaw—*ecce signum!*

—William SHAKESPEARE, *Romeo and Juliet*, (1596).

Pragmatographia, derived from the Greek words *pragma* ("that which has been done") and *graphe* ("to write"), is a kind of ENARGIA [055] —a generic term used to describe various types of description— solely concerned with the verbal description of actions or events. The subject of description can represent the actions of persons, feasts, wars, conquests, marriages, open ceremonies, burials, episodes, adventures, and so on.

This rhetorical description occurs when someone plainly depicts all circumstances of an event that is either happening or has already happened as if they were most lively painted. That is, the effectiveness of this color, as in any enargia, usually depends on the ability of the author (both in writing and speech) to narrate an event as if it were happening before one's eyes. Therefore, its transposition into the visual world may not be so surprising. However, the two notable visual examples of pragmatographia describe two events—a meal and a childrens' game jump rope— in a compelling, clear, lucid, and vivid way.

The four drawings of *Disorder of the Dining Table* by British architect Sarah Wigglesworth explores the idea of order in architecture. They depict the transformation of the plane of the ordered dining table into the plan of the house. From a rhetorical perspective, and focusing only on the description of the event, some elements need to be highlighted, making this four-drawing diagram unique. First of all, the composition of the drawing in four parts stands out, as the description of an event in a sequence provides more information than a single image could. The descriptive line begins with the table set for an evening meal for eight diners. This step gives information about the lay of the table, type of meal, host's or hostess's tastes, type of cutlery, and other matters. The second stage focuses on the meal, especially on movement and the interaction between the diners and the food. As the artist explains, it records the trace of occupation in time, and it is an excellent example of movement representation. The description of the event ends by depicting the table after the meal has finished, the dirty tablecloth and wrinkled napkins, leftovers on the plates, the position of the cutlery and chairs, glasses of wine and water, and so on. The details provided in these three moments are impossible without the juxtaposed visual scheme, making this drawing an excellent graphic transposition of pragmatographia.

Meagan VELLEMAN, *Jumprope Game: complex graphic narratives*, 2020, Melbourne, Australia.

"Children & Elders' Games" Advanced Design Studio and "Open Secrets" Studies Unit by Ciro Márquez and María Fullaondo, Monash Art Design Architecture (MADA), Monash University.

Courtesy of Meagan Velleman

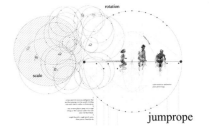

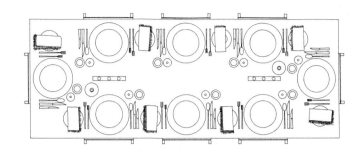

Sarah WIGGLESWORTH, *The Disorder of the Dining Table,* 1997.
© Sarah Wigglesworth, 1997

These four drawings are an exploration of the idea of order in architecture. They document the transformation of the plane of the ordered dining table into the plan of the house. The sequence begins with the table in readiness for an evening meal.

The Lay of the Table
An architectural ordering of place, status and function
A frozen moment of perfection.

The Meal
Use begins to undermine the apparent stability of the (architectural) order
Traces of occupation in time
The recognition of life's disorder.

The Trace
The dirty tablecloth, witness of disorder
Between space and time
The palimpsest.

The Lay of the Plan
Recognition of an/other system of order
Domestic clutter filling the plan(e).

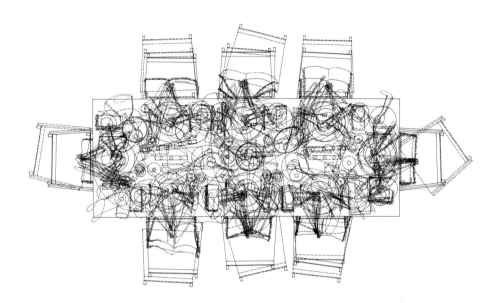

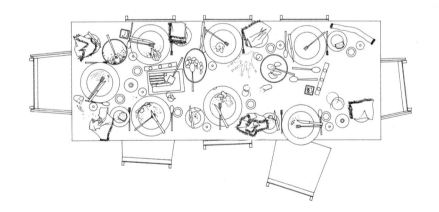

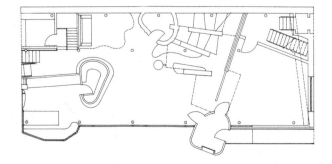

Operation:
SUBSTITUTION
Relation:
CONTIGUITY

—Conformatio
(L. "form,
configuration");
Counterfait in
Personation;
Personification:
Sermocinatio
(L. "conversation,
discussion").

See also
Fictio [063].

Prosopopoeia

An animal or inanimate object is represented as having human attributes and addressed or made to speak as if it were human.

The iron tongue of midnight hath told twelve:
Lovers, to bed; 'tis almost fairy time.

—William SHAKESPEARE, *A Midsummer Night's Dream*, (1596).

American photographer Joel Meyerowitz captures the magical moment of a man carrying a poodle in New York City in a street photograph that exemplifies **prosopopoeia** and **anastrophe** [017]. Instead of walking the dog in the usual way, the pet is in the man's arms as if it were a baby. The dog's size and the interaction between man and animal appear to have made the man forget how dogs are usually walked on the streets.

Dutch-artist Madelon Vriesendorp in 1972 began working on several sketches, drawings, and paintings under the name "Manhattan" that demonstrate the presence of this figure in the visual world. The most emblematic image in the series is *Flagrant Delit* (Flagrant Crime, 1975). It was the cover of *Delirious New York* in 1978 by Rem Koolhaas, and it depicts the post-coital Empire State and Chrysler Buildings caught in bed by the Rockefeller Building. Years later, Vriesendorp painted *10 Ans Après L'Amour* (10 Years After Love), the consequence of the love between the Empire State and the Chrysler building. The watercolor portrays a birthday party of two kid-buildings, the sons of this iconic couple.

Joel MEYEROWITZ, *New York City*, 1965, New York, United States.

(35mm B&W)
© Joel Meyerowitz. Courtesy of Howard Greenberg Gallery

METAPHORICAL
& METONYMIC
Substitution

● METAPHORICAL &
METONYMIC Substitution
● ENARGIA
● Techniques of argument
● AMPLIFICATIO(N)
● Balance
● Emotional appeals

Operation:
SUBSTITUTION
Relation:
CONTIGUITY

—Adage (L. "proverb");
Aphorismus
(G. "distinction,
definition"); Apothegm
(G. "terse saying");
Gnome (G. "thought,
judgment, opinion");
Maxim (L. "greatest
[proposition]");
Paroemia (G. "byword,
proverb"); Sententia
(L. "judgment,
sentiment, opinion").

G. "an old saying"

Proverb

A short, pithy statement of a general truth, one that condenses common experience into memorable form.

She puts the blue cloak on her husband.
—A DUTCH PROVERB

Pieter BRUEGEL the Elder (ca. 1525–1569), *The Netherlandish Proverbs*, 1559.
Berlin, Gemaeldegalerie -Staatliche Museen zu Berlin. Oil on oak panel, 46 x 64.17 in. (117 x 163 cm). Inv. 1720
Photo: Joerg P. Anders
© 2022. Photo Scala, Florence/bpk, Bildagentur fuer Kunst, Kultur und Geschichte, Berlin

The Netherlandish Proverbs (1559) by Peter Bruegel the Elder (ca. 1525–1569) portrays a collection of **proverbs** juxtaposed with everyday scenes. Also known as *The Dutch Proverbs*, *The Blue Cloak,* or *The Folly of the World,* this work is a detailed masterpiece that visually represents over a hundred Dutch proverbs. "She puts the blue cloak on her husband"—the saying that names the oil-on-oak-panel painting,—"To be on as gentle as a lamb," or "Watch out that a black dog does not come in between what seems" are just three of the proverbs represented in the painting. At first, the painting appears to be a simple village scene where each character performs their daily activities. However, it is soon revealed to be something more. Bruegel uses popular culture to criticize and question the false values of the society in which he lives. The artist's intention was not simply to illustrate traditional sayings but to show the universal stupidity of man.

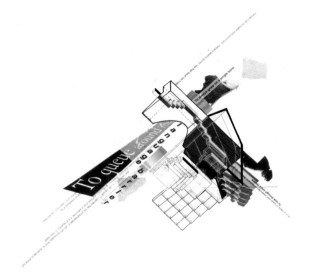

"Proverb Transcripts" was the first project of *Rear Window* Advanced Master design Studio at Monash University. The exercise focused on a set of actions, activities, and events presented in an urban scene. Expressed as contemporary visual proverbs or sayings, students were asked to invent and transcribe a collection of urban situations (scene events) to generate a city and construct society. The transcripts emphasized "space" in representational, formal, social, cultural, political, and economic terms. They were generated through collage, hybrid drawings, and rhetorical procedures.

Yoana Doleva proposed 10 contemporary proverbs extending on urban absurdities' ideas and emphasizing bodily performance in space. These urban actions are:

> To erect a language barrier, To escape through an entrance, To whisper into a microphone, To queue around the clock, To sit through an evacuation, To stall an accident, To trace a shadow, To model a monument in the image of its souvenir, To labour over a reflex, To halt a reflection.

As the Doleva explains in the process of establishing spatial and temporal interruptions, new events (proverbs) are generated:

> To queue around the language barrier, To escape through a microphone, To whisper into a shadow, To whisper into an evacuation, or To halt an evacuation.

> In this expression of the project, the wounds are drawn as a series of interruptions on space, time and event; an alternative city, no longer generic but still privileging the inherent democracy and freedoms of the Generic City...

> As the interruptions do not possess an intended interpretation, they allow alternative realities to take hold, establishing new relationships between space and event...

> This drawings demonstrate the scalable nature of the proposal, depicted simultaneously as a room and a theater. Infinitely replicable yet infinitely specific, as each interruption performed upon space, time and event would be unique (Yoana Doleva).

Yoana DOLEVA, *Spatialised Proverbs* and *Urban Theater*, 2019, Melbourne, Australia.

"Rear Window" Master Advanced Design Studio and Studies Unit by María Fullaondo, First Semester 2019, Monash Art Design Architecture (MADA), Monash University.

Courtesy of Yoana Doleva

[001] Accumulatio; [003] Adianoeta; [004] Adynaton; Aenos; [006] Allegory; [009] Alloiosis; [010] Amphibologia; [011] AMPLIFICATIO; [012] Anacoluthon; [014] Anamnesis; [017] Anastrophe; [018] ANATOMY; [028] Antiphrasis; [034] Apomnemonysis; [035] Appositio; [038] Asyndeton; Augendi Causa; [040] Bomphiologia; [045] Commoratio; [047] Congeries; Diaeresis; [049] Diallage; [050] Dinumeratio; [051] Disjunctio; [052] Ecphonesis; Emphasis; [054] ENALLAGE; [055] ENARGIA; [057] Epicrisis; [058] Epitheton; [060] Exergasia; [066] HYPERBATON; [067] Hyperbole; [068] Hysterologia; [068] Hysteron proteron; [070] IRONY; [071] Isocolon; [074] METAPHOR; [075] METONYMY; [079] PARADOX; [080] Parenthesis; PATHOPOEIA; Peristasis; [087] Proverb; [090] Scesis onomaton; [091] Significatio; [093] Syllepsis; [096] Synecdoche; [097] Synoeciosis; [098] Synonymia; [101] Topothesia.

(etymology uncertain)

PUN

A play on words.

To lose one parent, Mr. Worthing, may be
regarded as a misfortune; to lose both looks
like carelessness.

—Oscar WILDE, *The Importance of Being Earnest*, (1895).

A PUN is a rhetorical figure also known as a "play on words." It involves words with similar or identical sounds but different meanings. These wordplays also rely on a word or phrase having more than one meaning. Puns are generally intended to be humorous, like in the following Groucho Marx quote: "Time flies like an arrow. Fruit flies like a banana." However, in literary works, puns also have a serious purpose.

Visual puns play on the similar appearances of different and distant realities. *B 52 Lipstick Bomber* by Wolf Vostell (1932–1998) associates, replaces, and substitutes the dropping bombs of a warplane with tubes of lipstick. Many authors utilize both figures of double meaning and PARADOXES [079] to express critical commentaries on social and political issues to connect with the general public. Vostell often uses mass-media images of destruction to reflect on consumer culture. In this particular case, the parallelism between bombs and lipsticks condemns mindless consumerism and apathy toward contemporary injustices and violence.

Architect and cartoonist Saul Steinberg's collage constitutes an excellent example of a visual pun. *Chest of Drawers Cityscape*, like other works of the time, is created from cut-out photographs of antique home furniture. The furniture is removed from its original context, isolated, and introduced into a new environment generated by line drawing. The formal similarities detected by Steinberg between furniture and buildings in a big city generate a new reality. The magnificent drawing of this cityscape, which inserts drawers in the new context (a change of scale), immediately alters the meaning of the original element. It ceases to be furniture and becomes architecture, a skyscraper. On this occasion, the drawing provides the context for the photograph. However, in some of Steinberg's other works, photography provides the context for the line drawing. In this way, the assembly procedure and graphic composition stand out.

Between 1927 and 1930, American artist Edward Weston (1886–1958) initiated a series of photographs called "still-lifes" of individual ordinary objects such as seashells, peppers, and halved cabbages. *Pepper #30,* considered one of the most iconic modernist images, plays with peppers' shape and morphology, establishing a new formal association with the human body. The black and white image shows a solitary, oddly shaped bell pepper placed inside a tin funnel that reflects light from above.

However, as Esther Adler describes, "Weston almost elevates it [the pepper] to the status of a human figure. So you can kind of read these two forms of heads leaning in towards each other, or you can read the twisted form of the pepper body as someone's back." This anthropomorphic illustration depicts not only a vegetable but also a human's torso or two lovers intertwined. At least two realities are expressed and captured by a single form. What is seen is up to the viewer.

Wolf VOSTELL (1932–1998), *B 52 Lipstick Bomber*, 1968.

Multiplo, serigrafia con rossetti per labbra. Frame: 39.312 × 50.25 × 4.875 in. (99.9 × 127.7 × 12.4 cm). Publisher: Galerie Art Intermedia, Cologne. Printer: Kindermann and Giesen, Cologne. Edition: artist's proof outside the edition of 20. The Sue and Edgar Wachenheim III Endowment. Acc. no.: 609.2016. New York, Museum of Modern Art (MoMA).

© 2022. Digital image, The Museum of Modern Art, New York/Scala, Florence
© Wolf Vostell

Edward WESTON (1886–1958), *Pepper No. 30*, 1930.
Christie's Images Limited. Gelatin silver print.
9.6 x 7.5 in. (24.4 x 19.4 cm).
© 2022. Christie's Images, London/Scala, Florence
© [2022] Center for Creative Photography, The University of
Arizona Foundation / [VEGAP]

Saul STEINBERG (1914–1999), *Chest of Drawers Cityscape*, 1950.
Gelatin silver print, 8.75 x 6.875 in. (22.23 x 17.46 cm). © The Saul Steinberg
Foundation. Reproduced in *Flair*, September 1950, p. 81.

© Saul Steinberg

Operation:
AMPLIFICATION
Relation:
DOUBLE MEANING

—Amara irrisio
(L. "bitter laughing
at"); Bitter Taunt;
Exacerbatio
(L. "exasperation");

G. "mockery, sneering"

Sarcasmus

A bitter gibe or taunt.

However, General Joffre preserved his sangfroid amid these disastrous surprises to an extent which critics have declared almost indistinguishable from insensibility.

—Winston CHURCHILL, *The World Crisis: 1916–1918*, 1927.

Stanley Tigerman's provocative collage *The Titanic* depicts Mies van der Rohe's *Crown Hall* at the Illinois Institute of Technology sinking into Lake Michigan. Around that time, Tigerman, along with a group of Chicago architects (later known as "The Chicago Seven"), joined forces to start a postmodern group to fight the influence of Mies language in the architecture of Chicago. The **sarcasmus** of substituting the famous British luxury passenger liner that sank in 1912 with the Chicago Crown Hall is apparent in the context of this architectural battle.

Stanley TIGERMAN,
The Titanic, 1978.

Photomontage on paper,
Approx. 11.02 x 14.55 in.
(28 x 35.7 cm). Gift of Stanley
Tigerman, 1984.802

© 2022. The Art Institute of
Chicago / Art Resource, NY/
Scala, Florence

Operation:
AMPLIFICATION
Relation:
SIMILARITY

See also
Exergasia [060];
Synonymia [098].

For *Diamond
Series, see also*
Exergasia [060].

G. "relation of words"

Scesis onomaton

Using a string of synonymous expressions.

Ah sinful nation, a people laden with iniquity, a seed of evildoers, children that deal corruptly.

—ISAIAH 1:4

Oblique Projection for *Diamond* "House B"
Ink on cardboard overlaid with four color-separation positives. 30.31 x 20.07 in. (77 x 51 cm).
DR1998:0061 :003:001
John Hejduk fonds
Canadian Centre for Architecture ©CCA

Oblique Projection for *Diamond* "House A"
Graphite on translucent paper.
26.77 x 26.77 in. (68 x 68 cm).
DR 1998:0060:003:018
John Hejduk fonds
Canadian Centre for Architecture ©CCA

Oblique Projection for *Diamond* "Museum C"
Ink on translucent paper.
36.22 x 47.24 in. (92 x 120 cm).
DR1998:0062:007
John Hejduk fonds
Canadian Centre for Architecture ©CCA

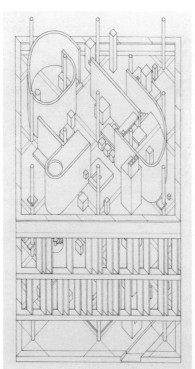

John HEJDUK (1929–2000), *Diamond Series:* "House A," "House B," "Museum C," 1963–1967.

Scesis onomaton has two meanings. It can refer to a sentence constructed of substantives and adjectives, as in

> A maid in conversation chaste, in speech mild, in countenance cheerful, in behavior modest, in beauty singular, in heart humble and meek, in honest mirth, merry with measure (Peacham).

It can also be presented as a series of successive, synonymous expressions, such as in "We sinned; we acted unjustly, we perpetrated evil." While it should be used carefully, this deliberate and obvious restatement can be effective.

As part of the Master architectural studio project "Rear Window," Sarah Mitchell works with this strategy to develop her *(Dis)continuous Theater* proposal. These four collages emphasize the idea of "anti-focus" through a string of synonymous drawings.

Hejduk's *Diamond Series* (1963–1967) is another excellent visual example of scesis onomaton. As explained in the pages devoted to **exergasia** [060], these projects are at the core of an investigation of the architectural implications of the "diamond configuration:" a 45-degree rotation of bounding elements relative to an orthogonal system. Three different conditions—columns, planes, biomorphic shapes—explore the formal consequences of Mondrian's diamond paintings in architecture. If the floor plans of the *Diamond Series* illustrate exergasia, the oblique projections of "House A," "House B," and "Museum C" express scesis onomaton. An oblique projection must be used to obtain this kind of drawing, a simultaneous presentation of plan and elevation. Usually, these drawings are known as "axonometrics." However, this is inaccurate since an axonometric uses an orthogonal projection.

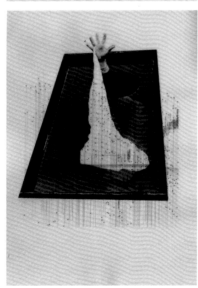

Sarah MITCHELL, *(Dis)continuous theater – Antifocus*, 2019, Melbourne, Australia.

"Rear Window" Master Advanced Design Studio and Studies Unit by María Fullaondo, First Semester 2019, Monash Art Design Architecture (MADA), Monash University. Courtesy of Sarah Mitchell

TECHNIQUES OF
ARGUMENT
● Techniques of argument
● AMPLIFICATIO(N)
● Omission
● Emotional appeals

Operation:
OMISSION
Relation:
DOUBLE MEANING

—Emphasis;
Reinforcer.

For *Running
Fence, see also*
Synoeciosis [097].

L. "sign; emphasis"

Significatio

To imply more than is actually stated.

Out of so great a patrimony, in so short a time,
this man has not laid by even an earthen pitcher
wherewith to seek fire for himself.

—Ad Herennium

Significatio, also known as *emphasis* or *reinforcer*, means
"to imply more than is actually stated." This strategy can be
used to have either a positive or negative impact. That is, a
powerful word or descriptive phrase (our common-sense
English meaning of "emphasis") can be used to intensify
meaning or an understatement can be made that implies
more than is said.

To enforce the sense of anything by a word of more than
ordinary efficacy is how Puttenham defines emphasis
(positive strategy). So, a fair lady is described as "O rare
beauty, O grace and courtesy."

[011] AMPLIFICATIO; [031] Antithesis; Antitheton; Augendi Causa;
Demonstratio; [052] Ecphonesis; Emphasis; [054] ENALLAGE;
[060] Exergasia; [064] Horismus; [067] Hyperbole; [070] IRONY;
[074] METAPHOR; [075] METONYMY; [079] PARADOX;
PATHOPOEIA; REPETITIO(N); [091] Significatio; [097] Synoeciosis;
[100] Topographia.

CHRISTO (1935–2020) and JEANNE-CLAUDE (1935–2009),
Running Fence, 1972–1976, Sonoma and Marin Counties,
California, United States.

Drawing in two parts. Top Panel: (39.5 x 245 x 3 cm). Text: (28.6 x
22.3 x 3 cm). Bottom Panel: (108 x 245 x 3 cm).

© 1976 Christo and Jeanne-Claude Foundation
© Centre Pompidou, MNAM-CCI, Dist. RMNGrand Palais /
Philippe Migeat

Meanwhile, Troilus says, "I am all patience" (W. Shakespeare, *Troilus and Cressida*). Here, the intensification is created by describing the person as abstract qualities rather than personal attributes.

In the negative strategy, something is emphasized by its omission, thus requiring the audience to fill in the meaning. As the *Ad Herennium* says, the negative strategy "permits the hearer himself to guess what the speaker has not mentioned." This can be accomplished by presenting ambiguity that invites complicitous completion (Lanham 1991, p. 138).

Intensification can also be accomplished through **hyperbole** [067]—specifically, by focusing on a single dramatic image as in *Running Fence*, one of Christo and Jeanne-Claude's most epic and amazing projects in California.

All Christo's and Jeanne-Claude's art installations are a distinct expression of visual hyperbole from a material point of view. *Running Fence* data clarifies this aspect, as it was 39.4 kilometers (24.5 miles) long and 5.5 meters (18 feet) high. It extended east-west near Freeway 101, north of San Francisco, on the private properties of 49 ranchers. It followed the rolling hills and dropped down to the Pacific Ocean at Bodega Bay. *Running Fence* crossed 14 roads and the town of Valley Ford, leaving a passageway for cars, cattle, and wildlife. It was designed to be viewed by following 64 kilometers (40 miles) of public roads in Sonoma and Marin Counties.

However, Christo and Jeanne-Claude's artwork is **paradoxical** from a conceptual perspective. The magnificent drawings and photographs of *Running Fence* reflect only a small part of its scope and transcendence. As Caitlin O'Hara affirms,

> *Running Fence* is more than the sum of its parts … Beyond its visual resplendence, the Fence is notable for opening a floodgate of interpretations and reactions. It conjures questions of ephemerality, intention, freedom, ownership, limitation, of what is deserving of the label "art," and of the creative process (Caitlin O'Hara, "The Journey to Running Fence" in UC Press Blog).

CHRISTO (1935–2020) and JEANNE-CLAUDE (1935–2009), *Running Fence*, 1972–1976, Sonoma and Marin Counties, California, United States.
Installation of Running Fence, California, 1976.
Photo: Wolfgang Volz
© 1976 Christo and Jeanne-Claude Foundation

The discussion of Running Fence *continues in the Synoeciosis [097] entry.*

L. "like"

Simile

Operation:
REPETITION
Relation:
SIMILARITY

—Homoeosis
(G. "likeness,
resemblance");
Similitude.

See also
METAPHOR [074].

An explicit comparison, often (but not necessarily) employing "like" or "as."

A library is like an island in the middle of a vast sea of ignorance, particularly if the library is very tall and the surrounding area has been flooded.
—Lemony SNICKET, *Horseradish*, 2007.

A **simile** is a figure of speech in which two unconnected objects or concepts are expressly compared with one another using "like" or "as." Similes and METAPHORS [074] are two tropes that can be difficult to differentiate since both devices are designed to create new meaning through comparison. In fact, a simile is a kind of metaphor. Similes make explicit comparisons as in "My love is like a red, red, rose" (Robert Burns). Meanwhile, the comparison is implicit in metaphors— that is, one of the terms being compared is omitted. This well-known literary device establishes a sense of equivalence and highlights a similarity with the help of the words "like" or "as."

> *Similitudo*, in Latin rhetoric, was a general term for similitude of various kinds; types, according to Puttenham, are **Exemplum**; **Icon**; **Parable**. **Fable** [062] is also sometimes reckoned part of this group. The modern reader may perhaps want to think of simile in the customary pairing with metaphor and leave the other terms to form a loose and informal group clustering around illustrative anecdote (Lanham 1991, 140).

Dr. Fritz Kahn (1888–1968), a German gynecologist and anatomy textbook author, published a five-volume set of books between 1922 and 1931 devoted to the human body's inner workings. Within these books, in 1926 Kahn produced a visual simile and one of the most iconic visualizations of all time. This lithograph depicting the human body as a modern factory, a chemical plant of sorts, is called *"Der Mensch als Industriepalast* (Man as Industrial Palace)."

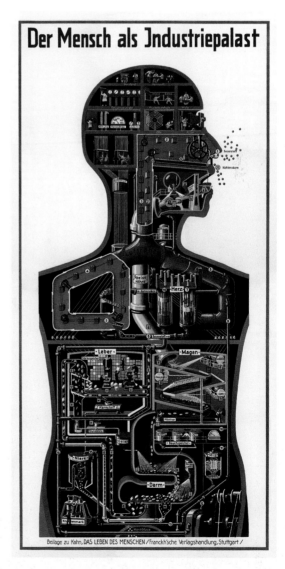

Fritz KAHN (1888–1968), *Der Mensch als Industriepalast* (Man as Industrial Palace), 1926.
© Franckh-Kosmos

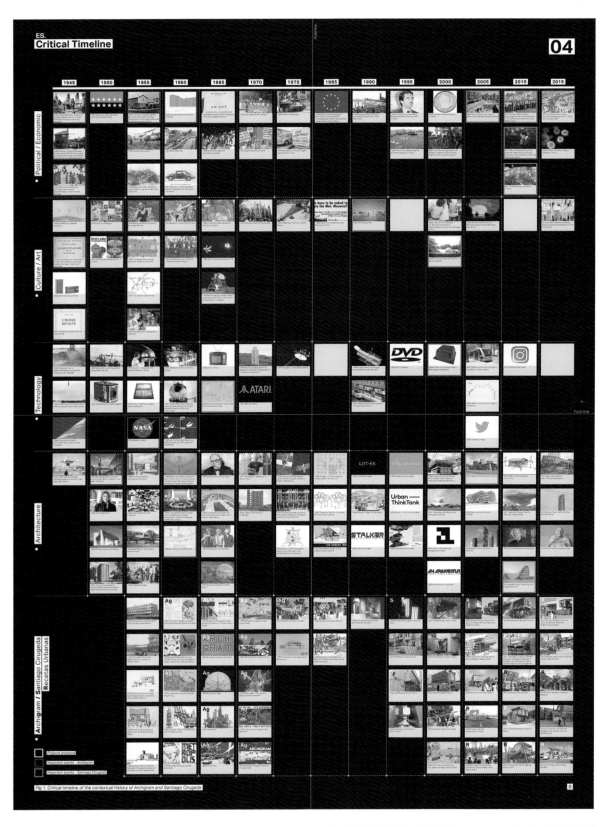

Patrick TRAN, *Existentialist Structures: A study of Archigram and Santiago Cirugeda,* "Critical timeline of the contextual history of Archigram and Santiago Cirugeda," 2020.

Courtesy of Patrick Tran

The critical timeline by Patrick Tran summarizes his research, which was based on a comparison between the architecture of Archigram and Santiago Cirugeda. As the author explains,

> The practices of Archigram and Cirugeda are perhaps antithetical to one another; whilst Archigram operated within the speculative realm of unbuilt projects, Cirugeda applies a practical ethos that results in built structures. However, a more profound underlying philosophical substructure may exist amongst the two practices; a subjective approach that emphasizes the possibility of choice within architecture and the urban space.

Jean Nouvel's entry for the Dolls' Houses architectural competition (held in 1983 by the British *Architectural Design Magazine*) creates at least two similes. In addition to the metaphor of the brief associating miniatures of modern dwellings to dollhouses, the French architect focused his proposal on transforming a toolbox into a dollhouse. While the first simile connects a toolbox to a dollhouse, the description of the project provides the second comparison: "A toolbox as a space for accommodating childhood memories."

Jean NOUVEL, *Doll House*, 1983.
1983 Architectural Design Dolls' Houses Competition.
Design: Jean Nouvel. Photo ©All Rights Reserved

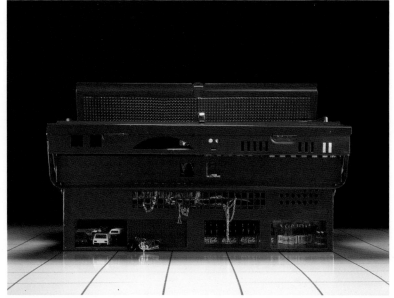

UNGRAMMATICAL,
ILLOGICAL, OR
UNUSUAL USES OF
LANGUAGE.

● Ungrammatical, illogical,
or unusual uses of language
● Techniques of argument
● AMPLIFICATIO(N)
● Emotional appeals

Operation:
SUBSTITUTION
Relation:
DIFFERENCE

—Double Supply.

Related to Zeugma
(G. "yoking").

G. "taking together"

Syllepsis

A verb lacks congruence with at least one subject that it governs.

The Nobles and the King was taken.

—Richard A. LANHAM, *A Handlist of Rhetorical Terms*, 1991.

Syllepsis is a rhetorical term for a kind of **ellipsis** [053] in which one word (usually a verb) is understood differently in relation to two or more other words that it modifies or governs.

These pages present two visual examples of syllepses. The first one is a photogram of the film *Schindler's List* by Steven Spileberg. While the film is shot primarily in black and white, the color red is introduced in two scenes. Spielberg uses a red coat to distinguish a little girl in the scene, thus depicting the liquidation of the Kraków ghetto. Later in the film, Schindler sees her exhumed dead body, recognizable only by the red coat she is still wearing. The director said the scene was intended to symbolize how members of the highest levels of government in the United States knew about the Holocaust but did nothing to stop it. This effective strategy of introducing color in a black and white film, as can be seen in the photograph, visually represents the mechanism of syllepsis.

Steven SPIELBERG,
Schindler's List, 1993.

AF archive / Alamy Foto de stock

American historical drama film directed and produced by Steven Spielberg and written by Steven Zaillian. Universal Pictures, release on December 15, 1993. It is based on the 1982 novel Schindler's Ark by Australian novelist Thomas Keneally.

The Solomon R. Guggenheim Museum of New York, designed by Frank Lloyd Wright (1867–1959) in 1956, is another excellent visual example of syllepsis based on the lack of congruence with at least one subject that it governs. The building is situated on Fifth Avenue between 88th and 89th Street facing Central Park. As the museum's website explains, Wright made no secret of his disenchantment with Guggenheim's choice of New York City for his museum: "I can think of several more desirable places in the world to build this great museum," the American architect wrote in 1949, "but we will have to try New York." Wright thought the city was overbuilt, overpopulated, and lacking architectural merit. However, the relationship between the building and Manhattan is one of many significant and surprising aspects of this work. The upper and middle parts of Manhattan follow a rectangular grid of blocks and streets where orthogonality presides over the architecture. However, Wright's curved, fluid building breaks the rigid pattern of the city. In other words, Wright takes advantage of the lack of unity within the city to make his architecture stand out.

Richard HAMILTON (1922–2011), *Guggenheim Collage* (detail), 1967, New York, United States.

Book cover *Fantastic Architecture* by Dick HIGGENIS and Wolf VOSTELL [Frank Lloyd WRIGHT, Solomon R. Guggenheim Museum, exterior, New York, United States, 1959.] Something Else Press, 1970. Reprint by Primary Information, 2015

© The Estate of Dick Higgins
© The Wolf Vostell Estate
© The Estate of Richard Hamilton
© R. Hamilton. All Rights Reserved, VEGAP, 2022
Courtesy of Primary Information

Operation:
SUBSTITUTION
Relation:
DIFFERENCE

Related to
Metaplasm
(G. "a change of
form"); Synalepha
(G. "coalescing of
two syllables into
one").

G. "drawing together, contraction"

Synaeresis

When two syllables are contracted into one.

Synaeresis (also known as *symphonesis*, *synecphonesis*, or *synizesis*) comes from Greek and literally means "contraction" or "drawing together." It is a kind of METAPLASM (a generic term meaning "a transformation of letters or syllables in single words, contrary to the common fashion of writing or speaking, either for cause of necessity, or else to make the verse more fine").

When synaeresis is used, two syllables or words are contracted into one, for example, when New Orleans is pronounced "Nawlins." This usually involves pronouncing two adjacent vowels that belong to different syllables within a single word as a diphthong— for example, Phaethon (Lanham 1991, 146).

This Hejduk drawing describing the "Animal Hospital," "Cross-Over House," and "Collector's House" for *The Lancaster/Hanover Masque* presents a visual transposition of synaeresis. Plans and sections of the hospital and these two houses of the masque are superimposed and juxtaposed to create a single, new hybrid projection for each structure.

For The Lancaster/ Hanover Masque see also Amphibologia [010]; Anoiconometon [019].

John HEJDUK (1929–2000), *The Lancaster/Hanover Masque*, 1980–1982.

Animal Hospital, Cross-Over House, and Collector's House.

Gray, brown, green, red, and yellow colored pencil over graphite on paper. 34 x 55.86 in. (86.6 x 141.9 cm). DR1988:0291 :047

John Hejduk fonds
Canadian Centre for Architecture
© Estate of John Hejduk

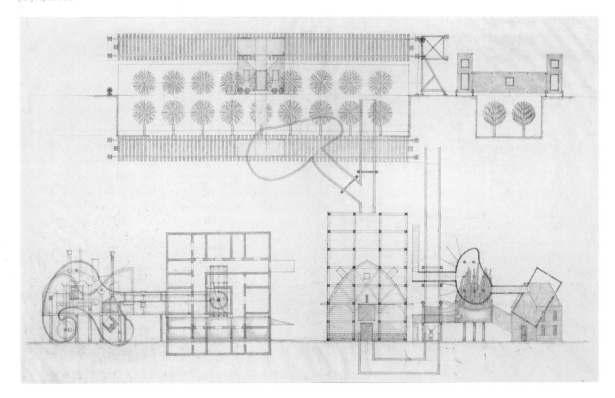

G. "comparison, combination"

Syncrisis

Comparison and contrast in parallel clauses.

The value of a life lies not in the length of days, but in the use we make of them. A man may live long, yet get little from life.

— Michel de MONTAIGNE, *Essais*, (1580-1595)

Syncrisis, that literally means "to separate" or "to compare," is a rhetorical device based on a parallel structure by which persons or things of similar or dissimilar qualities are compared and contrasted. The purpose of this device is to show either that the subjects are equal or that one is greater or lesser than the other—for instance, "Cowards die many times before their deaths; The valiant never taste of death but once." (W. Shakespeare).

A figure-ground drawing is any drawing that uses contrast to show the relationships between positive and negative spaces, solids and voids, built and unbuilt, or shadows and light. As such, this type of drawing is an excellent visual transposition of syncrisis.

Figure-ground map of New York.
© OpenStreetMap contributors

Giovanni Battista NOLLI (1701–1756),
Pianta Grande di Roma (plan of Rome),
1748, Rome, Italy.

Giovanni Battista NOLLI (1701–1756),
Pianta Grande di Roma (detail), 1748,
Rome, Italy.

In architecture, figure-ground drawings are called figure-ground diagrams and are used to analyze urban designs and plans. It is a technique for producing a two-dimensional map of an urban area that illustrates the relationship between built and unbuilt spaces. As in this figure-ground diagram of New York, the land coverage of buildings is visualized as solid black mass (figure), while the public spaces (for example, streets, parks, and plazas) are represented as white voids (ground). The solid black infill used for buildings is known as "poche," a term originating from the *École des Beaux-Arts* in Paris.

The most famous architectural example of a figure-ground drawing is the map of Rome produced by Italian architect Giambattista Nolli (1701–1756) in 1748 (now commonly known as the "Nolli Map"). Although a Nolli map is not the same as a figure-ground drawing, it is common for figure-ground drawings to be referred to as Nolli maps. However, a figure-ground diagram focuses on built and unbuilt spaces, whereas a Nolli map focuses on public and private spaces. A broader spectrum of colors replaces the binary color of the figure-ground diagrams.

G. "understanding one thing with another"

Synecdoche

Substitution of part for whole, genus for species, or vice versa.

I heard a Fly buzz — when I died —
The Stillness in the Room
Was like the Stillness in the Air —
Between the Heaves of Storm —
The Eyes around — had wrung them dry —
And Breaths were gathering firm
For that last Onset — when the King
Be witnessed — in the Room —

— Emily DICKINSON, *I heard a Fly buzz*, 1862.

Pablo PICASSO (1881–1973),
Nature morte à la chaise cannée (Still Life
with the Cane Chair), 1911–1912.
Paris, Musee Picasso. © 2022.
Photo Scala, Florence

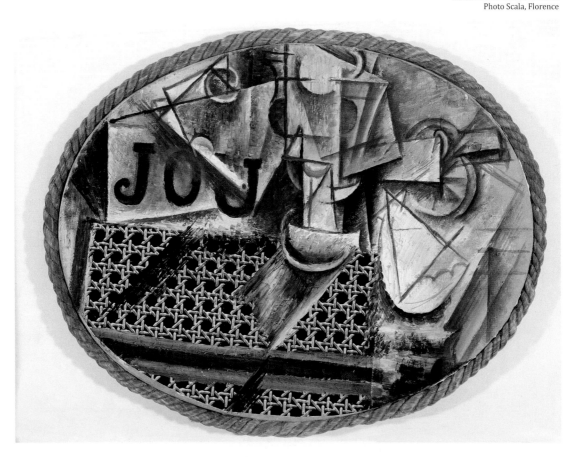

Synecdoche is a color of rhetoric that uses a part to represent the whole (for example, calling the alphabet "the ABCs"), or when the whole is represented by naming one of its parts, as in "England won the World Cup in 1966."

Synecdoche, which is a form of METONYMY [075], is a figure of substitution like the METAPHOR [074]. While metaphors substitute one element for a similar one and metonymic substitutions relate to different but contiguous elements, the elements in a synecdoche are related by inclusion. Different types of synecdoche involve relating a part to the whole, the universal to the specific, the genus to the species, the singular to the plural, matter to an object, abstract to concrete, and the species to the individual. All such relationships can be expressed from specific to general or from general to specific.

Walter DE MARIA (1935–2013),
Exhibition announcement for Walter De Maria at Nicholas Wilder Gallery, 1968, Los Angeles, United States.
© Estate of Walter De Maria, courtesy of the Walter De Maria Archive

These three works of art utilize synecdoche in different ways. In *Still Life with the Cane Chair,* Pablo Picasso (1881–1973) uses a part of the chair (caning chair) to express the whole chair. The fragments of a collage usually express an entity conceptually broader than its visual manifestation.

In the exhibition announcement of Walter de Maria (1935–2013), a man's torso is used to represent the artist.

The few elements of the *Sunken Garden* by Isamu Noguchi (1904–1988) in *Chase Manhattan Bank Plaza* represent the whole nature as in all Japanese dry or Zen gardens. Japanese gardens utilize ponds, streams, islands, hills, and other elements to create miniature reproductions of natural scenery. Dry gardens are comprised entirely of stones, with larger stones symbolizing mountains, islands, and waterfalls, while gravel and sand replace water.

PHOTO BOB BENSON

WALTER DE MARIA   APRIL 9-27   NICHOLAS WILDER GALLERY   814 N. La CIENEGA BLVD., LOS ANGELES, CALIFORNIA

Isamu NOGUCHI (1904–1988), *Sunken Garden
for Chase Manhattan Bank Plaza,* 1960–1965,
28 Liberty Street, New York, United States.

The Noguchi Museum Archives, 01935. Photo: Arthur
Lavine. © INFGM / ARS -VEGAP

G. "binding together"

Synoeciosis

PARADOX
● PARADOX
● AMPLIFICATIO(N)
● Emotional appeals

Operation:
SUBSTITUTION
Relation:
CONTRADICTION

Synaeceosis,
Syneciosis—
Cross-Couple.

See also
Oxymoron [077];
PARADOX [079].

For *Running Fence, see
also* Significatio [091].

An expanded oxymoron: a paradox.

Thus for your sake I dayly dye
And do but seem to live in deede:
Thus is my blisse but miserie,
My lucre losse without your meede.

—George Puttenham, *The Arte of English Poesie*, (1589).

CHRISTO (1935–2020) and JEANNE-CLAUDE
(1935–2009), *Running Fence*, 1972–1976,
Sonoma and Marin Counties, California,
United States.

Photo: Gianfranco Gorgoni
© 1976 Christo and Jeanne-Claude Foundation and
Estate of Gianfranco Gorgoni

CHRISTO (1935–2020) and
JEANNE-CLAUDE (1935–2009),
Installation of Running Fence, 1976,
Sonoma and Marin Counties, California,
United States.
Photo: Wolfgang Volz
© 1976 Christo and Jeanne-Claude Foundation

Synoeciosis is the coupling of contrary elements as in a quote from
Puttenham. The contrary pairs of words include "dye" and "live" in the
first two lines, "blisse" and "miserie" in the third line, and "lucre" [gain]
and "losse" in the last line. Thus, this example represents an extended
oxymoron [077] or PARADOX [079]. There are some connections between
synoecisosis and **antithesis** [031]; however, the terms do not directly oppose
one another as they do in antithesis.

Paradoxes can be found in most of the work by Christo and Jeanne-
Claude. As explained under the **significatio** [091] entry, paradox and
hyperbole [067] are the two main strategies utilized (both conceptually
and formally) to explain all Christo's and Jeanne-Claude's artwork—most
notably, *Running Fence*. From its conception, *Running Fence* met much
controversy and difficulty and became a reality only because of the effort and
determination of the authors. *Running Fence* presents many contradictions
and paradoxes. In addition to the paradox that involves limiting, fencing,
closing, and separating the unlimited as nature is, another contradiction
is characterized by the fact that Christo's and Jeanne-Claude's outdoor

installation in Northern California stood for only two weeks. *Running Fence*, an 18-foot-high white nylon "ribbon of light," as Christo described it, was first conceived in 1972, but the actual project took more than four years to plan and build. The artwork was removed 14 days after its installation, with no visible trace of it left behind. On the other hand, due to *Running Fence*'s short existence, relatively few people had the opportunity to see it in person.

The funding of the art piece was also very complex. The project cost three million dollars, with Christo and Jeanne-Claude paying all expenses for this temporary work of art through the sale of studies, preparatory drawings and collages, scale models, and original lithographs. The artists did not accept sponsorship of any kind.

As described on the artists' website, another ironic aspect is that all parts of this monumental structure were designed for complete removal; no visible evidence of the artwork remains on the hills of the Sonoma and Marin Counties. As had been agreed with the ranchers and country, state, and federal agencies, the removal of the fence started two weeks after its completion, and the ranchers received all the materials.

The project met heavy opposition, including lawsuits and 17 public hearings at the state and county level. The authors responded to many people, from environmentalists to local artists, who claimed that a nylon fence was not art. "Christo and Jeanne-Claude had an uphill battle to fight, but in that struggle lies their art's significance" (Caitlin O'Hara, "The Journey to Running Fence" in UC Press Blog).

Suzuki House by BOLLES+WILSON is another illustration of synoeciosis, as the architects made the most of the small plot of land in Tokyo. *Suzuki House* was built between 1990 and 1993 for Japanese architecture critic Akira Suzuki and his family. The project was described as follows:

> An asymmetrical concrete construction at the corner of a plot, the house is a classic expression of the architects' humor, who imagined it as being "glanced by a passing ninja." (... A suspended concrete box was expressly created for the child over the living space, an interpretation of the theme of the "house within the house."...)

The paradox lies in the response to the very small site on which this vertical house was built. The architects had to maximize their use of the surface area to create a comfortable home for four occupants and their dog Potato. *Suzuki House* comprises five levels with a staircase in the center that divides up each room. Also, each window is unique, adding to the peculiar character of this residential tower. As it has been stated,

> Small-scale protuberances, irregular windows, and a gantry crane for the delivery of furniture punctuate the facade, and a big black blob surrounds the main window (a ninja sign for the authors, the eye patch of a giant panda, in the adolescent mind of the client's daughter).

BOLLES+WILSON, *Suzuki House,*
1990–1993, Tokyo, Japan.
Oblique projections.
© BOLLES+WILSON

[BOLLES+WILSON: Peter L. WILSON
and Julia B. BOLLES-WILSON]

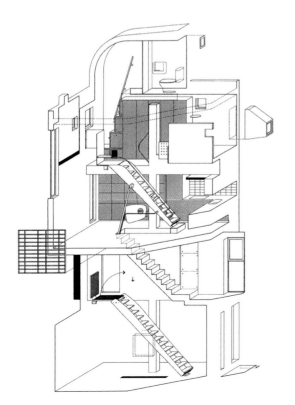

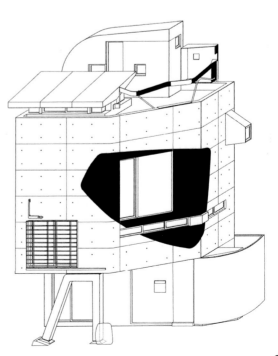

AMPLIFICATIO(N)
● Techniques of argument
● REPETITIO(N)
● AMPLIFICATIO(N)

Operation:
AMPLIFICATION
Relation:
SIMILARITY

—Communio;
Interpretatio; Store.

G. "name alike"

Synonymia

Amplification by synonym (words of like signification).

What is become of that beautiful face,
Those lovely looks, that favor amiable,
Those sweet features, and visage full of grace,
That countenance which is alonly able
To kill and cure?

— George PUTTENHAM, *The Arte of English Poesie*, (1589).

Synonymia combines words of similar signification (synonyms) in one sentence to amplify or explain a specific subject or term, such as in the following example: "Enter not into the path of the wicked, and go not in the way of evil men. Avoid it, pass not by it, turn from it, and pass away." This rhetoric device repeats a term to add emotional force or clarity.

This *Pleasure Palace*, or project at the scale of the city to facilitate a group of pleasures, follows the synonymia

technique. The second-year students who created it, opted for a palace composed of three laboratories of pleasures ("Race to the Top," "Jelly Tower," and "Motion Matrix") instead of creating a single structure. Three synonyms—in the form of hybrid structures—are generated from old industrial buildings and convey the same idea. The original industrial structures were decontextualized, transformed, and fragmented into sections of new realities to collect pleasures by working with collage techniques and searching for unexpected relationships.

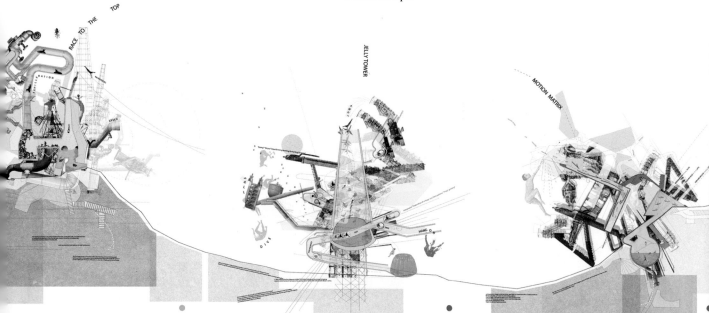

Jacob CUTRI, Francesca SANGUINETTI, and Jazelyn TAN, *The Pleasure Palace:*
"Race to the Top," "Jelly Tower," and "Motion Matrix," 2017, Melbourne, Australia.
"The Garden of Earthly Delights. A Social Condenser of Contemporary Pleasures," Second-Year Design Studio by
María Fullaondo and Joseph Gauci-Seddon, First Semester 2017, Monash Art Design Architecture (MADA), Monash University.
Courtesy of the Authors

AMPLIFICATIO
● METAPHORICAL &
METONYMIC Substitution
● ENARGIA
● Techniques of argument
● AMPLIFICATIO(N)
● Emotional appeals

Operation:
AMPLIFICATION
Relation:
DIFFERENCE

G. "collection"

Systrophe

Heaping up of descriptions of a thing without defining it.

Man is an example of imbecility, the spoil of time,
an image of unconstancy, a captive of calamity,
a prisoner to pains, a servant to covetousness,
finally, a food for worms.

—Henry PEACHAM, *The Garden of Eloquence*, (1577).

In rhetoric, listing many qualities or descriptions of someone or something without offering an explicit definition is called **systrophe**. This is the opposite of **horismus** [064] by which a clear and brief description is given to explain associated terms.

The Daily Members Only entry in the "2019 NGV Pavilion Architectural Competition" in Melbourne transposes this strategy to spatial and visual realms. Both a golden curtain and a six-month-long performance invite all museum visitors to experience and think about the segregation of public and private realms. Each day, a specific admission requirement limits visitors' access to the inner sector of the garden. More than 150 restrictions—an explicit acknowledgment of the infinite and diverse features that define each human being as a unique individual—describe and define the project. Some of the daily requirements that one needs to meet to enter the NVG garden through the golden

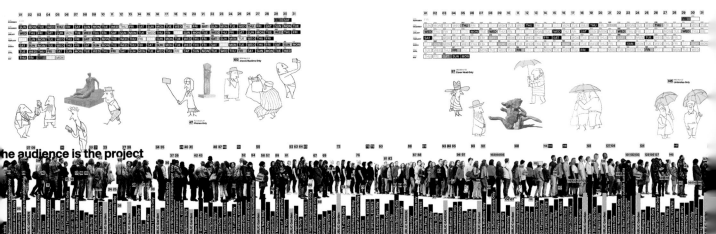

Diego FULLAONDO, María FULLAONDO, Ciro MÁRQUEZ, and Nicholas MILTOS, *The Daily Members Only*, 2019, Melbourne, Australia.
NGV (National Gallery of Victoria) Architecture Commission Competition 2019.
Courtesy of the Authors

[001] Accumulatio; [003] Adianoeta; [005] Aetiologia; [006] Allegory; [008] Alliteration; [009] Alloiosis; [011] AMPLIFICATIO; [018] ANATOMY; [022] Antenantiosis; [025] Antilogy; [029] Antiprosopopoeia; Antistasis; [031] Antithesis; Antitheton; [032] Antonomasia; [035] Appositio; Augendi Causa; [044] Climax; [045] Commoratio; [047] Congeries; Contrarium; Diaeresis; [049] Diallage; [050] Dinumeratio; [052] Ecphonesis; Emphasis; [058] Epitheton; [060] Exergasia; [061] Expeditio; [070] IRONY; [071] Isocolon; [074] METAPHOR; [075] METONYMY; [079] PARADOX; PATHOPOEIA; Peristasis; Progressio; [089] Sarcasmus; [091] Significatio; [096] Synecdoche; [099] Systrophe.

curtain were as follows: "Brands Only, Males Only, Manicure Only, Cameras Only, Bald Heads Only, Shirts Only, Tattoos Only." People's actions, reactions, and interactions constitute the proposal's core. Architecture steps back, allowing the broad spectrum of audiences of the NGV to become the project. Following the strategy of systrophe, the architectural definitions of the admission requirements are not straightforward.

In this hybrid drawing of *The Garden of Earthly Delights. A Social Condenser of Contemporary Pleasures*, Leanne Haidar also chooses to characterize her garden by a collection of pleasures that play with the dichotomy of public and private contexts and activities. This drawing depicts a set of real and invented pleasures with a robust private component that is exaggerated and exposed in the public setting. Some of the pleasures superimposed on the garden without an explicit definition include "Fart Room—a social condenser for farting flowers," "Foot Fetish—hidden sexual experiences exposed through direct interaction," "Picking Noses—a gigantic nose to be picked, climbed, popped, squeezed," "Running Naked—an enclosed apparatus that enables naked individuals to run freely in solidarity with a virtual human," "Mud Bath—nude beaches of caffeine," "Shaving Restaurant—a public context where individuals can groom together," "Naked Giant—sitting, sleeping, floating on a giant naked man," "Surprise Toilet—a toilet that bursts up into mid-air," "Sports on Sanitary Pads—boxing using pomegranate gloves on a bed of pads," and "Super Pee—an outdoor amusement park made out of pee on targets."

Leanne HAIDAR, *The Garden of Earthly Delights. A Social Condenser of Contemporary Pleasures*, 2017, Melbourne, Australia.

[Pleasures] Tactical proposal.

"The Garden of Earthly Delights. A Social Condenser of Contemporary Pleasures," Second-Year Design Studio by María Fullaondo and Joseph Gauci-Seddon, First Semester 2017, Monash Art Design Architecture (MADA), Monash University.

Courtesy of Leanne Haidar

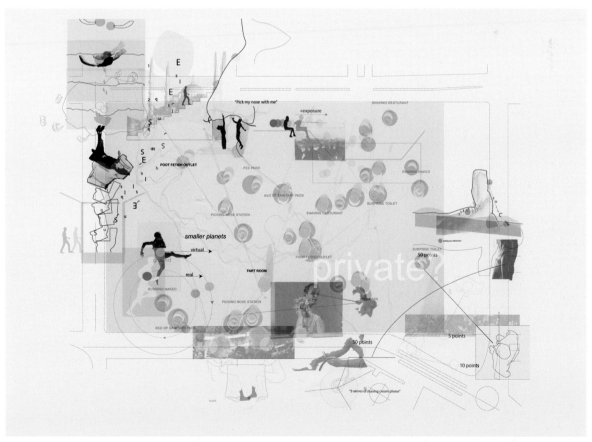

ENARGIA
- ●ENARGIA
- ● Techniques of argument
- ●AMPLIFICATIO(N)
- ● ANTITHESIS

Operation:
ADDITION
Relation:
DIFFERENCE

—Counterfait Place.

Juan DE SANDE,
Ruinas 4, 2000.
Courtesy of Juan de Sande

Topographia

Description of a place.

From a hill-top near by, where the wood had been recently cut off, there was a pleasing vista southward across the pond, through a wide indentation in the hills which form the shore there, where their opposite sides sloping toward each other suggested a stream flowing out in that direction through a wooded valley, but stream there was none.

—Henry David THOREAU, *Walden,* (1854).

G. "description of a place"

Topothesia

Description of imaginary, nonexistent places.

The island of the Utopians is two hundred miles across in the middle part where it is widest, and is nowhere much narrower than this except toward the two ends. These ends, drawn toward one another as if in a five-hundred-mile circle, make the island crescent-shaped like a new moon. Between the horns of the crescent, which are about eleven miles apart, the sea enters and spreads into a broad bay. Being sheltered from the wind by the surrounding land, the bay is never rough, but quiet and smooth instead, like a big lake. Thus, nearly the whole inner coast is one great harbor, across which ships pass in every direction to the great advantage of the people.

—Thomas MORE, *Utopia*, (1516).

Miquel SARQUELLA GÁZQUEZ, *The Garden of Earthly Delights. An urban condenser of contemporary pleasures within the city of instant gratification*, 2019, New York, United Sates.

Superimposed plan.

"The Garden of Earthly Delights. A Social Condenser of Contemporary Pleasures," Advanced Design Studio by María Fullaondo, The Bernard & Anne Spitzer School of Architecture, The City College of New York.

Courtesy of Miquel Sarquella Gázquez

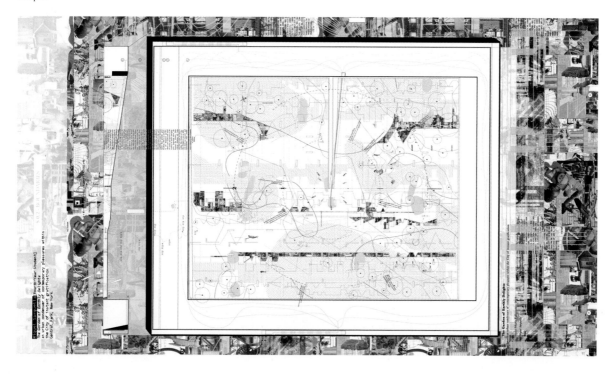

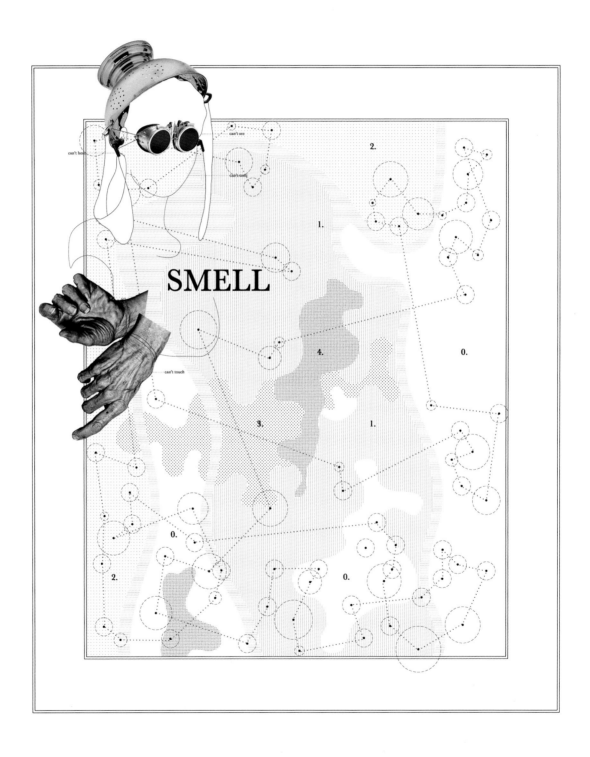

device vs. vegetation - E1:1000

Map of the different scents of the garden that will transport you to distant places and times.

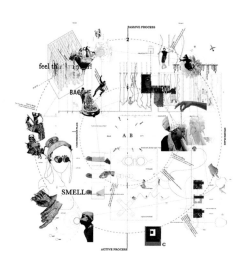

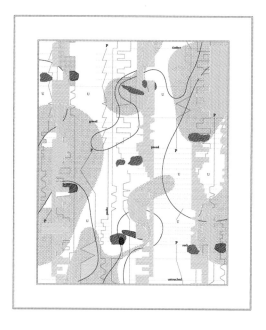

studio contents

Brief collection of A, B and C, the main ingredients for D.

textures - E1:1000

The paving materials create a map somewhere between the circulation and the scents, providing great texture stimulation.

Miquel SARQUELLA GÁZQUEZ, *The Garden of Earthly Delights. An urban condenser of contemporary pleasures within the city of instant gratification*, 2019, New York, United States.

Tactical proposals and snapshots.

"The Garden of Earthly Delights. A Social Condenser of Contemporary Pleasures," Advanced Design Studio by María Fullaondo, The Bernard & Anne Spitzer School of Architecture, The City College of New York.

Courtesy of Miquel Sarquella Gázquez

[001] Accumulatio; [006] Allegory; [009] Alloiosis; [011] AMPLIFICATIO; [014] Anamnesis; [018] ANATOMY; [034] Apomnemonysis; [035] Appositio; Augendi Causa; [045] Commoratio; [046] Conduplicatio; [047] Congeries; emonstratio; Diaeresis; [049] Diallage; [050] Dinumeratio; [051] Disjunctio; Distribution; [052] Ecphonesis; Emphasis; [054] ENALLAGE; Enantiosis; [055] ENARGIA; [056] Epexegesis; [057] Epicrisis; [060] Exergasia; [062] Fable; [067] Hyperbole; [070] IRONY; [074] METAPHOR; [075] METONYMY; [079] PARADOX; PATHOPOEIA; Peristasis; [083] Polyptoton; [087] Proverb; [088] PUN; REPETITIO(N); [091] Significatio; 096] Synecdoche; [097] Synoeciosis; [098] Synonymia; [101] Topothesia.

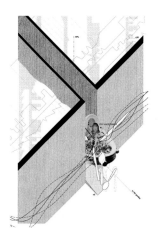

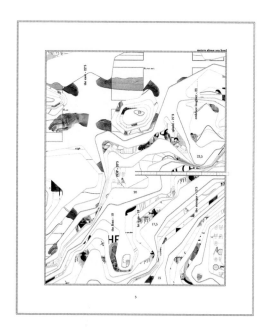

pleasures vs. topography - E1:1000

Each of the contemporary pleasures can be experienced exclusively at a certain altitude.

Part 3

Classifications, indexes, and bibliography

COLORS OF RHETORIC

[001] **Accumulatio:** Heaping up praise or accusation to emphasize or summarize points or inferences already made.

[002] **Acrostic:** A series of lines in which certain letters form a message when read in sequence.
acyrologia: The use of an inexact or illogical word; malapropism.

[003] **Adianoeta:** An expression that has an obvious meaning and an unsuspected secret one beneath.

[004] **Adynaton:** Stringing together of impossibilities.
aenos: Quoting wise sayings from fables.

[005] **Aetiologia:** Giving a cause or reason.

[006] **Allegory:** Extending a METAPHOR through an entire speech or passage.

[007] **Alleotheta:** Substitution of one case, gender, number, tense, or mood for another.

[008] **Alliteration:** Recurrence of an initial consonant sound, and sometimes of a vowel sound.

[009] **Alloiosis:** Breaking down a subject into alternatives.

[010] **Amphibologia:** Ambiguity, either intended or inadvertent.

[011] **AMPLIFICATIO:** Rhetorical device used to expand a simple statement.

[012] **Anacoluthon:** Ending a sentence with a different grammatical structure from that with which it began.

[013] **Analogy:** Reasoning or arguing from parallel cases.

[014] **Anamnesis:** Recalling ideas, events, or persons of the past.

[015] **Anantapodoton:** Omission of a correlative clause from a sentence.

[016] **Anaphora:** The repetition of the same word or phrase at the beginning of successive clauses.

[017] **Anastrophe:** Unusual arrangement of words or clauses within a sentence.

[018] **Anatomy:** The analysis of an issue into its constituent parts.

[019] **Anoiconometon:** Improper arrangement of words.

[020] **Antanaclasis:** Homonymic PUN.

[021] **Antapodosis:** A simile in which the objects compared correspond in several aspects.

[022] **Antenantiosis:** Positive statement made in a negative form.

[023] **Anthimeria:** Functional shift, using one part of speech for another.

[024] **Anthypallage:** Change of grammatical case for emphasis.

[025] **Antilogy:** Two or more opposed speeches on the same topic.

[026] **Antimetabole:** Inverting the order of repeated words.

[027] **Antinomy:** A contradiction between two beliefs or conclusions that are in themselves reasonable.

[028] **Antiphrasis:** IRONY of one word, often derisively, through obvious contradiction.

[029] **Antiprosopopoeia:** The representation of persons as inanimate objects.

[030] **Antiptosis:** Substituting one case for another.
antistasis: Repetition of a word in a different or contrary sense.

[031] **Antithesis:** Conjoining contrasting ideas.
antitheton: Antithesis.

[032] **Antonomasia:** Descriptive phrase for a proper name.
aphelia: Plainness of writing or speech.

[033] **Apodixis:** Confirming a statement by reference to generally accepted principles or experience.

[034] **Apomnemonysis:** The quotation of an approved authority from memory.
apophasis: Pretending to deny what is really affirmed.
aposiopesis: Stopping suddenly in midcourse, leaving a statement unfinished.

[035] **Appositio:** Two juxtaposed nouns, the second elaborating the first.

[036] **Assonance:** Identity or similarity in sound between internal vowels in neighboring words.

[037] **Asteismus:** Facetious or mocking answer that plays on a word.

[038] **Asyndeton:** Omission of conjunctions between words, phrases, or clauses.
augendi causa: Raising the voice for emphasis.

[039] **Auxesis:** Words or clauses placed in climactic order.

[040] **Bomphiologia:** Bombastic speech.
brachyologia: Brevity of diction; abbreviated construction; word or words omitted.
brevitas: Concise expression.
cacemphaton: Sounds combined for harsh effect.

[041] **Cacosyntheton:** Awkward transposition of the parts of a sentence.
Catacosmesis: Anticlimax, ordering words in descending importance.

[042] **Charientismus:** Clothing a disagreeable sense with agreeable expressions.

[043] **Chiasmus:** The ABBA pattern of mirror inversion.
chorographia: Description of a nation.

chronographia: Description of time.

[044] **Climax:** Mounting by degrees through linked words or phrases, usually of increasing weight and in parallel construction.

cohortatio: Amplification that moves the hearer's indignation.

[045] **Commoratio:** Emphasizing a strong point by repeating it several times in different words.

[046] **Conduplicatio:** Repetition of a word or words in succeeding clauses, (1) for amplification or emphasis; (2) to express emotion.

[047] **Congeries:** Piling up words of differing meaning but for a similar emotional effect.

consonance: Resemblance of stressed consonant-sounds where the associated vowels differ.

contrarium: One of two opposite statements is used to prove the other.

[048] **Correctio:** Correction of a word or phrase.

demonstratio: Vivid description.

diaeresis: Dividing the genus into species in order to amplify.

[049] **Diallage:** Bringing several arguments to establish a single point.

digestion: An orderly enumeration of the points to be discussed, the implications of a question, etc.

[050] **Dinumeratio:** Dividing a subject into subheadings. A summary or recapitulation, intended to refresh the hearer's memory.

[051] **Disjunctio:** Use different verbs to express similar ideas in successive clauses.

distinctio: Explicit reference to various meanings of a word, thereby removing ambiguities.

distribution: Dividing the whole into its parts.

[052] **Ecphonesis:** Exclamation expressing emotion.

[053] **Ellipsis:** Omission of a word or short phrase easily supplied.

emphasis: Implying more than is actually stated.

[054] **ENALLAGE:** Substitution of one case, person, gender, number, tense, mood, part of speech, for another.

enantiosis: IRONY.

[055] **ENARGIA:** A general term for visually powerful, vivid description.

epanodos: (1) A general statement is expanded by discussing it part by part. (2) Ploce.

[056] **Epexegesis:** Adding words or phrases to further clarify or specify a statement already made.

[057] **Epicrisis:** The speaker quotes a passage and comments on it.

[058] **Epitheton:** Qualifying the subject with an appropriate adjective.

[059] **Erotesis:** A "rhetorical question," one which implies an answer but does not give or lead us to expect one.

ETHOS: The emotions or character which a speaker re-enacts in order to affect the audience.

euphemismus: Euphemism; circumlocution to palliate something unpleasant.

exemplum: An example cited, either true or feigned; illustrative anecdote.

[060] **Exergasia:** Repeating the same thought in many figures.

[061] **Expeditio:** Rejection of all but one of various alternatives.

[062] **Fable:** A short, allegorical story.

[063] **Fictio:** Attributing rational actions and speech to nonrational creatures.

[064] **Horismus:** A definition by opposites.

[065] **Hypallage:** Awkward or humorous changing of agreement or application of words.

[066] **HYPERBATON:** A generic figure of various forms of departure from ordinary word order.

[067] **Hyperbole:** Self-conscious exaggeration.

hypozeuxis: Every clause in a sentence has its own subject and verb.

[068] **Hysterologia:** A phrase is interposed between a preposition and its object.

[068] **Hysteron proteron:** Syntax or sense out of normal logical or temporal order.

icon: Painting resemblance by imagery.

[069] **Image:** A thing that represents something else; a symbol, emblem, representation.

indignatio: Arousing the audience's scorn and indignation.

[070] **IRONY:** Implying a meaning opposite to the literal meaning.

[071] **Isocolon:** Phrases of approximately equal length and corresponding structure.

[072] **Litotes:** Denial of the contrary; understatement that intensifies.

macrologia: Long-winded speech; using more words than necessary.

[073] **Meiosis:** To belittle, often through a trope of one word; use a degrading epithet.

merismus: Dividing the whole into its parts.

metalepsis: Present effect attributed to a remote cause.

metanoia: Qualification of a statement by recalling it and expressing in a better way, often by using a negative.

[074] **METAPHOR**

METAPLASM: A generic term. A transformation of letters or syllables in single words, contrary to the common fashion of writing and speaking.

[075] **METONYMY:** Replacement of one word for another that has a spatial, temporal, or causal contiguity with the first.

MIMESIS: Imitation of gesture, pronunciation, or utterance.

occultatio: Emphasizing something by pointedly seeming to pass over it.

[076] **Onomatopoeia:** Use or invention of words that sound like their meaning.

[077] **Oxymoron:** A condensed PARADOX.

paeanismus: An exclamation of joy.

[078] **Palindrome:** Words, phrases, or sentences which make sense read backwards as well as forwards.

parable: Teaching a moral by means of an extended METAPHOR.

[079] **PARADOX:** A seemingly self-contradictory statement, which yet is shown to be true.

parataxis: Clauses or phrases arranged independently.

[080] **Parenthesis:** A word, phrase, or sentence inserted as an aside in a sentence complete in itself.

[081] **Paronomasia:** Playing on the sounds and meanings of words.

PATHOPOEIA: A generic term for arousing passion or emotion.

periphrasis: Circumlocution.

peristasis: Amplifying by describing attendant circumstances.

[082] **Ploce:** Repetition of a word or a name with a new signification after the intervention of another word or words.

[083] **Polyptoton:** Repetition of words from the same root but with different endings.

[084] **Polysyndeton:** Use of a conjunction between each clauses.

[085] **Pragmatographia:** Vivid description of an action or event.

progressio: Building a point around a series of comparisons.

[086] **Prosopopoeia:** An animal or inanimate object is represented as having human attributes.

[087] **Proverb:** A short, pithy statement of a general truth.

[088] **PUN:** Play on words.

REPETITIO(N): In classical rhetoric this is the repetition of the same sound, the same word, or the same group of words.

[089] **Sarcasmus:** A bitter gibe or taunt. Use of mockery, verbal taunts, or bitter IRONY.

[090] **Scesis onomaton:** Using a string of synonymous expressions.

[091] **Significatio:** To imply more than is actually stated.

[092] **Simile:** Explicit comparison.

[093] **Syllepsis:** A verb lacks congruence with at least one subject that it governs.

[094] **Synaeresis:** Pronouncing as diphthong two adjacent vowels that belong to different syllables within a single word.

synchisis: Confused word order in a sentence.

[095] **Syncrisis:** Comparison and contrast in parallel clauses.

[096] **Synecdoche:** Substitution of part for whole, genus for species, or vice versa.

[097] **Synoeciosis:** An expanded oxymoron: a PARADOX.

[098] **Synonymia:** Amplification by synonym.

[099] **Systrophe:** Heaping up of descriptions of a thing without defining it.

tautology: Repetition of the same idea in different words.

[100] **Topographia:** Description of a place.

[101] **Topothesia:** Description of imaginary, nonexistent places.

zeugma: A kind of ellipsis in which one word, usually a verb, governs several congruent words or clauses.

COLORS BY TYPE

AMPLIFICATION

[001]   **Accumulatio:** Heaping up praise or accusation to emphasize or summarize points or inferences already made.

[005]   **Aetiologia:** Giving a cause or reason.

[011]   **AMPLIFICATIO:** Rhetorical device used to expand a simple statement.
        apophasis: Pretending to deny what is really affirmed.

[035]   **Appositio:** Two juxtaposed nouns, the second elaborating the first.
        augendi causa: Raising the voice for emphasis.

[039]   **Auxesis:** Words or clauses placed in climactic order.

[040]   **Bomphiologia:** Bombastic speech.

[044]   **Climax:** Mounting by degrees through linked words or phrases, usually of increasing weight and in parallel construction.
        cohortatio: Amplification that moves the hearer's indignation.

[045]   **Commoratio:** Emphasizing a strong point by repeating it several times in different words.

[046]   **Conduplicatio:** Repetition of a word or words in succeeding clauses, (1) for amplification or emphasis; (2) to express emotion.

[047]   **Congeries:** Piling up words of differing meaning but for a similar emotional effect.
        diaeresis: Dividing the genus into species in order to amplify.

[049]   **Diallage:** Bringing several arguments to establish a single point.

[050]   **Dinumeratio:** Dividing a subject into subheadings. A summary or recapitulation, intended to refresh the hearer's memory.
        distinctio: Explicit reference to various meanings of a word, thereby removing ambiguities.
        distribution: Dividing the whole into its parts.

[052]   **Ecphonesis:** Exclamation expressing emotion.
        epanodos: A general statement is expanded by discussing it part by part.

[056]   **Epexegesis:** Adding words or phrases to further clarify or specify a statement already made.

[057]   **Epicrisis:** The speaker quotes a passage and comments on it.

[058]   **Epitheton:** Qualifying the subject with an appropriate adjective.

[061]   **Expeditio:** Rejection of all but one of various alternatives.

[067]   **Hyperbole:** Self-conscious exaggeration.

[072]   **Litotes:** Denial of the contrary; understatement that intensifies.
        macrologia: Long-winded speech; using more words than necessary.

[080]   **Parenthesis:** A word, phrase, or sentence inserted as an aside in a sentence complete in itself.
        periphrasis: Circumlocution.
        peristasis: Amplifying by describing attendant circumstances.

[098]   **Synonymia:** Amplification by synonym.

[099]   **Systrophe:** Heaping up of descriptions of a thing without defining it.

ANTITHESIS

[025]   **Antilogy:** Two or more opposed speeches on the same topic.

[031]   **Antithesis:** Conjoining contrasting ideas.
        antitheton: Antithesis.
        contrarium: One of two opposite statements is used to prove the other.

[064]   **Horismus:** A definition by opposites.

[072]   **Litotes:** Denial of the contrary; understatement that intensifies.

[095]   **Syncrisis:** Comparison and contrast in parallel clauses.

BALANCE

[026]   **Antimetabole:** Inverting the order of repeated words.

[043]   **Chiasmus:** The ABBA pattern of mirror inversion.

[044]   **Climax:** Mounting by degrees through linked words or phrases, usually of increasing weight and in parallel construction.

[051]   **Disjunctio:** Use different verbs to express similar ideas in successive clauses.

[071]   **Isocolon:** Phrases of approximately equal length and corresponding structure.

[084]   **Polysyndeton:** Use of a conjunction between each clauses.

BREVITY

        brachyologia: Brevity of diction; abbreviated construction; word or words omitted.
        brevitas: Concise expression.

[062]   **Fable:** A short, allegorical story.

[077]   **Oxymoron:** A condensed PARADOX.

[087]   **Proverb:** A short, pithy statement of a general truth.

DESCRIPTION {ENARGIA}

[018]   **Anatomy:** The analysis of an issue into its constituent parts.
        chorographia: Description of a nation.
        chronographia: Description of time.
        demonstratio: Vivid description.

[055]   **ENARGIA:** A general term for visually, powerful, vivid description.
        icon: Painting resemblance by imagery.
        MIMESIS: Imitation of gesture, pronunciation, or utterance.

[076]   **Onomatopoeia:** Use or invention of words that sound like their meaning.

[085]   **Pragmatographia:** Vivid description of an action or event.

[100]   **Topographia:** Description of a place.

[101]   **Topothesia:** Description of imaginary, nonexistent places.

EMOTIONAL APPEALS

        augendi causa: Raising the voice for emphasis.

[040]   **Bomphiologia:** Bombastic speech.

[046]   **Conduplicatio:** Repetition of a word or words in succeeding clauses, (1) for amplification or emphasis; (2) to express emotion.

[052]   **Ecphonesis:** Exclamation expressing emotion.
        emphasis: Implying more than is actually stated.
        ETHOS: The emotions or character which a speaker re-enacts in order to affect the audience.
        euphemismus: Euphemism; circumlocution to palliate something unpleasant.
        indignatio: Arousing the audience's scorn and indignation.
        paeanismus: An exclamation of joy.
        PATHOPOEIA: A generic term for arousing passion or emotion.

[089]   **Sarcasmus:** A bitter gibe or taunt. Use of mockery, verbal taunts, or bitter IRONY.

ENALLAGE

[007]   **Alleotheta:** Substitution of one case, gender, number, tense, or mood for another.

[023]   **Anthimeria:** Functional shift, using one part of speech for another.

[024]   **Anthypallage:** Change of grammatical case for emphasis.

[030]   **Antiptosis:** Substituting one case for another.

[054]   **ENALLAGE:** Substitution of one case, person, gender, number, tense, mood, part of speech, for another.

[065]   **Hypallage:** Awkward or humorous changing of agreement or application of words.

EXAMPLE, ALLUSION, AND CITATION OF AUTHORITY

[013]   **Analogy:** Reasoning or arguing from parallel cases.

[014]   **Anamnesis:** Recalling ideas, events, or persons of the past.

[027] **Antinomy:** A contradiction between two beliefs or conclusions that are in themselves reasonable.

[033] **Apodixis:** Confirming a statement by reference to generally accepted principles or experience.

[034] **Apomnemonysis:** The quotation of an approved authority from memory.

[057] **Epicrisis:** The speaker quotes a passage and comments on it.
exemplum: An example cited, either true or feigned; illustrative anecdote.

[062] **Fable:** A short, allegorical story.
parable: Teaching a moral by means of an extended METAPHOR.

[092] **Simile:** Explicit comparison.

HYPERBATON

[017] **Anastrophe:** Unusual arrangement of words or clauses within a sentence.

[019] **Anoiconometon:** Improper arrangement of words.

[041] **Cacosyntheton:** Awkward transposition of the parts of a sentence.

[066] **HYPERBATON:** A generic figure of various forms of departure from ordinary word order.

[068] **Hysterologia:** A phrase is interposed between a preposition and its object.

[068] **Hysteron proteron:** Syntax or sense out of normal logical or temporal order.

[080] **Parenthesis:** A word, phrase, or sentence inserted as an aside in a sentence complete in itself.
synchisis: Confused word order in a sentence.

IRONY

[028] **Antiphrasis:** IRONY of one word, often derisively, through obvious contradiction.

[042] **Charientismus:** Clothing a disagreeable sense with agreeable expressions.
enantiosis: IRONY.

[070] **IRONY:** Implying a meaning opposite to the literal meaning.

[089] **Sarcasmus:** A bitter gibe or taunt. Use of mockery, verbal taunts, or bitter IRONY.

METAPHORICAL & METONYMIC SUBSTITUTIONS

[003] **Adianoeta:** An expression that has an obvious meaning and an unsuspected secret one beneath.

[006] **Allegory:** Extending a METAPHOR through an entire speech or passage.

[021] **Antapodosis:** A simile in which the objects compared correspond in several aspects.

[029] **Antiprosopopoeia:** The representation of persons as inanimate objects.

[031] **Antithesis:** Conjoining contrasting ideas.

[032] **Antonomasia:** Descriptive phrase for a proper name.

[052] **Ecphonesis:** Exclamation expressing emotion.
euphemismus: Euphemism; circumlocution to palliate something unpleasant.

[062] **Fable:** A short, allegorical story.

[063] **Fictio:** Attributing rational actions and speech to nonrational creatures.

[067] **Hyperbole:** Self-conscious exaggeration.
icon: Painting resemblance by imagery.

[069] **Image:** A thing that represents something else; a symbol, emblem, representation.

[070] **IRONY:** Implying a meaning opposite to the literal meaning.

[073] **Meiosis:** To belittle, often through a trope of one word; use a degrading epithet.
metalepsis: Present effect attributed to a remote cause.

[074] **METAPHOR**

[075] **METONYMY:** Replacement of one word for another that has a spatial, temporal, or causal contiguity with the first.

parable: Teaching a moral by means of an extended METAPHOR.

[086] **Prosopopoeia:** An animal or inanimate object is represented as having human attributes.

[087] **Proverb:** A short, pithy statement of a general truth.

[089] **Sarcasmus:** A bitter gibe or taunt. Use of mockery, verbal taunts, or bitter IRONY.

[092] **Simile:** Explicit comparison.

[096] **Synecdoche:** Substitution of part for whole, genus for species, or vice versa.

PARADOX

[005] **Aetiologia:** Giving a cause or reason.

[025] **Antilogy:** Two or more opposed speeches on the same topic.

[027] **Antinomy:** A contradiction between two beliefs or conclusions that are in themselves reasonable.

[077] **Oxymoron:** A condensed PARADOX.
paeanismus: An exclamation of joy.

[079] **PARADOX:** A seemingly self-contradictory statement, which yet is shown to be true.

[097] **Synoeciosis:** An expanded oxymoron: a PARADOX.

PUN

[002] **Acrostic:** A series of lines in which certain letters form a message when read in sequence.

[010] **Amphibologia:** Ambiguity, either intended or inadvertent.

[020] **Antanaclasis:** Homonymic PUN.
antistasis: Repetition of a word in a different or contrary sense.

[037] **Asteismus:** Facetious or mocking answer that plays on a word.
cacemphaton: Sounds combined for harsh effect.

[078] **Palindrome:** Words, phrases, or sentences which make sense read backwards as well as forwards.

[081] **Paronomasia:** Playing on the sounds and meanings of words.

[088] **PUN:** Play on words.

REPETITION: Letters, Syllables, Sounds, Words, Clauses, Phrases, and Ideas

[008] **Alliteration:** Recurrence of an initial consonant sound, and sometimes of a vowel sound.

[016] **Anaphora:** The repetition of the same word or phrase at the beginning of successive clauses.

[026] **Antimetabole:** Inverting the order of repeated words.
antistasis: Repetition of a word in a different or contrary sense.

[036] **Assonance:** Identity or similarity in sound between internal vowels in neighboring words.

[043] **Chiasmus:** The ABBA pattern of mirror inversion.

[045] **Commoratio:** Emphasizing a strong point by repeating it several times in different words.

[046] **Conduplicatio:** Repetition of a word or words in succeeding clauses, (1) for amplification or emphasis; (2) to express emotion.
consonance: Resemblance of stressed consonant-sounds where the associated vowels differ.

[048] **Correctio:** Correction of a word or phrase.
demonstratio: Vivid description.
diaeresis: Dividing the genus into species in order to amplify.

[051] **Disjunctio:** Use different verbs to express similar ideas in successive clauses.
epanodos: (1) A general statement is expanded by discussing it part by part. (2) Ploce.

[060] **Exergasia:** Repeating the same thought in many figures.
metanoia: Qualification of a statement by recalling it and expressing in a better way.

[082] **Ploce:** Repetition of a word or a name with a new signification after the intervention of another word or words.

[083] **Polyptoton:** Repetition of words from the same root but with different endings.

[084] **Polysyndeton:** Use of a conjunction between each clauses.
REPETITIO(N): In classical rhetoric this is the repetition of the same sound, the same word, or the same group of words.

[090] **Scesis onomaton:** Using a string of synonymous expressions.

[098] **Synonymia:** Amplification by synonym.
tautology: Repetition of the same idea in different words.

SUBTRACTION/OMISSION

[015] **Anantapodoton:** Omission of a correlative clause from a sentence.
aposiopesis: Stopping suddenly in midcourse, leaving a statement unfinished.

[038] **Asyndeton:** Omission of conjunctions between words, phrases, or clauses.
brachyologia: Brevity of diction; abbreviated construction; word or words omitted.

[053] **Ellipsis:** Omission of a word or short phrase easily supplied.

[072] **Litotes:** Denial of the contrary; understatement that intensifies.

[073] **Meiosis:** To belittle, often through a trope of one word; use a degrading epithet.
METAPLASM: A generic term. A transformation of letters or syllables in single words, contrary to the common fashion of writing and speaking.

[091] **Significatio:** To imply more than is actually stated.

[094] **Synaeresis:** Pronouncing as diphthong two adjacent vowels that belong to different syllables within a single word.
zeugma: A kind of ellipsis in which one word, usually a verb, governs several congruent words or clauses.

TECHNIQUES OF ARGUMENT

[004] **Adynaton:** Stringing together of impossibilities.
aenos: Quoting wise sayings from fables.

[005] **Aetiologia:** Giving a cause or reason.

[009] **Alloiosis:** Breaking down a subject into alternatives.

[013] **Analogy:** Reasoning or arguing from parallel cases.

[021] **Antapodosis:** A simile in which the objects compared correspond in several aspects.

[022] **Antenantiosis:** Positive statement made in a negative form.
aphelia: Plainness of writing or speech.

[033] **Apodixis:** Confirming a statement by reference to generally accepted principles or experience.

[034] **Apomnemonysis:** The quotation of an approved authority from memory.
catacosmesis: Anticlimax, ordering words in descending importance.
cohortatio: Amplification that moves the hearer's indignation.

[045] **Commoratio:** Emphasizing a strong point by repeating it several times in different words.

[048] **Correctio:** Correction of a word or phrase.
diaeresis: Dividing the genus into species in order to amplify.

[049] **Diallage:** Bringing several arguments to establish a single point.

[050] **Dinumeratio:** Dividing a subject into subheadings. A summary or recapitulation, intended to refresh the hearer's memory.

[051] **Disjunctio:** Use different verbs to express similar ideas in successive clauses.
distinctio: Explicit reference to various meanings of a word, thereby removing ambiguities.
distribution: Dividing the whole into its parts.

[056] **Epexegesis:** Adding words or phrases to further clarify or specify a statement already made.

[059] **Erotesis:** A "rhetorical question," one which implies an answer but does not give or lead us to expect one.
ETHOS: The emotions or character which a speaker re-enacts in order to affect the audience.
euphemismus: Euphemism; circumlocution to palliate something unpleasant.
exemplum: An example cited, either true or feigned; illustrative anecdote.

[061] **Expeditio:** Rejection of all but one of various alternatives.

[063] **Fictio:** Attributing rational actions and speech to nonrational creatures.
indignatio: Arousing the audience's scorn and indignation.

[073] **Meiosis:** To belittle, often through a trope of one word; use a degrading epithet.
merismus: Dividing the whole into its parts.
metanoia: Qualification of a statement by recalling it and expressing in a better way.
occultatio: Emphasizing something by pointedly seeming to pass over it.
parable: Teaching a moral by means of an extended METAPHOR.
parataxis: Clauses or phrases arranged independently.
periphrasis: Circumlocution.
progressio: Building a point around a series of comparisons.

[089] **Sarcasmus:** A bitter gibe or taunt. Use of mockery, verbal taunts, or bitter IRONY.

[090] **Scesis onomaton:** Using a string of synonymous expressions.

[091] **Significatio:** To imply more than is actually stated.

UNGRAMMATICAL, ILLOGICAL, OR UNUSUAL USES OF LANGUAGE

acyrologia: The use of an inexact or illogical word; malapropism.

[010] **Amphibologia:** Ambiguity, either intended or inadvertent.

[012] **Anacoluthon:** Ending a sentence with a different grammatical structure from that with which it began.

[017] **Anastrophe:** Unusual arrangement of words or clauses within a sentence.

[019] **Anoiconometon:** Improper arrangement of words.

[023] **Anthimeria:** Functional shift, using one part of speech for another.

[024] **Anthypallage:** Change of grammatical case for emphasis.

[030] **Antiptosis:** Substituting one case for another.
cacemphaton: Sounds combined for harsh effect.

[041] **Cacosyntheton:** Awkward transposition of the parts of a sentence.

[054] **ENALLAGE:** Substitution of one case, person, gender, number, tense, mood, part of speech, for another.

[065] **Hypallage:** Awkward or humorous changing of agreement or application of words.

[066] **HYPERBATON:** A generic figure of various forms of departure from ordinary word order.

[068] **Hysterologia:** A phrase is interposed between a preposition and its object.

[068] **Hysteron proteron:** Syntax or sense out of normal logical or temporal order.
METAPLASM: A generic term. A transformation of letters or syllables in single words, contrary to the common fashion of writing and speaking.

[093] **Syllepsis:** A verb lacks congruence with at least one subject that it governs.

[094] **Synaeresis:** Pronouncing as diphthong two adjacent vowels that belong to different syllables within a single word.
synchisis: Confused word order in a sentence.

No.	Term	Definition	Amplification	Antithesis	Balance	Brevity	Description	Emotional appeals	ENALLAGE	Citation	HYPERBATON	IRONY	Substraction	Substitutions	PARADOX	PUN	Repetition: Letters	Repetition: Words	Repetition: Ideas	Techniq. of argument	Unusual uses of language
[001]	**Accumulatio**	Heaping up praise to emphasize points already made.	•																•		
[002]	**Acrostic**	A series of lines in which certain letters form a message.	•														•			•	
	acyrologia	The use of an inexact or illogical word; malapropism.																			•
[003]	**Adianoeta**	An expression with several meanings.	•									•		•							
[004]	**Adynaton**	Stringing together of impossibilities.	•								•			•	•	•				•	•
	aenos	Quoting wise sayings from fables.								•											
[005]	**Aetiologia**	Giving a cause or reason.	•																		
[006]	**Allegory**	Extending a METAPHOR through an entire speech.	•									•		•					•		
[007]	**Alleotheta**	Substitution of one case, gender, number, etc. for another.						•	•					•						•	•
[008]	**Alliteration**	Recurrence of an initial consonant and vowel sound.					•				•						•				
[009]	**Alloiosis**	Breaking down a subject into alternatives.					•		•						•						
[010]	**Amphibologia**	Ambiguity, either intended or inadvertent.	•													•					
[011]	**AMPLIFICATIO**	Rhetorical device used to expand a simple statement.	•						•												
[012]	**Anacoluthon**	Different grammatical structure.	•																		•
[013]	**Analogy**	Reasoning or arguing from parallel cases.			•					•										•	
[014]	**Anamnesis**	Recalling ideas, events, or persons of the past.							•	•											
[015]	**Anantapodoton**	Omission of a correlative clause from a sentence.	•										•								
[016]	**Anaphora**	The repetition of the same word or phrase.	•															•	•		
[017]	**Anastrophe**	Unusual arrangement of words.							•		•										
[018]	**Anatomy**	The analysis of an issue into its constituent parts.					•														
[019]	**Anoiconometon**	Improper arrangement of words.							•		•										
[020]	**Antanaclasis**	Homonymic PUN.	•			•										•					
[021]	**Antapodosis**	A simile.			•									•							
[022]	**Antenantiosis**	Positive statement made in a negative form.		•					•				•								
[023]	**Anthimeria**	Functional shift, using one part of speech for another.							•												
[024]	**Anthypallage**	Change of grammatical case for emphasis.							•												
[025]	**Antilogy**	Two or more opposed speeches on the same topic.	•	•											•					•	
[026]	**Antimetabole**	Inverting the order of repeated words.	•		•													•	•		
[027]	**Antinomy**	Contradiction between two beliefs.							•	•					•					•	
[028]	**Antiphrasis**	IRONY of one word through obvious contradiction.	•			•						•								•	
[029]	**Antiprosopopoeia**	The representation of persons as inanimate objects.	•						•					•						•	
[030]	**Antiptosis**	Substituting one case for another.							•				•								•
	antistasis	Repetition of a word in a different or contrary senses.														•		•			
[031]	**Antithesis**	Conjoining contrasting ideas.	•	•										•							
	antitheton	Antithesis.		•																	
[032]	**Antonomasia**	Descriptive phrase for a proper name.					•	•		•				•							
	aphelia	Plainness of writing or speech.																		•	
[033]	**Apodixis**	Reference to generally accepted principles or experience.	•							•										•	
[034]	**Apomnemonysis**	The quotation of an approved authority from memory.	•							•										•	
	apophasis	Pretending to deny what is really affirmed.	•																		
	aposiopesis	Stopping suddenly in midcourse.											•								
[035]	**Appositio**	Two juxtaposed nouns, the second elaborating the first.	•																	•	
[036]	**Assonance**	Identity or similarity in sound between vowels.	•														•				
[037]	**Asteismus**	Facetious or mocking answer that plays on a word.	•			•						•				•					
[038]	**Asyndeton**	Omission of conjunctions.											•							•	•
	augendi causa	Raising the voice for emphasis.	•					•													
[039]	**Auxesis**	Words or clauses placed in climactic order.	•		•															•	
[040]	**Bomphiologia**	Bombastic speech.	•					•												•	
	brachyologia	Brevity of diction.				•							•								
	brevitas	Concise expression.				•															
	cacemphaton	Sounds combined for harsh effect.														•					•
[041]	**Cacosyntheton**	Awkward transposition of the parts of a sentence.									•										•
	catacosmesis	Ordering words in descending importance.																		•	
[042]	**Charientismus**	Clothing a disagreeable sense with agreeable expressions.	•										•								
[043]	**Chiasmus**	The ABBA pattern of mirror inversion.			•													•	•		
	chorographia	Description of a nation.					•														
	chronographia	Description of time.					•														
[044]	**Climax**	Mounting by degrees through linked words or phrases.	•		•			•													
	cohortatio	Amplification that moves the hearer's indignation.	•					•												•	
[045]	**Commoratio**	The repetition of a strong point in different words.	•																•	•	
[046]	**Conduplicatio**	Repetition of a word or words in succeeding clauses.	•					•										•			
[047]	**Congeries**	Piling up words of differing meaning.	•																•		
	consonance	Resemblance of stressed consonant-sounds.															•				
	contrarium	One of two opposite statements is used to prove the other.		•																	
[048]	**Correctio**	Correction of a word or phrase.																•	•	•	
	demonstratio	Vivid description.					•														
	diaeresis	Dividing the genus into species in order to amplify.	•																	•	
[049]	**Diallage**	Bringing several arguments to establish a single point.	•																	•	
[050]	**Dinumeratio**	Dividing a subject into subheadings.	•																	•	
[051]	**Disjunctio**	Use different verbs to express similar ideas.			•															•	
	distinctio	Explicit reference to various meanings of a word.	•																	•	
	distribution	Dividing the whole into its parts.	•																	•	
[052]	**Ecphonesis**	Exclamation expressing emotion.	•			•		•						•							
[053]	**Ellipsis**	Omission of a word or phrase easily supplied.	•										•								
	emphasis	Implying more than is actually stated.						•													

	Term	Definition	Amplification	Antithesis	Balance	Brevity	Description	Emotional appeals	ENALLAGE	Citation	HYPERBATON	IRONY	Substraction	Substitutions	PARADOX	PUN	Repetition: Letters	Repetition: Words	Repetition: Ideas	Techniq. of argument	Unusual uses of language
[054]	**ENALLAGE**	Substitution of one case, person, etc. for another.	∘				∘		●											∘	∘
	enantiosis	IRONY.										∘									
[055]	**ENARGIA**	A general term for visually, powerful, vivid description.	∘				●													∘	
	epanodos	A statement is expanded by discussing it part by part. Ploce.	●																●		
[056]	**Epexegesis**	Adding words or phrases to clarify.	●																	●	
[057]	**Epicrisis**	The speaker quotes a passage and comments on it.	●					∘		●											
[058]	**Epitheton**	Qualifying the subject with an appropriate adjective.	●																		
[059]	**Erotesis**	A rhetorical question.	∘			●		∘				∘	∘	∘						●	
	ETHOS	The emotions which a speaker re-enacts.						●												●	
	euphemismus	Circumlocution to palliate something unpleasant.						●						●						●	
	exemplum	An example cited, either true or feigned.								●										●	
[060]	**Exergasia**	Repeating the same thought in many figures.	∘																●	●	
[061]	**Expeditio**	Rejection of all but one of various alternatives.	●										●							●	
[062]	**Fable**	A short, allegorical story.	∘				∘	∘		∘				●						●	
[063]	**Fictio**	Attributing rational actions to nonrational creatures.	∘							∘										●	
[064]	**Horismus**	A definition by opposites.		●										∘						●	
[065]	**Hypallage**	Awkward application of words.	∘					∘	●		∘			∘						∘	●
[066]	**HYPERBATON**	Various forms of departure from ordinary word order.	∘					∘			●									∘	
[067]	**Hyperbole**	Self-conscious exaggeration.	●					∘				∘		∘						∘	
[068]	**Hysterologia**	A phrase is interposed.	∘								●									∘	
[068]	**Hysteron proteron**	Syntax or sense out of normal logical or temporal order.									●										
	icon	Painting resemblance by imagery.					●							●							
[069]	**Image**	A thing that represents something else.					∘	∘		∘				●						∘	
	indignatio	Arousing the audience's scorn and indignation.						●												●	
[070]	**IRONY**	Implying a meaning opposite to the literal meaning.	∘									●	●							∘	
[071]	**Isocolon**	Phrases of equal length and corresponding structure.	∘		●															∘	
[072]	**Litotes**	Understatement that intensifies.	●	●									●							∘	
	macrologia	Using more words than necessary.	●																		
[073]	**Meiosis**	To belittle, Use a degrading epithet.											●							∘	
	merismus	Dividing the whole into its parts.																		●	
	metalepsis	Present effect attributed to a remote cause.												●							
	metanoia	Qualification of a statement by expressing it in a better way.																	●	●	
[074]	**METAPHOR**		∘	∘	∘	∘	∘	∘	∘	∘	∘	∘	∘	●	∘	∘	∘	∘	∘	∘	∘
	METAPLASM	A transformation of letters or syllables in single words.											●								●
[075]	**METONYMY**		∘	∘	∘	∘	∘	∘	∘	∘	∘	∘	∘	●	∘	∘	∘	∘	∘	∘	∘
	MIMESIS	Imitation of gesture, pronunciation, or utterance.					●														
	occultatio	Emphasizing by pointedly seeming to pass over.																		●	
[076]	**Onomatopoeia**	Use or invention of words that sound like their meaning.	∘		∘	●	●							∘							∘
[077]	**Oxymoron**	A condensed PARADOX.		∘		●									●						
	paeanismus	An exclamation of joy.					●														
[078]	**Palindrome**	Words which make sense read backwards.			∘	●										●					
	parable	Teaching a moral by means of an extended METAPHOR.								●				●						●	
[079]	**PARADOX**	A seemingly self-contradictory statement.	∘											∘	●					∘	
	parataxis	Clauses or phrases arranged independently.																		●	
[080]	**Parenthesis**	A word inserted as an aside in a sentence complete in itself.	●								●									∘	∘
[081]	**Paronomasia**	Playing on the sounds and meanings of words.	∘											∘		●				∘	
	PATHOPOEIA	A generic term for arousing passion or emotion.						●													
	periphrasis	Circumlocution.	●																	●	
	peristasis	Amplifying by describing attendant circumstances.	●																		
[082]	**Ploce**	Repetition of a word with a new signification .												∘		∘		●		∘	
[083]	**Polyptoton**	Repetition of words from the same root.																●			
[084]	**Polysyndeton**	Use of a conjunction between each clause.			●													●			
[085]	**Pragmatographia**	Vivid description of an action or event.	∘				●													∘	
	progressio	Building a point around a series of comparisons.																		●	
[086]	**Prosopopoeia**	Inanimate object as having human attributes.					∘							●							
[087]	**Proverb**	A short, pithy statement of a general truth.				●	∘			∘		●								∘	
[088]	**PUN**	Play on words.	∘							∘						●					
	REPETITIO(N)	The repetition of the same sound, word or words.															●	●	●		
[089]	**Sarcasmus**	A bitter gibe or taunt.						●				●		●						●	
[090]	**Scesis onomaton**	Using a string of synonymous expressions.	∘		∘									∘					∘	●	
[091]	**Significatio**	To imply more than is actually stated.											●							∘	
[092]	**Simile**	Explicit comparison.	∘							●				●						∘	
[093]	**Syllepsis**	A verb lacks congruence.	∘					∘												∘	●
[094]	**Synaeresis**	Incorrect pronunciation.	∘										●								∘
	synchisis	Confused word order in a sentence.									●										●
[095]	**Syncrisis**	Comparison and contrast in parallel clauses.	∘	●	∘									∘	∘					∘	
[096]	**Synecdoche**	Substitution of part for whole or vice versa.								∘				●							
[097]	**Synoeciosis**	An expanded oxymoron.	∘												●						
[098]	**Synonymia**	Amplification by synonym.	●																●	∘	
[099]	**Systrophe**	Heaping up of descriptions of a thing without defining it.	●				∘							∘							
	tautology	Repetition of the same idea in different words.																	●		
[100]	**Topographia**	Description of a place.	∘				●													∘	
[101]	**Topothesia**	Description of imaginary, nonexistent places.	∘				●													∘	
	zeugma	An ellipsis in which one word governs several clauses.				●								●							

COLORS

ARTWORKS

AUTHORS

BIBLIOGRAPHY

Anyhow. New York: Cambridge, Mass.: Anyone Corp.; MIT Press, 1998.

Anyplace. New York, N.Y.: London,: Anyone Corp.; MIT Press, 1995.

Architecture (CCA), Canadian Centre https://www.cca.qc.ca/en/archives.

Aristóteles. "Aristóteles RETORICA," n.d.

Aristotle. *Ars Rhetorica*. Edited by W. D. Ross. Oxford: Oxford University Press, 1959.

——. "Rhetorica." In *The Works of Aristotle Translated into English*, translated by W. Rhys Roberts, W. D. Ross. Vol. 11. Oxford: Clarendon Press, 1924.

Armitage, John. *Virilio for Architects*. Thinkers for Architects; 12, 2015.

Atzmon, Leslie. *Visual Rhetoric and the Eloquence of Design Artifacts*. Visual Rhetoric Series. Anderson, S.C.: Parlor Press, 2011.

Barthes, Roland. "Rhetoric of the Image." In *Image-Music-Text: Essays*, translated by Stephen Heath, 32–51. London: Fontana, 1977.

Betsky, A., and P. Sartogo. *Roma Interrotta: Twelve Interventions on the Nolli's Plan of Rome: In the MAXXI Architettura Collections*.

Bizzell, Patricia, and Bruce Herzberg. *The Rhetorical Tradition: Readings from Classical Times to the Present*. Bedford/St. Martin's, 2000.

Bonsiepe, Gui. "Visuell-verbale Rhetorik /Visual-verbal Rhetoric." *Ulm (Journal of the Ulm School of Design)*, Journal of the Ulm School of Design, no. 14–16 (1965): 23–40.

Bonsiepe, Gui, Richard Buchanan, Paul Chamberlain, Nigel Cross, Joep Frens, Wolfgang Jonas, Ianus Keller, et al. *Design Research Now: Essays and Selected Projects/Ralf Michel. Design Research Now: Essays and Selected Projects*. Board of International Research in Design. Basel: Birkhäuser, 2012.

Bouissac, Paul, ed. *Encyclopedia of Semiotics. Encyclopedia of Semiotics*. Oxford University Press, 2007.

Buchanan, Richard. "Declaration by Design: Rhetoric, Argument, and Demonstration in Design Practice." *Design Issues* 2, no. 1 (1985): 4–22.

Buckley, Craig. *Graphic Assembly*. Minneapolis, London: Univeristy of Minnesota Press, 2019.

——, ed. "Manifesto Architecture." In *After the Manifesto*, 40–81. Columbia Books on Architecture and the City, 2015.

Burke, Kenneth. *A Grammar of Motives, and A Rhetoric of Motives*. Meridian Books, M143. Cleveland: World Pub. Co, 1962.

Burton, Gideon O. "Silva Rhetoricae: The Forest of Rhetoric." The Forest of Rhetoric. Accessed September 3, 2020. http://rhetoric.byu.edu.

Cicero. *Brutus*. Translated by G. L. Hendrickson. *Orator*. Translated by H. M. Hubbell LCL, 1939.

——. *De inventione and Topica*. Translated by H. M. Hubbell. LCL, 1949.

——. *De oratore*. Translated by E. W. Sutton and H. Rackham. 2 vols. LCL, 1942.

——. *Philippics*. Edited and translated by D. R. Shackleton Bailey. Chapel Hill: University of North Carolina Press, 1986.

[Cicero] *Ad C. Herennium: De Ratione Dicendi (Rhetorica Ad Herennium)*, Translated by Harry Caplan. LCL, 1954.

Colomina, Beatriz, "Manifesto Architecture," in *After the Manifesto*, Craig Buckley, ed., Columbia Books on Architecture and the City, 2015, 40–81.

Cook, Peter. "Strange Pavilions of the Mind. The Work of Diploma Unit 10, 1973–1983." *AA Files*, no. 4 (1983): 102–107.

Diller, Elizabeth, Ricardo Scofidio, Georges Teyssot, and Diller + Scofidio. *Flesh. The Mutant Body of Architecture: Architectural Probes*. New York: Princeton Architectural Press, 1994.

Duffy, William. "Defining Rhetoric, 50+ Modern Takes." Medium, October 10, 2016.

Durand, Jacques. "Rhetoric and the Advertising Image." *Australian Journal of Cultural Studies* 1, no. 2 (December 1983): 29–61.

——. "Rhetorical Figures in the Advertising Image." In *Marketing and Semiotics*, edited by Jean Umiker-Sebeok, 295–318. Approaches to Semiotics. De Gruyter Mouton, 1987.

Dyer, Gillian. *Advertising as Communication*. Studies in Communication (London, England). London; New York: Methuen, 1982.

Eco, Umberto. *A Theory of Semiotics*. Advances in Semiotics. Indiana University Press, 1976.

——. *La estructura ausente*. Penguin Random House Grupo Editorial España, 2011.

——. *Obra abierta: forma e indeterminación en el arte contemporáneo*. Seix Barral, 1962.

——. *The Open Work*. Translated by A. Cancogni. Harvard University Press, 1989.

——. *The Role of the Reader: Explorations in the Semiotics of Texts*. Advances in Semiotics. Indiana University Press, 1984.

Eisenman, Peter. "In My Father's House Are Many Mansions (Inside Out)," n.d.

——. *Eisenman Inside Out: Selected Writings, 1963-1988*. Yale University Press, 2004.

Evans, Robin. "Translations from Drawing to Building." *AA Files*, no. 12 (1986): 3–18.

——. *Translations from Drawing to Building*. AA Ducuments; 2. Cambridge, Mass.: MIT Press, 1997.

Foss, Sonja K. "Theory of Visual Rhetoric." In *Communication: Theory, Methods, and Media*. Routledge Communication Series. New York, NY: Routledge, 2004.

Fraser, Professor Murray, ed. *Design Research in Architecture: An Overview*. Design Research in Architecture, 2013.

Fullaondo, María, and Joseph Gauci-Seddon. "The Garden of Earthly Delights: A Social Condenser of Contemporary Pleasures in Pedagogical Design Strategies." *Journal of Architectural Education* 72, no. 1 (January 2, 2018): 105–119.

Fullaondo, María, and Ciro Márquez. *The Drawing Bazaar*. First edition (English). Colección Manuales/Escuela de Arquitectura Ingeniería y Diseño 2. Madrid: Escuela de Arquitectura de la Universidad Europea de Madrid: Editorial Rueda, 2015.

Hauser, Gerald A. *Introduction to Rhetorical Theory*. 2nd Edition. Prospect Heights, Ill: Waveland Pr Inc, 2002.

Hauser, Gerard A. "Aristotle on Epideictic: The Formation of Public Morality." *Rhetoric Society Quarterly* 29, no. 1 (January 1999): 5–23.

"Hennepin: The Future of an Avenue." *Design Quarterly*, no. 78/79 (1970): 59–63. https://doi.org/10.2307/4047408.

Hill, Jonathan. *Actions of Architecture Architects and Creative Users*. London; New York: Routledge, 2003.

——. "Building a Drawing and Drawing a Building." *Nordisk Arkitekturforskning (NA Nordic Journal of Architectural Research)* 15, no. 4 (April 19, 2013). http://arkitekturforskning.net/na/article/view/325.

——. "Building the Drawing." *Architectural Design* 75, no. 4 (2005): 13–21. https://doi.org/10.1002/ad.98.

——. "Design Research: The First 500 Years." In *Design Research in Architecture: An Overview*, 15–34, n.d.

——. "Drawing Research." *The Journal of Architecture* 11, no. 3 (June 1, 2006): 329–333. https://doi.org/10.1080/13602360600931342.

——. *Immaterial Architecture*. [1st ed.]. London; New York: Routledge, 2006.

Hollein, Hans, and Cooper-Hewitt Museum. *MAN TransFORMS: An International Exhibition on Aspects of Design*. Exhibition Catalogue Series. Smithsonian Institution, 1976.

Isaac, Victor, and Gift Essien. "Ifioque.Com | Online Hub for Educational Resources." https://ifioque.com/.

John Hoskyns, "Directions for Speech and Style [ca. 1599]," in *Life, Letters, and Writtings of John Hoskyns, 1566–1638*, ed. Louise Brown Osborn, 103–166. Yale Studies in English, 87. New Haven: Yale University Press, 1937.

Jakobson, R., and M. Halle. *Fundamentals of Language*. Janua Linguarum: Series Minor, v. 10. Mouton, 1956.

Josephson, S., J. Kelly, and K. Smith. *Handbook of Visual Communication: Theory, Methods, and Media*. Second. Routledge Communication Series. New York, NY: Taylor & Francis, 2020.

Judovitz, Dalia. *Unpacking Duchamp. Art in Transit*. Univeristy of California Press, n.d.

Kaufer, David S. *Rhetoric and the Arts of Design*. Mahwah, N.J.: L. Erlbaum Associates, 1996.

Klingmann, A. *Brandscapes: Architecture in the Experience Economy*. MIT Press, 2007.

Korn, Samuel. "An Environment of Environments: MAN TransFORMS—Curatorial Modes, Designs, Structures." *Architectural Theory Review* 23, no. 1 (2019): 59–89.

Kress, Gunther R, and Theo van Leeuwen. *Reading Images: The Grammar of Visual Design*. 2nd ed. London; New York: Routledge, 2006.

Krippendorff, Klaus. "Design Research, an Oxymoron?" In *Design Research Now: Essays and Selected Projects*, 67–80. Zürich: Birkhäuser Verlag, n.d.

Lanham, Richard A. *A Handlist of Rhetorical Terms*. Second Edition. University of California Press, 1991.

Lehtonen, Kimmo. "Rhetoric of the Visual: Metaphor in a Still Image." *Jyväskylä Studies in Humanities*, 2011.

Leith, Sam. *You Talkin' To Me?: Rhetoric from Aristotle to Obama*. Profile, 2011.

Rhetorical figures. "List of Rhetorical Figures." https://rhetfig.appspot.com/.

LitCharts. "Literay Devices and Terms." https://www.litcharts.com/literary-devices-and-terms.

Lucarelli, Fosco, and Mariabruna Fabrizi. "Socks." Online magazine. https://socks-studio.com/introducing-socks/.

MAXXI architettura (Museum). "Roma Interrotta: Twelve Interventions on the Nolli's Plan of Rome: In the MAXXI Architettura Collections - UQ ESpace."

McKeon, Richard. *Rhetoric: Essays in Invention & Discovery*. Woodbridge: Ox Bow, 1987.

McQuarrie, Edward F., and David Glen Mick. "Figures of Rhetoric in Advertising Language." *Journal of Consumer Research* 22, no. 4 (1996): 424–438.

McQuarrie, Edward F., and Barbara J. Phillips. *Go Figure! New Directions in Advertising Rhetoric*. M.E. Sharpe, 2008.

Mick, David, and Edward Mcquarrie. "On Resonance: A Critical Pluralistic Inquiry Into Advertising Rhetoric." *Journal of Consumer Research* 19 (1992): 180–197.

Migayrou, Frédéric. *Bernard Tschumi: Architecture: Concept & Notation*, 2014.

"New Taipei City Museum of Art Proposal / Federico Soriano Pelaez | ArchDaily." Accessed September 8, 2020. https://www.archdaily.com/178460/new-taipei-city-museum-of-art-proposal-federico-soriano-pelaez.

O'Toole, Michael. *The Language of Displayed Art*. Rutherford: Fairleigh Dickinson University Press, 1994.

Patton, Tracey Owens. "Visual Rhetoric." In *Handbook of Visual Communication: Theory, Methods, and Media*. Routledge Communication Series. New York, NY: Taylor & Francis Group, n.d.

Peacham, Henry. *The Garden of Eloquence* [1577]. Facsimile reproduction. Menston, England: Scolar Press, 1971.

Petit, Emmanuel. *Irony, or, the Self-Critical Opacity of Postmodern Architecture*. New Haven: Yale University Press, 2013.

———. *Reckoning with Colin Rowe: Ten Architects Take Position*. New York: New York: Routledge, 2015.

Puttenham, George. *The Arte of English Poesie* [1589]. Edited by Gladys Doige Willcock and Alice Walker. Cambridge: Cambridge University Press, 1936.

Quintilian. *Insitituto Oratoria*. Translated by H.E Butler. Vol. 3. 12 vols. LCL, 1920.

Rodríguez Cedillo, Carmelo. "Arqueología Del Futuro." E.T.S. Arquitectura (UPM), 2016.

———."Arqueología Del Futuro," Arqueología Del Futuro (blog), 2016, http://arqueologiadelfuturo.blogspot.com

Rowe, C., and F. Koetter. *Collage City*. The MIT Press. MIT Press, 1983.

Ruwet, Nicolas. *Introduction à La Grammaire Générative*. Librairie PLON, 1969.

Saint-Martin, Fernande. *Semiotics of Visual Language*. Advances in Semiotics. Bloomington: Indiana University Press, 1990.

Savic, Selena. "Event and Movement in Architecture The Manhattan Transcripts: Theoretical Projects," n.d.

Sherry, Richard. *A Treatise of Schemes and Tropes.*, 1550.

Site: Identity in Density. The Master Architect, VI. Australia: iMAGES, 205AD.

Sloane, Thomas O. *Encyclopedia of Rhetoric*. Oxford Digital Reference Shelf. Oxford University Press, 2001.

Smith, K.L., S. Moriarty, K. Kenney, and G. Barbatsis, eds. *Handbook of Visual Communication: Theory, Methods, and Media*. Routledge Communication Series. New York, NY: Taylor & Francis, 2004.

Soby, Thrall. "René Magritte." Museum of Modern Art (New York, N.Y.), 1965. https://assets.moma.org/documents/moma_catalogue_1898_300062306.pdf.

Sonesson, Göran. "An Essay Concerning Images." *Semiotica* 109, no. 1–2 (1996): 41–140.

———. *Pictorial Concepts: Inquiries into the Semiotic Heritage and Its Relevance to the Interpretation of the Visual World*. Lund: Lund University Press, 1989.

———. "Rhetoric of the Image." In *Encyclopedia of Semiotics*. Oxford University Press, 2007.

Spier, Steven. "Dancing and Drawing, Choreography and Architecture." *The Journal of Architecture* 10, no. 4 (2005): 349–364.

Spirn, A.W. *The Language of Landscape*. Yale University Press, 1998.

Šuvaković, Miško. "Cognitive importance and functions of: Readymade, Metaphor, Allegory and Simulation." *Filozofski Vestnik* 9, no. 1 (January 2016).

Takac, Balasz. "The Origin of the World and Scandal - Gustave Courbet's Provocative Painting." *Widewalls* (blog). https://www.widewalls.ch/magazine/the-origin-of-the-world-courbet-painting.

Tapia, Alejandro. "El Árbol de La Retórica: Retórica y Arquitectura." *El Árbol de La Retórica* (blog). http://elarboldelaretorica.blogspot.com/2007/03/retrica-y-arquitectura.html.

"The Journal of Architecture — Vol. 11 Issue 3 — Monash University — BrowZine."

Tschumi, Bernard. "Advertisements for Architecture. 1976-1977," n.d. http://www.tschumi.com/projects/19/.

Ungers, Oswald Mathias. *City Metaphors*. Walther König, 2011.

Wallace, Karl R. "Topoi and the Problem of Invention." *Quarterly Journal of Speech* 58, no. 4 (1972): 387–95.

Zimmerman, Brett. *Edgar Allan Poe: Rhetoric and Style*. McGill-Queen's University Press, 2005.

Wilson, Peter. "The Park and the Peak — Two International Competitions. Parc de La Villette, Paris / The Peak, Hong Kong." *AA Files*, no. 4 (1983): 75–87.

ACKNOWLEDGMENTS

First, I want to thank Diego Fullaondo and Ciro Márquez for providing inspiration, guidance, and feedback throughout this project. Without them, this project would not have been possible.

To Hugo Fullaondo and Ashkhen Manukyan for helping me with the design of this book and for tracing the copyright holders of the images.

To María López, Esther Moreno, María Asunción Salgado, and Titina Serrano for all the support received and the numerous conversations and discussions held on the subject during these years.

To Iñigo Aguirre, Emilio Alarcón, Iciar Alguero, Santiago Álvarez, Susana Antón, María Bances, Chris Brasher, Hayden Brown, Almudena Burkhalter, Natalia Cazcarra, Marina Crespo, Carolina Cuevas, Iciar de Basterrechea, Iñigo de Basterrechea, Guillermo Caruana, Elena del Río, Juan de Sande, Paco Díaz, Raquel Díaz, Ana Díez López, Concha Díez Garcillan, Casilda Epeldegui, Fernando Espada, Ana Fernández-Cárdenas, Conchita Fernández Gutiérrez, Patricia Fullaondo, Pía Fullaondo, Sofía Fullaondo, Teresa García Larrache, Luis Galiana, Mónica García-Murillo, José María García-Pablos Ripoll, Joseph Gauci-Seddon, Alicia Gimeno Blanco, Joaquín Gimeno López-Dóriga, Alicia Gimeno, Belén Gómez Lorenzo, Fernando G. Valderrama, María Gordon, Verónica Gross, Mónica Guillot, José Luis Guillot, Mar Illán, Eduardo Kairuz, Lee-Ann Khor, Alazne Larrinaga, Mirjana Lozanovska, Lola Lucena, Gorka Magallón, Antonio Marín Hernández, Eva Márquez Salmerón, Victor Márquez Reviriego, Lourdes Martín Fernández-Cárdenas, Francisco Montero, Rodrigo y María Moreno, Helena Moretti, Matilde Moro, Sofía Moro, Borja Moronta, Pilar Muñoz, Ana Parada, José Parada, Mauro Parada, Alfonso Parada, Ramón Parada, Fernando Quesada, Eva Rasines, Anne-Françoise Raskin, Arancha Rodríguez de Buen, Francisco Roibal Feal, Nacho Rupérez, Rosa Ana, María Luisa Sáez Gutiérrez, Ana Sala, Mariasun Salgado, Pilar Salmerón, Marco Sánchez, Carmen Sánchez, Yolanda Sánchez, Michele Sanguinetti, Francesca Sanguinetti, Loli Serrano, Witerico Solís, Naomi Stead, Jeannette Stoffregen, Marcin Strzala, Ngawang Tenzin, Hella Wigge, Tara Wood, and Rosana Yagüe for all their contributions.

To Luis Cuesta, Jaime Fullaondo, and Ricardo Porras.

To Iñaki Ábalos, Takefumi Aida, Francis Alÿs, BOLLES+WILSON, Daniel Canogar, Francesca Carr, Isaac Catón Rasines, Anna Chan, Junhao Chen, Georgia Collins, Jacob Cutri, Saskia Daale-Setiady, Sophie Davis, Walter de Maria, Juan de Sande, Diller Scofidio + Renfro, Yoana Doleva, Olafur Eliasson, Leandro Erlich, Federico Soriano & Asociados, Irena Galanos, Zaha Hadid, Leanne Haidar, Haus-Rucker-Co, Juan Herreros, Steven Holl, Madison Horth, Wes Jones, Chun Keong Ng, Christian Kerez, Wan Chee Kit, Kari Kleinmann, Anna Lekanidis, Yixuan Li, Ash Manukyan, George Mellos, Nicholas Miltos, Sarah Mitchell, mmmm...., Helena Moretti, Jean Nouvel, Marcella Palma, Renzo Piano, Reiser + Umemoto, Samantha Romana, Francesca Sanguinetti, Miquel Sarquella Gázquez, Ryoji Suzuki, Jazelyn Tan, Ngawang Tenzin, Alex Thelan, Patrick Tran, Oswald Mathias Ungers, Meagan Velleman, Peter Wegner, Peter Weibel, Allan Wexler, Sarah Wigglesworth, and Günther Zamp Kelp for their generosity.

To all design students, the reason and purpose for *Colors of Rhetoric*.